Accounting Control Best Practices

Steven M. Bragg

WILEY

John Wiley & Sons, Inc.

*To my parents, who exercised just enough control over me
as a child to mitigate the risk of such dreadful occurrences
as poor grades, car accidents, and entering politics*

Library of Congress Cataloging in Publication Data

ISBN–13: 978–0–471–35639–4 (cloth)
ISBN–10: 0–471–35639–5 (cloth)

Printed in the United States of America

10 9 8 7 6 5 4 3 2 1

Contents

Preface

This book addresses one of the primary concerns in accounting today—how to develop a comprehensive system of accounting and operational controls. This concern has been exacerbated by the provisions of the Sarbanes-Oxley Act, which requires public companies to report an assessment of their internal control structures and which has led to comprehensive control examinations by all types of companies.

Accounting Control Best Practices describes a complete set of controls for both a paper-based accounting process and a computerized system and then describes controls for more advanced best practices that are layered onto the basic computerized system. By reviewing the more than 400 controls for the various systems presented here, the accountant or systems analyst can devise a set of controls that is precisely tailored to the needs of his or her system.

Accounting Control Best Practices encompasses all of the major accounting and operational processes, including:

Billing	Manufacturing resources planning
Cash receipts	Order entry
Credit management	Payroll
Evaluated receipts	Perpetual inventory recordkeeping
Fixed assets transactions	Petty cash
Inventory transactions and valuation	Procurement cards
Investments	Purchasing
Just-in-time manufacturing	Shipping

In addition, each chapter includes control flowcharts for all major processes, as well as a comprehensive set of corporate policies designed to support the system of controls. Further, to ensure that only enough controls are applied so that process efficiency is not reduced excessively, the controls are divided into primary and ancillary ones. This in-depth treatment makes *Accounting Control Best Practices* the guidebook needed to ensure that a company has constructed a durable and efficient set of controls.

This book is intended to be a reference handbook for accountants and systems analysts who design, monitor, and revise accounting systems, as well as for the internal and external auditors who review those systems for control weaknesses. It is also useful for accounting managers who must be aware of the control issues associated with any best practices they wish to install in their accounting systems.

Steven M. Bragg
Centennial, Colorado
December 2005

About the Author

Steven Bragg, CPA, CMA, CIA, CPIM, has been the chief financial officer or controller of four companies, as well as a consulting manager at Ernst & Young and auditor at Deloitte & Touche. He received a master's degree in finance from Bentley College, an MBA from Babson College, and a bachelor's degree in economics from the University of Maine. He has been the two-time president of the Colorado Mountain Club, is an avid alpine skier and mountain biker, and is a certified master diver. Mr. Bragg resides in Centennial, Colorado, with his wife and two daughters. He has published the following books through John Wiley & Sons:

Accounting and Finance for Your Small Business

Accounting Best Practices

Accounting Reference Desktop

Billing and Collections Best Practices

Business Ratios and Formulas

Controller's Guide to Costing

Controller's Guide to Planning and Controlling Operations

Controller's Guide: Roles and Responsibilities for the New Controller

Controllership

Cost Accounting

Design and Maintenance of Accounting Manuals

Essentials of Payroll

Fast Close

Financial Analysis

GAAP Guide

GAAP Implementation Guide

Inventory Accounting

Inventory Best Practices

Just-in-Time Accounting

Managing Explosive Corporate Growth

Outsourcing

Payroll Accounting

Payroll Best Practices

Sales and Operations for Your Small Business

The Controller's Function

The New CFO Financial Leadership Manual

The Ultimate Accountants' Reference

Also:

Advanced Accounting Systems (Institute of Internal Auditors)

Run the Rockies (CMC Press)

> Subscribe to Steve's FREE accounting best practices newsletter, blog, and podcast at www.stevebragg.com.

Chapter 1

Introduction

Introduction

This book contains hundreds of very specific controls over the basic processes of a business—order entry, shipping, billing, purchasing, and the like. These controls are presented in layers, beginning with those needed for a very basic paper-based system and progressing through computerized systems and the use of selected best practice enhancements to the computerized systems. Thus, users can find within these pages a variety of control systems for different levels of system complexity. As a supplement to the many controls detailed in later chapters, this chapter contains additional comments about the overall system of controls, high-risk areas, the segregation of duties, implied controls, the impact of the Sarbanes-Oxley Act, and the occasional need to deinstall controls.

Control Point

This book is entirely about the control point, which is an activity within a business process that will prevent or detect a process breakdown. For example, the requirement to have a supervisor sign checks is a control point; the key element in this control point is not the actual signing of the check, but rather the assumption that the manager will not sign the check without first reviewing the attached payment documentation to ensure that the payment is necessary. However, this control point is necessary only in a relatively disorganized purchasing environment where many people can authorize purchases. If a company were to impose a rigid requirement that all acquisitions must involve an authorizing purchase order, there is no longer a need for a control point represented by the check signer, since the purchasing department has taken over this role. Thus, control points can be activated or discarded, depending on the structure of the underlying process.

A control point itself can break down through inattention, lack of formal training or procedures, or intentionally, through fraud. To mitigate these issues, some processes involving especially high levels of asset loss are more likely to require two controls to attain a single control objective, thereby reducing the risk that the control objective will not be attained. However, double controls are not recommended in most situations, especially if the controls are not automated, since they can increase the cost and duration of the processes they are designed to safeguard.

The controls outlined in the chapters that follow are broken into two types: primary controls that usually are highlighted on a control flowchart and ancillary controls that can be added to the primary controls to provide an additional layer of security. For example, detective controls designed to find errors after they have occurred are rarely designated as primary controls (which are intended to prevent control breaches from initially occurring) and instead are to be found in the list of ancillary controls. Primary controls are more likely to be an authorization, whereby a supervisor reviews a key aspect of a transaction before it is completed, or corrective, so that an error is spotted at or close to its source and fixed immediately.

Besides the detective controls already noted, verification controls usually can be considered supplemental. For example, an inventory audit or review of a petty cash box is a verification control, but because it is not conducted as an integral part of a process flow, it is considered supplemental to the primary set of controls. For the same reason, a passive control, such as installing a surveillance camera near a cash register, is considered a supplemental control.

There are many supplemental controls to choose from. However, just having a large selection of supplemental controls does not mean that they must all be used. Quite the contrary. Most controls add to a company's costs and clutter the work required of employees, so it is best to first determine exactly what risks must be addressed and what controls are required to do so, and to avoid using all other controls to the greatest extent possible.

To some degree, the use of ancillary controls is driven by a company's control environment, which includes these elements:

- *The enforcement of ethical standards.* A company that promulgates a written ethical standard, informs employees about it regularly, and enforces its parameters has established an excellent mind-set throughout the organization that a certain ethical standard is expected. This standard should be supported by the board of directors, while the board's audit committee should be active in investigating ethical (as well as control) breaches.

- *The operating style of management.* If the management team sets unrealistic goals for bonus payments or tells employees to meet stretch targets by whatever means possible, then it is creating an environment in which employees are indirectly encouraged to breach the control system. Alternatively, a focus on long-term results and reasonable short-term objectives tends to enforce compliance with the existing control system. Further, the establishment of free lines of communication between management and staff, so that control problems can be quickly and easily communicated throughout the corporate hierarchy, is an essential element of management's operating style.

- *Structure of the organization.* If a company is highly decentralized, with minimal overview of operations by the corporate staff, then controls will likely be enforced locally with minimal rigor. Conversely, a strong interest in control compliance by corporate management, with attendant auditing reviews, will assist in achieving a strong controls environment.

- *Assignment of control responsibility.* Controls will be followed with considerably greater enthusiasm when local managers are assigned direct responsibility for their consistent application. Without local assignment of control responsibility, controls tend to be looked on as hindrances to the efficient completion of processes and so are circumvented where possible.

- *Experience and expertise of employees.* If employees have a fundamental understanding of company systems, which comes from a combination of experience and intensive training by the company, then they will understand why controls are used, as well as the ramifications of their absence. Conversely, the lack of experience or training tends to result in the lapsing of controls.

Thus, the presence of a strong control environment is directly related to a reduced need for ancillary control points.

High-Risk Areas

All areas of a company contain some control weaknesses, but some harbor key risk areas, especially the diversion of company assets or misrepresentation of financial results. Of primary concern are those areas where these two issues coincide. The paragraphs that follow note how this book's controls can mitigate these risks, but also point out areas in which problems will still exist.

A major risk area is revenue recognition, for there are a variety of ways to manipulate it to accelerate revenues improperly, thereby reporting excessively profitable financial results. The bulk of the revenue recognition controls described in this book address the mechanics of ensuring that suppliers receive an accurate invoice in a timely manner—which unfortunately addresses only part of the revenue recognition control problem. Management still may have the capability to adjust revenue with a few well-placed journal entries or by altering the timing of transactions.

Another area of significant risk is the capitalization of assets. Chapter 8 addresses the basic controls needed to properly record expenditures large enough to exceed the corporate capitalization limit. However, once again (as has been proved at WorldCom), expenses can be capitalized on a massive scale by management, completely avoiding the intentions of the existing capitalization control system.

Yet another high-risk area is the valuation of reserves, such as for bad debts, warranty claims, or product returns. Anyone responsible for these valuations can easily adjust them (within limits) to arrive at enhanced financial results. Since reserve valuations fall entirely outside of any normal process flow, they can be more easily abused.

Several other high-risk areas are also unrelated to basic process flows—the valuation of acquired assets, related-party transactions, contingent liabilities, and special-purpose entities. Thus, even with in-depth and comprehensive controls over such key processes as purchasing, billings, and cash receipts, significant areas that can be circumvented easily—usually by management—still lie outside the traditional control systems.

Consequently, this book provides only part of the controls solution: It shows how to control both basic business processes and best practice improvements to those processes, but it does not provide a control system for management. That level of control requires a different set of approaches, such as tight board oversight of operations, an active and well-funded internal audit team that reports directly to the board of directors, good recruitment procedures, clear lines of authority, constant attention to ethics training throughout the organization, a fraud hotline, and the imposition of a corporate code of ethics. Unfortunately, these approaches are much fuzzier than the precise control points laid out in this book, which still leaves room for control breaches by management. In short, all manner of controls over management can be attempted, but there will always be a higher risk of control breaches by them.

Segregation of Duties

One of the fundamental concepts of control systems is that the level of control increases when duties are segregated among employees—and the more employees, the better. By segregating duties, one person typically is responsible for handling an asset (i.e., cash), while another records the transaction and a third approves the transaction, with no one being responsible for more than one of the handling, recording, or authorization tasks. If a process flows through multiple departments, the use of duty segregation can lead to the involvement of a dozen or more people in the process.

The advantage of using segregation of duties is that a massive level of collusion would be required to commit fraud. A typical case of fraud involving collusion results in a loss averaging six times the amount lost when a single person is involved, so there is certainly a valid point behind the use of duty segregation. However, it is also an extremely expensive proposition, for the involvement of many people in a process results in lengthy wait and queue times that yield a highly inefficient operation.

Due to the exceptional cost of duty segregation, it is increasingly common to find corporate risk managers evaluating the cost and benefit of such systems and sometimes deciding against an excessive level of segregation. The deciding factor is typically the size of the potential loss; for example, the handling of corporate securities will always call for the use of a considerable degree of duty segregation, while petty cash management will not.

Implied Controls

This book contains few references to automated data entry accuracy checks, since it is assumed that they are already present. Such controls include these validations:

- *Completeness.* A transaction is not considered complete until a specific set of required fields are completed. For example, the entry of a supplier invoice requires a supplier invoice number, invoice date, and dollar amount, and the computer system should not record an entry unless all of these fields have been completed.

- *Duplication.* The computer warns of the existence of a duplicate record already containing the same information. For example, the computer should reject a supplier invoice number that has already been entered.

- *Limit.* A transaction is flagged for supervisory review or rejected outright by the computer if a numerical value is too high. An example is a payroll application where the entry of an hourly wage rate is rejected if it is higher than a predetermined amount or lower than the minimum wage.

- *Table lookups.* The computer employs table lookups to determine the validity of entered data. For example, an entered part number will be compared to the item master file and rejected if the part number does not exist.

These automated controls are extremely useful for enhancing the completeness and accuracy of entered information.

Impact of the Sarbanes-Oxley Act on Controls

The Sarbanes-Oxley Act (Sarbanes) requires that an internal control report be included in a public company's annual report that contains an assessment of the effectiveness of the company's internal control structure and procedures for financial reporting. To determine if the control system meets this requirement, it is useful to complete these five steps:

1. Determine which accounts feed into the financial statements and which disclosures are key to the overall accuracy of the statements.
2. Document the process flows that materially impact the accounts and disclosures identified in the first step.
3. Identify the key risk elements in each if the highlighted process flows.
4. Document the effectiveness of existing preventive and detective controls in mitigating the identified risks.
5. Identify the need for alternative controls to mitigate the key risk elements down to targeted levels, and implement those changes.

Since this book is a broad-based source of control concepts, it is useful for completing steps 4 and 5 of the Sarbanes review process just noted. Within these pages, readers can locate controls for many key risk elements identified during their process reviews. To accomplish step 5 in the review process, it may be useful to audit a process once the controls described in this book have been installed, in order to identify any residual risk and then to adjust the control points to achieve the targeted risk level.

Deinstalling Controls

Though this book is concerned entirely with the selection and installation of controls to a process, a further consideration is when to deinstall a control. By its nature, a control usually involves non–value-added work, which either directly or indirectly increases company expenses. Therefore, you should conduct a periodic review of the existing control structure to determine which controls are no longer needed. A good time for this is just prior to the annual audit, when the external auditors likely will want to see some documentation of the company's system of controls. Another trigger for a controls review is whenever a process flow is altered, perhaps due to the installation of a new best practice. Whatever the reason for the review, all controls should be formally documented, thereby making subsequent reviews substantially easier.

Summary

The increased emphasis on controls that is mandated by the Sarbanes-Oxley Act makes it necessary to determine carefully what risks must be guarded against throughout a company's systems and to construct a set of controls to mitigate those risks. However, a company should not be ruled by a vast array of multilayered controls, unless it wants to see its operating efficiencies vanish. A better approach is to review the need for controls continually, both on regularly scheduled dates and as new best practices are installed, to ensure that only the correct controls are used in precisely measured amounts. This book is designed for such an approach, since it describes different sets of controls, depending on what best practices are being used. The reader can then assemble and disassemble controls as needed to match the specific systems in use.

An important concept to remember when reading this book is that even the most intricate, interlocking set of controls will not ensure the complete elimination of risk from a process. On the contrary, it creates only a reasonable expectation of that achievement. The reasons that risk cannot be completely eliminated are a combination of unforeseen circumstances for which controls were not installed, the occasional breakdown of the control system, and the presence of collusion, which effectively undermines many controls.

A final thought: It is possible to continue past the scope of this book and experiment with new types of controls, which can become best practices in their own right. This endeavor is particularly useful if controls can be created that require no capital or labor cost, and that do not interfere with the natural flow of a process.

Chapter 2

Controls for Accounts Payable Best Practices

Overview

This chapter covers three general sets of controls. First, it addresses the system of controls needed for an entirely paper-based accounts payable system, with descriptions for a supporting set of controls. Second, it reveals the controls needed for a basic, computerized accounts payable system, such as is installed in most companies today. Finally, it shows how to modify the controls for a computerized system in order to incorporate a number of payables best practices, including evaluated receipts, procurement cards, the replacement of checks with electronic payments, and more. Each set of controls includes a flowchart, showing necessary control points, as well as an itemization of supplemental control points.

2–1 Basic Accounts Payable Controls

Though it may seem unlikely that some companies still use entirely paper-based systems to conduct their accounts payable processes, this is still the case for some smaller businesses. The flowchart in Exhibit 2.1 shows the basic process flow for these organizations, with the minimum set of controls needed to ensure that it operates properly. The small black diamonds on the flowchart indicate the location of key control points in the process, with descriptions next to the diamonds.

The controls noted in the flowchart are described at greater length next, in sequence from the top of the flowchart to the bottom.

- *Manually review for duplicate invoices.* A noncomputerized accounting system has no way to automatically verify a supplier's invoice number

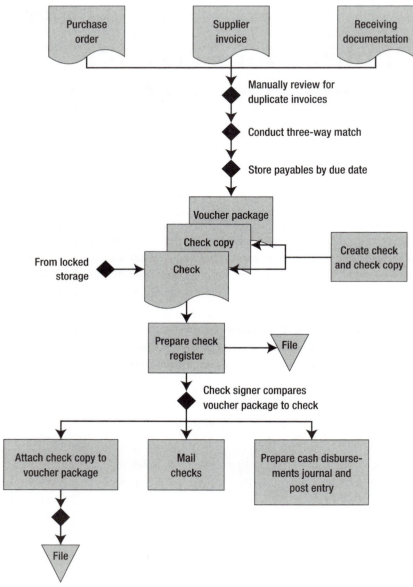

Exhibit 2.1   System of Controls for Paper-Based Accounts Payable

against the invoice number of invoices previously paid. Consequently, the payables staff must compare each newly received supplier invoice against invoices in two files: both those in the unpaid invoices file and those in the paid invoices file.

- *Conduct three-way match.* The payables staff must compare the pricing and quantities listed on the supplier invoice to the quantities actually received, as per receiving documents, and the price originally agreed to, as noted in the company's purchase order.

- *Store payables by due date.* The company must pay its bills on time, which calls for proper filing of unpaid supplier invoices by payment due date. Otherwise, suppliers can give the company a lower credit score or charge late fees. This control assumes that unpaid invoices will be stored based on the dates when the company can take early-payment discounts.

- *Check stock from locked cabinet.* Unused check stock should always be kept in a locked storage cabinet. In addition, the range of check numbers used should be stored in a separate location and cross-checked against the check numbers on the stored checks, to verify that no checks have been removed from the locked location.

- *Check signer compares voucher package to check.* The check signer must compare the backup information attached to each check to the check itself, verifying the payee name, amount to be paid, and the due date. This review is intended to spot unauthorized purchases, payments to the wrong parties, or payments being made either too early or too late. This is a major control point for companies not using purchase orders, since the check signer represents the only supervisory-level review of purchases.

- *Perforate voucher package.* The voucher package can be reused as the basis for an additional payment unless the package is perforated with the word "Paid" or some other word that clearly indicates the status of the voucher package.

Though the preceding controls are the basic ones needed for a paper-only accounts payable system, the next controls can also be used to bolster the level of control over the process.

- *Prenumber receiving reports.* A key part of the three-way matching process is to ensure that the items being paid for have actually been received, and in the correct quantities. It is easier to ensure that all receiving reports are being transferred to the accounts payable department by prenumbering the receiving reports and tracking down any reports whose numbers are missing.

- *Lock up blank receiving reports.* If three-way matching is used, then the receiving report is considered evidence that the quantity of an item contracted for has arrived at a company location. If someone were to steal a blank receiving report, he or she could take the goods and still submit a completed receiving report, resulting in undetected theft. Consequently, it may be useful to lock up unused receiving reports.

- *Prenumber purchase orders.* The purchase order is a key part of many accounts payable systems, since it provides the central authorization to pay. Consequently, if the purchasing system is paper-based, it makes sense to keep track of the stock of purchase orders by prenumbering them.

- *Lock up blank purchase orders.* The purchase order represents a company's official authorization to acquire goods and services. If someone could obtain blank purchase orders and fraudulently affix a company officer's signature to it, that person could obligate the company to a variety of purchases with relative impunity. Consequently, in cases where purchase orders are printed in advance, they should be stored in a locked cabinet.

- *Maintain a register of unapproved supplier invoices.* If a company issues new supplier invoices to those empowered to authorize the invoices, then there is a significant chance that some invoices will be lost outside of the accounting department and will not be paid. To avoid this, update a register of unapproved supplier invoices on a daily basis, adding invoices to the register as they are sent out for approval and crossing them off the list upon their return. Any items remaining on the list after a predetermined time limit must be located.

- *Conduct a daily review of unmatched documents.* The three-way matching process rarely results in a perfect match of all three documents (purchase order, receiving report, and supplier invoice), so these documents tend to pile up in a pending file. To keep the associated supplier payments from extending past early-payment discount dates or from incurring late-payment penalties, there should be a daily review of the pending file as well as ongoing, active measures taken to locate missing documents.

- *Reconcile supplier credit memos to shipping documentation.* If a company negotiates the return of goods to a supplier, then it should deduct the amount of this return from any obligation owed to the supplier. To do so, it should maintain a register of returned goods and match it against supplier credits. If no credits arrive, then use the register to continually remind suppliers to issue credit memos.

- *Only fund the checking account sufficiently to match outstanding checks.* If someone were to fraudulently issue a check or modify an existing check, a company could lose a large part of the funds in its bank account. To avoid this, only transfer into the checking account an amount sufficient to cover the total amount of all checks already issued.

- *Destroy or perforate and lock up cancelled checks.* Once a check is created, even if it is cancelled on the in-house accounting records, there is still a chance that someone can steal and cash it. To avoid this problem, either perforate it with the word "cancelled" and store it in a locked cabinet or shred it with a cross-cut shredder.

- *Add security features to check stock.* A wide array of security features are available for check stock, such as watermarks and "Void" pantographs, that make it exceedingly difficult for a forger to alter a check. Since the cost of these features is low, it makes sense to add as many security features as possible.

- *Verify that all check stock ordered has been received.* It is possible for both inside and outside parties to intercept an incoming delivery of check stock and to remove some checks for later, fraudulent use. To detect such activity, always compare the number of checks ordered to the number that has arrived. Also, verify that the first check number in the new delivery is in direct numerical sequence from the last check number in the last delivery. In addition, flip through the check stock delivery to see if any check numbers are missing. Further, if the check stock is of the continuous feed variety, see if there are any breaks in the delivered set, indicating that some checks were removed.

- *Limit the number of check signers.* If there are many check signers, it is possible that unsigned checks will be routed to the person least likely to conduct a thorough review of the accompanying voucher package, thereby rendering this control point invalid. Consequently, it is best to have only two check signers—one designated as the primary signer to whom all checks are routed and a backup who is used only when the primary check signer is not available for a lengthy period of time.

- *Restrict check signer access to accounting records, cash receipts, and bank reconciliations.* The check signer is intended to be a reviewer of a nearly complete disbursement transaction, which requires independence from all the payables activities leading up to the check signing for which this person is responsible. Consequently, the check signer should not have access to cash receipts, should not perform bank reconciliations, and should not have access to any accounting records. It is best if the check signer is not even a member of the accounting department and is not associated with it in any way.

- *Never sign blank checks.* Though an obvious control, this should be set up as a standard corporate policy, and reiterated with all check signers.

- *Separate disbursement and bank account reconciliation duties.* If a person involved in the disbursement process were to have responsibility for bank reconciliations, that person could improperly issue checks and then hide the returned checks. Consequently, always separate the disbursement function from the reconciliation function.

2–2 Controls for a Computerized Accounts Payable Environment

The accounts payable process flow most familiar to readers is the one shown in Exhibit 2.2. This process flow takes advantage of the basic features of a computerized accounting system, including the minimum set of controls needed to ensure that it operates properly. The small black diamonds on the flowchart indicate the location of key control points in the process, with descriptions next to the diamonds.

The process flow in Exhibit 2.2 includes many steps already seen in the paper-based payables process flow. By consolidating some accounting information into a central accounting database, the accounting staff now has access to more online information for the three-way matching task, but most computer-enabled users still conduct a manual matching, rather than attempting to automate the process. There is also no need to review the system

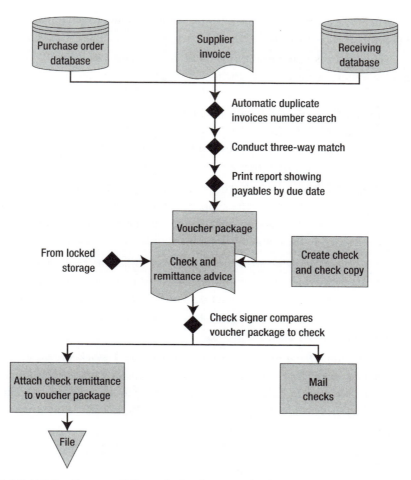

Exhibit 2.2   System of Controls for Computerized Accounts Payable

for duplicate supplier invoices manually, since this can be done by the accounting database. Further, the system will inform users when payables are due for payment, so no manual tracking of due dates is necessary. In addition, since checks are usually printed on a laser printer, there is only a single page printed, one portion of which is used as the in-house check copy. Thus, a separate page is no longer used as the check copy. Finally, there is no need to construct or print a check register or cash disbursements journal, since these documents are created automatically by the accounting software. Thus, computerization of the accounts payable process results in a number of efficiencies, though the overall process bears numerous similarities to the original paper-based system.

The controls noted in the flowchart are described in the bullet points that follow, in sequence from the top of the flowchart to the bottom.

- *Automatic duplicate invoice number search.* The accounting software automatically checks to see if a supplier's invoice number has already been entered and warns the user if this is the case, thereby avoiding the need for manual investigation of potentially duplicate invoices.
- *Conduct three-way match.* The payables staff must compare the pricing and quantities listed on the supplier invoice to the quantities actually received, as per receiving documents, and the price originally agreed to, as noted in the company's purchase order.
- *Print report showing payables by due date.* Since the computer system stores the invoice date and number of days allowed until payment, it can report to the user the exact date on which payment must be made for each invoice, thereby eliminating the need to manually monitor this information.
- *Check stock from locked storage.* Unused check stock should always be kept in a locked storage cabinet. In addition, the range of check numbers used should be stored in a separate location, and cross-checked against the check numbers on the stored checks, to verify that no checks have been removed from the locked location.
- *Check signer compares voucher package to check.* The check signer must compare the backup information attached to each check to the check itself, verifying the payee name, amount to be paid, and the due date. This review is intended to spot unauthorized purchases, payments to the wrong parties, or payments being made either too early or too late. This is a major control point for companies not using purchase orders, since the check signer represents the only supervisory-level review of purchases.

Perforating the voucher package after a check has been signed was one of the controls needed in a manual system, since it is an effective way to keep the same backup materials from being used a second time to authorize an additional payment. Though this control can still be used in a computerized system, there is less need for it, since the software automatically warns users of the presence of duplicate invoice numbers.

The preceding list of controls constitutes the basic controls needed for a computerized accounts payable system, but the controls that follow can also be used to bolster the level of control over the process.

- *Restrict access to the vendor master file.* For a variety of reasons that are enumerated in the next bullet points, it is unwise to allow unrestricted access to the vendor master file. Instead, use password access to restrict access to the smallest possible number of people, and only to those people who have no other responsibilities within the accounts payable and bank reconciliation areas.

- *Separate the supplier record creation and payment approval functions.* A strong risk of fraud arises when the same person can create a supplier record in the vendor master file and approve payments to the same suppliers, since this person is capable of creating a fake supplier and approving payments to it. Instead, split these two responsibilities among different employees.

- *Use a standard naming convention to create supplier names in the vendor master record.* Having multiple supplier records for the same supplier presents a problem when attempting to locate duplicate supplier invoices, since the same invoice may have been charged multiple times to different supplier records. One of the best ways to address this problem is to adopt a standard naming convention for all new supplier names, so that it will be readily apparent if a supplier name already exists. For example, the file name might be the first seven letters of the supplier name, followed by a sequential number. Under this sample convention, the file name for Smith Brothers would be recorded as SMITHBR001

- *Review daily changes to the vendor master file.* An employee with access to the vendor master file could alter a supplier's remit-to address, process checks having a revised address that routes the checks to him or her, and then alter the vendor master record again, back to the supplier's remit-to address. If this person can also intercept the cashed check copy when it is returned by the bank, there is essentially no way to detect this type of fraud. The solution is to run a report listing all changes to the vendor master record, which includes the name of the person making changes. A second control that provides evidence of this type of fraud is to only use a bank that creates an electronic image of all checks processed, so there is no way for an employee to eliminate all traces of this type of crime.

- *Require independent review of additions to vendor master file.* To reduce the risk of having an employee create a shell company to which payments are made by the company, have a person not associated with the payables process review all additions to the vendor master file and confirm that they are acceptable prior to any payments being made. Under this approach, only collusion that involves the reviewer will result in shell company fraud.

- *Purge the vendor master file.* The vendor master file within the accounting software can become clogged with multiple versions of the same supplier information, if not regularly reviewed and cleaned up. Having multiple supplier records presents a problem when attempting to locate duplicate supplier invoices, since the same invoice may have been charged multiple times to different supplier records. The solution is to conduct a regularly scheduled review and purge of the vendor master file.

- *Run a credit report on every new supplier added to the vendor master file.* A clear sign of fraud is when a shell company is set up specifically to receive fraudulent payments from someone within the accounts payable department. By running a credit report on every new supplier, it is possible to see how long a supplier has been in business and investigate further as necessary.

- *Run a report listing identical remit-to addresses for multiple suppliers.* Sometimes even the best manual review of the vendor master file will not detect all instances of duplicate records, because the variety of names used for a single supplier may be widely separated within the vendor master file. A good way to spot this problem is to sort the vendor master file by remit-to address, which tends to cluster multiple instances of the same supplier close together in the report.

- *Match supplier addresses to employee addresses.* Employees can create shell companies and fraudulently have checks sent to themselves. To detect this issue, create a computer report that matches supplier addresses in the vendor master file to employee addresses in the employee master file (assuming that the payroll function has also been computerized).

• *Reconcile supplier statements to payment detail.* When a supplier's monthly statement reveals that some payments are overdue, this can be evidence of a diverted payment by an employee. Consequently, the timely comparison of any supplier statements containing overdue payment notices to the vendor ledger in the computer system can be a good way to detect fraud. This control is also possible for a paper-based payables system, but requires considerably more review time, since payment records must be manually assembled for comparison purposes.

• *Access the vendor history file when paying from a copy.* There is a greatly increased chance of duplicate payment when paying from a document copy, since the document original may already have been processed for payment. To mitigate this risk, always review the vendor history file to see if the same invoice number or an identical dollar amount has already been paid. An additional control is to require more approval signatures whenever a document copy is used.

• *Match quantities ordered to MRP requirements.* When the purchasing department orders more materials than are required by the material requirements planning (MRP) system, this may represent fraud by the purchasing staff, which may be diverting the excess materials for their own uses. Using the computer to match quantities ordered to actual requirements needed will spot this problem.

• *Match purchase order records to actual quantities received.* If a company has a policy of paying the full amount of the purchase order if the delivered quantity is within a small percentage of the ordered amount, a canny supplier can continually short-ship deliveries by a small amount and never be caught. To detect this problem, run a computer report comparing the purchased amount to the delivered amount to see if there are any suppliers who have an ongoing pattern of delivering less than the ordered quantity.

• *Track changes in customer complaints related to suppliers.* A supplier can improve its profits by selling low-quality goods to the company. Though this problem is difficult to detect, an indication is a sudden increase in customer complaints related to the materials provided by the supplier. Running a summary-level report itemizing customer complaints by supplier or type of complaint can spot this problem.

- *Track short-term price changes by suppliers.* There is a possibility that suppliers will offer a kickback to a person in the purchasing department in exchange for allowing price increases by the supplier. To detect at least the possibility of this type of fraud, run a report listing short-term price changes by suppliers. By screening the report to show only significant price increases, the probability of the report showing evidence of fraud will increase. However, if a canny supplier increases prices only by a small amount, such a report will still not detect the problem, unless the filter is set to report on price changes of any size.

- *Audit acquisitions made within authorized purchase levels.* Employees sometimes attempt to circumvent maximum purchase authorization levels by having suppliers split invoices into multiple smaller-dollar invoices. To detect this control circumvention, have the internal auditors run a report listing multiple small payments to suppliers within a short time period, and see if these payments are related to a single acquisition.

- *Investigate payments made for which there are no purchase orders.* If the purchase order is the primary control over the payables process, then it is critical to ensure that all payments made (above a minimum-dollar threshold) are supported by an authorizing purchase order. To locate control failures in this area, run a report comparing the payables file to the purchase order file, and list all payments for which there is no authorizing purchase order record.

- *Use varying font sizes for each character in a check payment.* Using a computer to print checks has the advantage of allowing for a wide array of printing techniques that makes it more difficult for someone to alter a printed check. One approach is to have the computer use a different font size and type for each character of the written payment amount listed on the face of a check. This type of printing is extremely difficult to modify.

- *Restrict access to check-signing equipment.* If a company uses any form of computerized check-printing equipment, it may be necessary to lock down all access to it. This can include any printers in which check stock is maintained, signature plates, and signature stamps.

- *Require a manual signature on checks exceeding a predetermined amount.* This control is useful when signature plates are used for smaller check amounts. When signature plates are used, there is no longer a final review of payments before they are mailed. Therefore, requiring a "real" signature for large checks adds a final review point to the payment process.

*   *Implement positive pay.* A strong control that virtually eliminates the risk of an unauthorized check being cashed is "positive pay." Under this approach, a company sends a list of all checks issued to its bank, which only clears checks on this list, rejecting all others. However, this approach also calls for consistent use of the positive pay concept, since any manual checks issued that are not included on the daily payments list to the bank will be rejected by the bank.

*   *Use electronic payments.* There are several types of fraud that employees can use when a company pays with checks, while outside parties can also modify issued checks or attempt to duplicate them. This problem disappears when electronic payments are made instead. In addition, the accounts payable staff no longer has to follow up with suppliers on uncashed checks or be concerned about remitting payments to state governments under local escheat laws, since there are no checks.

*   *Reconcile the checking account every day.* An excellent detective control, this approach ensures that any fraudulently modified checks or checks not processed through the standard accounting system, will be spotted as soon as they clear the bank and are posted on the bank's Web site. This control is not available to companies not having Internet access.

As is readily apparent from the number of controls associated with the vendor master file, this is an area requiring restricted access and regular review in order to reduce the risk of multiple payments and fraudulent payments. Also, a computerized accounting environment allows for a panoply of additional controls that are not cost-effective in an entirely paper-based environment, allowing for cross-checking of accounting records against the purchasing, production planning, receiving, and customer complaints databases to unearth control problems.

2–3 Automated Check Signing

The central problem with the accounts payable system is that the primary control point—supervisory review of the purchase—occurs *after* the service or product has already been delivered, so a company typically is obligated to pay for whatever was purchased, even if it has no need for it or management did not initially authorize it. In essence, a lack of up-front control over the purchasing process results in an excessively late approval process just before payment is due to be made to the supplier.

This problem is exacerbated if supervisors are not asked to approve supplier invoices, so that the sole control point becomes the check signer. This person is now obligated to sort through the voucher package that accompanies all unsigned checks and investigate any suspicious payments. In reality, this person is usually a senior-level manager who has many other activities to accomplish and so conducts no more than a cursory review of the accompanying voucher packages and then signs the checks. The result is the almost total lack of any real control over the purchases that a company makes.

Many larger companies have recognized the futility of the control represented by the check signer and have eliminated this control through the use of a signature stamp, signature plate, electronic signature image, or some similar device. However, by doing so, they must ensure that a sufficient level of control has been added earlier in the purchasing and payables process to compensate for this loss of control. As shown in the flowchart in Exhibit 2.3, the check signer control point has been cancelled, while a new control has been added at the top of the flowchart for purchase order authorization, as well as another that rejects any materials received at the receiving dock if there is no authorizing purchase order. The use of a purchase order is a better control point than a check signer, since purchases must now be approved in advance, rather than after receipt, thereby giving the company greater control over what materials are allowed to be received at the receiving dock.

The new controls noted in the flowchart that are specific to automated check signing are described in the bullet points that follow, in sequence from the top of the flowchart to the bottom.

- *Mandatory purchase order authorization.* The key control point for automated check signing is requiring the purchasing staff to issue a purchase order for every purchase made by the company. This means that the purchasing staff must also forward a copy of each purchase order to the receiving dock, where it is used to verify the purchasing authorization for each item received (see next item).

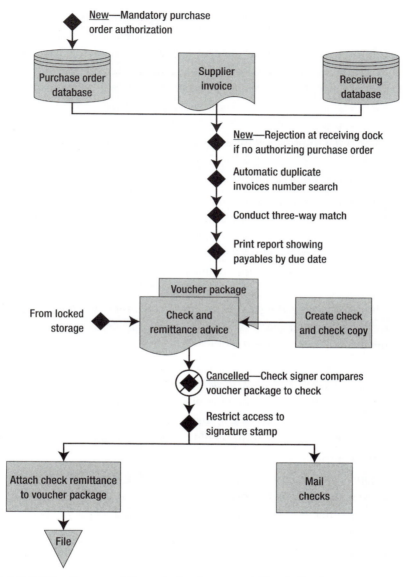

Exhibit 2.3 System of Controls for Automated Check Signing

- *Rejection at receiving dock if no authorizing purchase order.* Requiring a purchase order for every purchase does not represent much of a control if the receiving department accepts all arriving deliveries. Instead, the receiving staff must ensure that an authorizing purchase order is on file for every item that arrives at the dock. If there is no purchase order for a delivery, the receiving staff must reject it. This control can be quite time-consuming for the receiving department, which must research purchase order information for every delivery. To ease the workload, suppliers should be asked to prominently tag their deliveries with the authorizing purchase order number.

- *Restrict access to signature stamp.* This control actually applies to any form of automated check-signing equipment, not just the signature stamp. This is a critical control, since anyone gaining access to both check stock and the check-signing equipment could create authorized checks in any amount with impunity.

Though the preceding list of controls constitutes the basic controls needed for automated check signing, the next controls can be used to bolster the level of control over the process.

- *Restrict access to purchase order documents.* If the purchasing department uses paper-based purchase orders, then it must restrict access to the purchase orders by locking them in a storage cabinet when not in use. Otherwise, blank forms could be used by unauthorized parties to order goods.

- *Prenumber purchase orders and track missing documents.* If the purchasing department uses paper-based purchase orders, it can more easily determine if blank forms have been removed by prenumbering all purchase orders, keeping track of the numbers used, and investigating any missing numbers. This approach makes it less likely that blank forms will be removed from the department.

- *Restrict access to the purchase order database.* If the purchasing department creates all of its purchase orders through a computer database, then it must restrict access to that database to guard against the unauthorized creation of purchase orders. Typical controls include password protection, regular password changes, access being limited to a small number of purchasing staff, and a human resources check-off list for departing employees that calls for the immediate cancellation of their database access privileges.

- *Compare payments to authorizing purchase orders.* This detective control is used to spot payments made without a supporting purchase order, which constitutes evidence of a breach in the purchase order control requirement.

- *Review old open purchase orders.* This detective control is useful for determining which outstanding purchase orders are no longer needed and can be cancelled. Taking this step makes it less likely that someone could use an old, open purchase order to order goods inappropriately.

Though the use of purchase orders can provide a very effective level of control over purchases, it also results in a great deal of "paper-pushing" labor by the purchasing staff, which must create a purchase order for every item that a company acquires. To reduce the amount of purchasing labor while still retaining a high level of control over purchases, it is logical to implement procurement cards, which are described in the next section.

2–4 Use Procurement Cards[1]

Procurement cards are essentially credit cards that are used by designated employees to purchase small-dollar items without any prior authorization. Their use greatly reduces the labor of the purchasing department, which can instead focus its purchasing efforts on large-dollar items. However, because the use of procurement cards falls completely outside the normal set of controls used for the procurement cycle, an entirely different set of controls is needed. In addition, new procedures are needed to ensure that procurement cards are properly used. As a result, this section contains far more than a new set of control points—it also itemizes the procedures and forms needed to ensure that a procurement card program functions correctly.

The procedures and forms in this section enumerate the role of the purchasing card manager and how employees: apply for purchasing cards, buy items with the cards, reconcile their monthly statements of items purchased

---

[1]Adapted with permission from Steven M. Bragg, *Design and Maintenance of Accounting Manuals, 2005,* Cumulative Supplement (Hoboken, NJ: John Wiley & Sons, 2005), pp. 81–97.

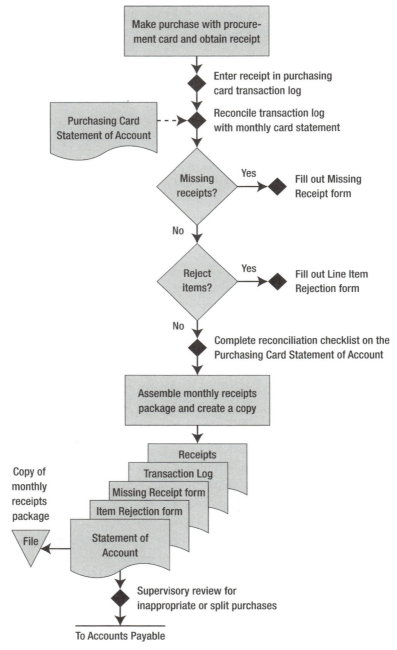

Exhibit 2.4   System of Controls for Procurement Cards

to detailed records, account for missing receipts, reject purchases they claim not to have made, request alterations to their spending limits, report lost cards, and handle card user terminations. Thus, the procedures presented here are intended to address all aspects of the procurement card process.

The key procurement card controls are enumerated in Exhibit 2.4, where controls are summarized next to the small black diamonds. The first control calls for card users to itemize each of their purchases in a separate log, which they then reconcile against the monthly card statement, noting missing receipts and rejected line items as part of the reconciliation. They then assemble this information into a packet of receipts and forms, and have a supervisor review it for inappropriate or split purchases. Then the supervisor forwards the packet to the accounts payable department for payment.

The controls noted in the flowchart are described in the bullet points that follow, in sequence from the top of the flowchart to the bottom.

- *Enter receipt in procurement card transaction log.* When employees use procurement cards, there is a danger that they will purchase a multitude of items and not remember all of them when it comes time to approve the monthly purchases statement. By maintaining a log of purchases, the card user can tell which statement line items should be rejected. A sample procurement card transaction log is shown later in Exhibit 2.9.

- *Reconcile transaction log with monthly card statement.* All card holders must review their monthly purchases, as itemized by the card issuer on the monthly card statement. The procedure for this reconciliation is noted later in Exhibit 2.10. A sample of the statement of account used for this reconciliation is shown in Exhibit 2.11, where it is assumed that the company obtains an electronic feed of all procurement card transactions from the card provider and dumps this information into individualized reports for each card user. This approach provides each user with a convenient checklist of reconciliation activities within the statement of account; the same result can be obtained by stapling a reconciliation activity checklist to a copy of the bank statement.

- *Fill out missing receipt form.* All card users should attach original receipts to the statement of account, in order to verify that they have made every purchase noted on the statement. If they do not have a receipt, they should fill out a missing receipt form, which itemizes each line item on the statement of account for which there is no receipt. The department manager must review and approve this document, thereby ensuring that all purchases made are appropriate. A sample missing receipt form is shown later in Exhibit 2.12.

- *Fill out line item rejection form.* There must be an organized mechanism for card holders to reject line items on the statement of account. A good approach is to use a procurement card line item rejection form (see Exhibit 2.14 for the form and Exhibit 2.13 for the related procedure), which users can send directly to the card issuer.

- *Complete reconciliation checklist.* The statement of account reconciliation process requires multiple steps, some of which card holders are likely to skip inadvertently from time to time. Accordingly, having them sign a standard reconciliation checklist is a useful way to ensure that the procedure is followed. A sample checklist is shown at the bottom of Exhibit 2.11.

- *Supervisory review for inappropriate or split purchases.* There must be a third-party review of all purchases made with procurement cards. An effective control is to hand this task to the person having budgetary responsibility for the department in which the card holder works. By doing so, the reviewer is more likely to conduct a detailed review of purchases that will be charged against his or her budget.

The preceding set of controls relate only to the process of tracking receipts and reconciling them against the monthly card statement. A number of additional controls can be used to keep excessive or inappropriate purchases from being made. The next controls address these additional issues.

- *Restrict purchasing levels.* A major control over the use of procurement cards is the restriction of amounts that can be purchased. This may be a maximum amount of daily purchases, a limitation on the total purchased over a month, or restriction to purchases only from suppliers having certain Standard Industry Classification (SIC) codes. This approach is extremely useful for ensuring that card holders do not run amuck with their card purchases, while also ensuring that losses are restricted if cards are stolen and used by a third party to make purchases.

- *Require supervisory approval of changes in spending limits.* The initial spending limitation on a procurement card is intended to meet the purchasing needs of the user. Consequently, any request for an increase in the spending limit may mean that the user fraudulently intends to purchase beyond the budgeted spending level. To ensure that spending limits do not result in a significant level of overspending, all spending limit changes should be closely monitored and approved by a supervisor. A sample spending limit change request form is shown in Exhibit 2.15.

- *Restrict use for cash advances.* A good control is to restrict procurement cards from being used to obtain cash advances, thereby keeping employees from being tempted to obtain cash for personal use or for purchases in areas outside the preapproved SIC codes for their cards. This control may not apply if cards are also given to employees who travel frequently and may need cash advances.

- *Restrict the number of card users.* Any procurement card in the wrong hands represents a risk of excessive purchases. While one approach for controlling this problem is to restrict the spending limit per card, another option is to be very restrictive in deciding who is allowed to use a procurement card. Possibilities for ensuring the minimum level of risk in issuing a procurement card include employee background checks as well as initially granting very small spending limits and expanding the limits based on evidence of responsible use.

- *Have card users sign an agreement.* Procurement card users can be required to sign an agreement stating their responsibilities in using the card. If the agreement also states the sanctions to be imposed on the card user if the card is misused, this may act as a deterrent to anyone who might otherwise be tempted to misuse a card.

- *Obtain Level III reporting by the card provider.* It is easier to control purchases if there is a greater level of detail regarding what card users are buying. Thus, it is useful to obtain from the card provider an electronic download of all Level III data relating to purchases, which includes the quantity, product code, product description, and freight/duty cost associated with each purchase.

- *Verify that purchases are made through an approved supplier.* The purchasing staff may have negotiated special volume pricing deals with selected suppliers, so it may be necessary to review statements of account to ensure that card users are making purchases from those suppliers. This control can be made more robust by issuing an approved supplier "Yellow Pages" to all card holders, so they know where they are supposed to make purchases.

- *Investigate any card purchases made for MRP items.* A properly installed material requirements planning system will automatically generate purchase orders for materials needed for the production process, which are either issued automatically to suppliers or through an intermediary in the purchasing department. Therefore, there is no reason for a procurement card user to buy any materials that are already being ordered by the MRP system. If a card user is doing so, this is probably evidence of a breakdown in the MRP system involving a sudden materials shortage that called for a rush purchase by a card user. All such purchases should be investigated at once to determine why the MRP system failed and to repair the underlying problem.

- *Track card expenditures on a trend line.* A simple way to determine the likelihood of inappropriate expenditures with procurement cards is to monitor purchasing totals by expense type for each card user. This detective method is useful for spotting sudden expense spikes that may call for a detailed investigation.

- *Report missing cards promptly.* There should be a mechanism in place that allows users to report that a card is missing. Though the use of a hotline number is the most obvious control, it is also useful to have users complete a missing card form, such as the one shown in Exhibit 2.18. By doing so, the company has evidence of when the card provider was notified, in case there is a dispute regarding who is responsible for charges made against a card.

The remainder of this section addresses the system of procedures and forms needed to ensure that all aspects of a procurement card program are controlled properly. An overview of the procurement card procedures is shown in Exhibit 2.5, which identifies the responsibilities of both card users and the manager of the card program, while also identifying all additional procedures.

The procurement card application process is itemized in the application procedure shown in Exhibit 2.6. By using the detailed process flow noted in

Exhibit 2.5 Procurement Card Program Overview

Policy/Procedure Statement   Retrieval No.: PCM-01

Subject: Procurement Card Program Overview

1. PURPOSE AND SCOPE

This document provides an overview of the procurement card program as well as the range of related procedures and forms associated with the program.

2. OVERVIEW

The corporate procurement card program is intended to simplify the purchasing of low-cost items that would otherwise require a purchase requisition and the involvement of the purchasing department. Purchases under $2,500 generally fall into this category. Card users are nominated by department managers and approved by the purchasing card manager. Expanded purchasing limits require the approval of successively higher levels of company managers, depending on the desired limits.

3. CARD USER RESPONSIBILITIES

Inappropriate procurement card use can result in significant losses for a company, so the designation of their use is a serious matter. Users are expected to use these cards with the highest sense of ethics. The following rules apply to users of company purchasing cards:

- Do not use procurement cards for personal transactions.
- Do not use procurement cards for purchases on Internet auction sites, even if the purchases are intended for company use.
- Do not use procurement cards to acquire capital items, such as machinery, computer hardware, or vehicles.
- Do not share the card with any other person.
- Only use a procurement card to purchase items for which your department is responsible for payment.
- Do not receive cash back for procurement card credit transactions; all credits must be processed through the purchasing card.
- Do not split charges into smaller amounts in order to stay within the purchasing restrictions of your purchasing card.
- Promptly forward monthly account statements with attached receipts to the procurement card manager.
- Promptly report transaction discrepancies or a lost procurement card to the processing bank.
- Improper use of purchasing cards will result in revocation of one's card and possible additional disciplinary action.

(continues)

Exhibit 2.5   *(Continued)*

4.   PROCUREMENT CARD MANAGER RESPONSIBILITIES

The procurement card program is managed by the procurement card manager (PCM). This position is responsible for a payment method that may cover more than 25% of all company expenditures; for that reason, this is a highly responsible position. The following rules apply to the PCM:

- Carefully investigate nominated procurement card users prior to authorizing card issuances to them.
- Monitor the results of disputed transaction charges to ensure that the company does not pay for items for which it is not responsible.
- Monitor card usage to ensure that cards are being used appropriately.
- Monitor remaining unused department budgets to ensure that managers are aware of approaching budgetary limits.
- Ensure that procurement cards used by departing or transferring employees are properly cancelled and related receipts forwarded to department managers.

5.   DESCRIPTION OF PROCEDURES

The following procedures apply to the procurement card program:

Retrieval No.	Procedure Name	Description
PCM-02	Application for Purchasing Card	Used to apply for a corporate procurement card from the purchasing department
PCM-03	Purchasing with the Purchasing Card	Used to instruct in the daily use of the procurement card
PCM-04	Monthly Statement Reconciliation	Used to reconcile the monthly procurement card statement to one's payment records
PCM-05	Purchasing Card Line Item Rejection	Used to reject specific transaction line items on monthly billing statements
PCM-06	Request Altered Spending Limits	Used to request changes to the spending limits on procurement cards
PCM-07	Report Lost Purchasing Card	Used to provide necessary information to the processing bank regarding a lost or stolen procurement card
PCM-08	Moved or Terminated Card User	Used to describe the correct procedures for handling procurement cards if their users either change departments or leave the company

Exhibit 2.6 Procurement Card Application Procedure

Policy/Procedure Statement Retrieval No.: PCM-02

Subject: Application for Procurement Card

1. PURPOSE AND SCOPE

This procedure is used by company employees to apply for a corporate procurement card from the purchasing department.

2. PROCEDURES

2.1 Access the Procurement Card Application Form (Employee)

Go to the corporate intranet site and access the "Employee Forms" button. Print the "Procurement Card Application" form. The form is stored in Adobe PDF format, so download the Adobe Acrobat Reader from *www.adobe.com* if your computer cannot read the PDF document. The form is shown in Exhibit 2.7.

2.2 Complete the Procurement Card Application Form (Employee)

1. In Section A of the form, complete all fields containing information about your name, title, department, department code, and department mailing address. Also include your contact information: e-mail address, phone number, and fax number. In addition, enter your date of birth and social security number. Further, enter the default expense account number to which you would like to have your procurement card charges debited. Finally, sign and date where indicated at the bottom of the section, and have the department manager do the same.

2. Section B contains the authorized spending limits for your procurement card, as assigned by the Procurement Card Manager. These include the maximum single purchase amount, total monthly purchase amount, and total number of authorization transactions allowed per day.

3. Section C of the form contains approval and processing information, which is for use by the Procurement Card Manager.

4. Forward the completed form to the procurement card manager at the address noted at the bottom of the form.

2.3 Process Application (Procurement Card Manager)

1. Verify that the default expense account number listed on the form is a valid account number for the applying department, with budgeted funding assigned to it.

2. Verify that the manager approval signature is by an authorized department manager.

3. Verify that the applicant is applying for a procurement card for the first time. If there have been multiple applications, determine why a rejection occurred in the past, or if a credit card was issued and then revoked.

(continues)

Exhibit 2.6 *(Continued)*

4. Enter the single purchase, monthly purchase total, and number of authorizations allowed per day in Section B of the form, based on company policy regarding purchasing volumes for the position held by the applicant.

5. Sign and date the form in Section C.

6. Enter the date when the form is sent to the procurement card provider, and fax the form to the provider. File the form in the pending file.

2.4 Issue Procurement Card (Procurement Card Manager)

1. Upon receipt of the procurement card, withdraw the associated form from the pending file and note on it in Section C the date when the card was received.

2. Notify the applicant of the next procurement card orientation meeting.

3. Make a copy of the procurement card application and retain it. File the original in the permanent procurement card file.

4. At the orientation meeting, issue the procurement card to the applicant as well as the copy of the procurement card application.

---

the procedure, it is less likely that a procurement card will be issued inappropriately. Exhibit 2.7 shows the application form.

The procedure shown in Exhibit 2.8 walks procurement card users through the process of making ongoing purchases with their cards, including the important control step of entering each purchase in a transaction log (a sample of which is shown in Exhibit 2.9).

The monthly statement reconciliation procedure shown in Exhibit 2.10 encompasses several of the most important control points used in a procurement card program, including controls for reconciliation, missing receipts, rejected line items, and supervisory approval of the completed reconciliation.

The sample procurement card account statement shown in Exhibit 2.11 is a custom-designed statement. The company has received from the procurement card supplier an electronic feed of all purchases and has integrated it into the account statement. This format is useful for presenting to card users a combination of spending limits, detail on purchases made, and a reconciliation checklist.

The procurement card missing receipt form shown in Exhibit 2.12 is especially useful for establishing documentation that card users have incurred expenses for legitimate business uses, which may become evidential

Exhibit 2.7 Procurement Card Application Form

Procurement Card Application

[Company Name]

Applicant Information: ⒜

    Applicant Name/Title: _____ / _____

    Department Name/Number: _____ / _____

    Department Mailing Address: _____

    _____

    Applicant Contact Information:

      E-mail: _____

      Phone: _____

      Fax: _____

    Applicant Identification Information:

    Date of Birth: _____

    S/S Number: _____

    Default Expense Account Number: ☐☐☐☐☐☐

    Applicant Signature: _____ Date: _____

    Manager Signature: _____ Date: _____

Do Not Write Below This Line

Ⓑ | Single Purchase | Monthly Purchase Total | Authorizations Allowed/Day

Spending Limits: $_____ $_____ #_____

Processing and Approval Information: Ⓒ

    Procurement Card Manager Approval/Date: _____ / _____

    Date Sent to Card Provider/Received From: _____ / _____

Mail To:

    Procurement Card Manager
    Company Name
    Street
    City, State, Zip Code   Form No. PUR-193

Exhibit 2.8   Purchasing with the Procurement Card

Policy/Procedure Statement   Retrieval No.:   PCM-03

Subject: Purchasing with the Procurement Card

1.   PURPOSE AND SCOPE

This procedure is used by company employees to determine the correct processing of daily purchases with a procurement card.

2.   PROCEDURES

2.1   Pay with Procurement Card (Employee)

1. When first making a purchase with a procurement card, inquire if the supplier accepts credit card payments. If so, pay with the card if the purchase is less than the per-transaction purchasing maximum for the card. When making the transaction, give the supplier the address listed on the purchasing card billing statement.

2. If a purchase is declined by the supplier, refer the matter to the procurement card manager. This may call for an increase in the authorized spend limit on the card. (See the "Request Altered Spending Limits" procedure.)

3. Always obtain an itemized receipt for all purchases made with the procurement card. Receipts will be used at month-end to verify purchases listed on the procurement card statement.

4. Log all receipts into the procurement card transaction log, which is shown in Exhibit 2.9. The "Trans. No." is a sequential numbering of the transactions on the page. The "Date" field is for the date of the purchase transaction as noted on the supplier's receipt. Also fill in the remaining descriptive information as noted in the form. This form is available on the company intranet site.

5. Verify that items ordered are actually received. It is easiest to do this by requiring that all purchases be delivered directly to you. If there is evidence of nonreceipt, dispute supplier billings as noted later in the "Procurement Card Line Item Rejection" procedure in Exhibit 2.13.

Exhibit 2.9   Procurement Card Transaction Log

Trans. No.	Date	Supplier Name	Purchased Item Description	Total Price	Comments
1	5/1/06	Acme Electric Supply	200w floodlights	$829.00	
2	5/2/06	Wiley Wire Supply	Breaker panels	741.32	
3	5/5/06	Coyote Electrical	12 gauge cable	58.81	Returned for credit
4	5/7/06	Roadrunner Electric	Foot light trim	940.14	

Exhibit 2.10 Monthly Statement Reconciliation Procedure

Policy/Procedure Statement   Retrieval No.:   PCM-04
Subject: Monthly Statement Reconciliation

1. PURPOSE AND SCOPE

This procedure is used by company employees to reconcile the monthly procurement card statement to their payment records.

2. PROCEDURES

2.1 Review Monthly Billing Statement (Employee)

1. You will receive a procurement card account statement at the end of each month. (A sample statement is shown in Exhibit 2.11.) When it arrives, compare the line items on the statement to your manual Procurement Card Transaction Log (as shown earlier in Exhibit 2.9). Verify all matching items and attach receipts to the statement for those items.

2. If any receipts are missing, contact the supplier and attempt to obtain a replacement receipt.

3. If any receipts are still missing, list them on the Procurement Card Missing Receipt form (as shown in Exhibit 2.12), which is located on the company intranet site. In Section A of this form, list your contact information, including your name, address, phone number, and fax number. In Section B, list the month and year of the procurement card account statement and reference number in which the item is listed for which you have no receipt. Then list in the expense matrix the statement line item number for each missing receipt, as well as the date and dollar amount of the expense as listed on the statement. Also fill in the supplier name and the description of the expense. Sign in Section C to certify that the expenditures with missing receipts were legitimate business expenses, and also obtain the signature of the department manager.

4. Once all line items have been reviewed, go back to Section C of the statement and write the expense account number in the "Account Number" column next to any line items that are different from the default expense account used for the card.

5. If you are disputing any line items, circle them in Section C of the statement and write "in dispute" next to them.

6. Sign and date the billing statement.

7. Make a copy of the entire expense packet and store it in a safe place. Company policy requires that you retain this document for three years. This is useful for researching possible double billings that may appear on multiple account statements.

8. Review and check off the reconciliation checklist in Section D of the statement to ensure that you have completed all reconciliation tasks.

9. Forward the statement, with attached receipts and Procurement Card Missing Receipt form, to the procurement card manager for review.

(continues)

Exhibit 2.10   *(Continued)*

Note: If you do not forward the completed packet to the accounts payable department by the required date, all charges made during the month will be charged to a default departmental expense account and the department will be charged a $100 processing fee by the accounting department.

2.2   Review Forwarded Expense Packet (Procurement Card Manager)

1. Upon receipt of each employee's expense packet, scan the list of purchased items to determine if any inappropriate purchases were made, or if there is any evidence of split purchases being made. If so, discuss the issue with the employee's manager to see if further action should be taken.

2. Promptly forward the expense packet to the accounts payable department for payment.

matter if it later becomes evident that purchases were not made for business purposes.

The procurement card line item rejection procedure noted in Exhibit 2.13 is an excellent control tool, because it identifies a number of problems caused by suppliers—unauthorized charges, altered charges, duplicate billings, credit offsets, lack of product receipt, and so on. By using this rejection procedure to monitor the types of problems encountered by card users, the purchasing department can identify which suppliers are causing problems and locate issues with the procurement card process that require improvement. Exhibit 2.14 shows the line item rejection form.

A key control over procurement cards is the purchasing limit assigned to each card, which can be divided into limits for single purchases and monthly total purchases, and the number of purchasing transactions allowed per day. The procedure shown in Exhibit 2.15 is designed to restrict the amount of spending limits granted, since it requires a large number of authorizations, depending on the spending level requested. Exhibit 2.16 shows the change request form.

The procedure in Exhibit 2.17 and the related form in Exhibit 2.18 address the notification system needed to report on a lost procurement card. It is especially useful for providing a record of exactly when a card was lost and how the replacement card is to be delivered to the card user.

Terminating a procurement card in a timely manner is another crucial control, which is addressed in the procedure shown in Exhibit 2.19. This

Exhibit 2.11 Sample Monthly Procurement Card Account Statement

Procurement Card Statement of Account

[Company Name]

A

Statement Date: May 2006   **Statement Reference Number:** 12345678

Cardholder: Mary Follett

123 Sunny Lane

Anywhere, USA 01234

Monthly Purchase Authorizations

B

	Single Purchase	Total	Allowed per Day
Spending Limits:	$2,500	$25,000	10

C **Transaction Detail:**

Transaction Date	Reference Number	Supplier	SIC Code	Account Number	Amount
5/1/06	1234567AB043	Acme Electric Supply	7312	—	$829.00
5/2/06	2345678CD054	Wiley Wire Supply	7312	—	741.32
5/5/06	3456789DE065	Coyote Electrical	7312	040-1720	58.81
5/7/06	4567890EF076	Roadrunner Electric	7312	—	940.14
				Total	$2,569.27

D **Reconciliation Checklist:**

☐ I have reconciled this statement of account.

☐ I have attached all receipts to this statement of account.

☐ I have completed and attached the Procurement Card Missing Receipt form for all line items for which I have no receipts.

☐ I have entered account numbers in the "Account Number" column for those line items that vary from the default expense account number.

☐ I have circled any items currently under dispute with suppliers.

☐ I have signed and dated this statement of account.

☐ I have retained a copy and understand that it must be retained for three years.

Card Holder Signature: _____ Date: _____

Exhibit 2.12   Procurement Card Missing Receipt Form

Procurement Card Missing Receipt Form

[Company Name]

A **Your Contact Information:**

Name: _____   Address Line 1: _____

Phone Number: _____   Address Line 2: _____

Fax Number: _____

B **Account Statement Information:**

Statement Month/Year: _____ / _____

Statement Reference Number: _____

Line Item Number	Line Item Date	Line Item Amount	Supplier Name	Description

C I certify that the above expenditures were legitimate business expenditures on behalf of the company.

Card Holder
Signature: _____   Date: _____

Department Manager
Signature: _____   Date: _____

Form PUR-196

Exhibit 2.13 Procurement Card Line Item Rejection Procedure

Policy/Procedure Statement Retrieval No.: PCM-05

Subject: Procurement Card Line Item Rejection

1. PURPOSE AND SCOPE

This procedure is used by company employees to reject specific transaction line items on their monthly billing statements.

2. PROCEDURES

2.1 Review Monthly Billing Statement (Employee)

When you receive the monthly billing statement from the procurement card provider, carefully review all line items and verify that all charges match your purchasing records. If there are any discrepancies calling for rejection of specific line items, go to the following step.

2.2 Complete the Line Item Rejection Form (Employee)

1. Go to the corporate intranet site and access the "Procurement Card Line Item Rejection" form (shown in Exhibit 2.14).

2. In Section A of the form, fill in your contact information under the "Your Contact Information" heading. Also specify your card number under the "Dispute Information" heading, as well as the number, date, dollar amount, and supplier name for the line item you are disputing. Please note that a separate form must be used for each line item.

3. In Section B of the form, check off the box next to the dispute description most closing matching the problem you have encountered. Please follow the instructions next to the checked box, either to attach a receipt or to include additional detail regarding the nature of the problem.

4. In Section C of the form, sign and date the form. Make a copy of the form. Send the original to the purchasing card provider in accordance with the mailing or fax instructions noted at the bottom of the section, and send the copy to the procurement card manager.

Exhibit 2.14   Procurement Card Line Item Rejection Form

Procurement Card Line Item Rejection Form

| **A** | **Your Contact Information: Dispute Information:** |

Name: _____	Card Number: _____
Phone Number: _____	Line Item Number: _____
Fax Number: _____	Line Item Date: _____
Address Line 1: _____	Line Item Amount: _____
Address Line 2: _____	Supplier Name: _____

B   Please check the box next to the reason for your line item rejection, and add explanations as requested. Please sign and mail **or** fax the completed form to the location indicated at the bottom of this form.

☐ I did not authorize the purchasing transaction represented by this line item.

☐ I have a receipt indicating a different amount than was charged in this line item.
(Attach a copy of the receipt.)

☐ I have already been billed for this amount in a previous account statement.
Date of the previous charge: _____

☐ I have a credit voucher offsetting this line item, but it does not appear on the account statement.
(Attach a copy of the credit voucher.)

☐ I have not received the goods ordered or have returned them.
Details of the dispute:
_____
_____

☐ I am disputing this line item for other reasons.
Details of the dispute:
_____
_____

C   Signature: _____   Date: _____

Mail To: **Fax To: (111) 111-1111**
 Bank Name
 Bank Address
 City, State, Zip

Form No. PUR-194

Exhibit 2.15 Altered Spending Limits Request Procedure

Policy/Procedure Statement Retrieval No.: PCM-06

Subject: Request Altered Spending Limits

1. PURPOSE AND SCOPE

This procedure is used by company employees to request changes to the spending limits on their procurement cards.

2. PROCEDURES

2.1 Review Monthly Billing Statement (Employee)

1. Each procurement card is limited in terms of the total monthly allowable spending as well as smaller daily limits and in terms of the number of authorized purchases per day. If your regular purchasing patterns are being impacted by these limits, fill out the Procurement Card Spending Limit Change Request form (shown in Exhibit 2.16).

2. In Section A of the form, enter your name, phone number, fax number, and address.

3. In Section B of the form, enter the procurement card number in the squares provided.

4. In Section C of the form, enter the requested spending limit changes. If you are not requesting a change in all three of the limitation areas, enter "N/A" in the unused fields.

5. In Section D of the form, obtain approval signatures in accordance with the approval policy in the signature table.

6. Retain a copy of the form and forward the original to the procurement card manager.

2.2 Complete the Procurement Card Spending Limit Change Request Form (Procurement Card Manager)

1. Verify that the signed approval level on the form matches the requested spending limit, as per the company policy on procurement card monthly spending limits, which follows:

   - $10,000 limit—department manager approval
   - $10,001–$25,000 limit—Operations Vice President approval
   - $25,000+ limit—Chief Operating Officer approval

2. If the required signatures are missing, return the form to the relevant department manager with an explanatory note. Otherwise, sign and date the form and make a copy. Forward the original to the procurement card bank to have the revised purchasing levels updated for the procurement card.

3. At month-end, request from the bank a summary statement of authorization levels for all procurement cards. Verify that the requesting employee's card spending limits have been changed. If not, follow up with the bank.

Exhibit 2.16   Procurement Card Spending Limit Change Request Form

---

Procurement Card Spending Limit Change Request Form
[Company Name]

| A |

Your Contact Information:

Name: _____   Address Line 1: _____

Phone Number: _____   Address Line 2: _____

Fax Number: _____

| B |

Procurement Card Number:

▢▢▢▢ - ▢▢▢▢ - ▢▢▢▢ - ▢▢▢▢

| C |

Requested Spending Limits:

Single Purchase	Monthly Purchase Total	Authorizations Allowed per Day
$ _____	$ _____	$ _____

| D |

Authorization Signatures:

Monthly Spending Limit	Authorized Approver	Signature	Print Name	Date
$10,000	Dept. Manager	_____	_____	_____
$10,001–$25,000	Operations Vice President	_____	_____	_____
$25,000+	Chief Operating Officer	_____	_____	_____

| E |

Procurement Card Manager Approval:

Signature	Print Name	Date

Form PUR-195

Exhibit 2.17 Lost Procurement Card Reporting Procedure

Policy/Procedure Statement   Retrieval No.:   PCM-07

Subject: Report Lost Procurement Card

1. PURPOSE AND SCOPE

This procedure is used by company employees to provide necessary information to the processing bank regarding a lost or stolen procurement card.

2. PROCEDURES

2.1 Notify Bank Regarding Lost Card (Employee)

Notify the card-issuing bank as soon as you realize that your procurement card is missing. Write down the name of the person you contact as well as the date and time when the contact was made.

2.2 Complete Missing Procurement Card Form (Employee)

1. Download the Missing Procurement Card form from the company intranet site (as shown in Exhibit 2.7).
2. Complete the contact information shown in Section A of the form.
3. In Section B, check off the appropriate box to indicate what happened to the card.
4. In Section C, enter the card number in the boxes provided. If you do not have this information, check the box immediately below the spaces provided for the card number.
5. Based on your notification call to the bank, enter in Section D the name of the person contacted as well as the date and time when the call occurred.
6. In Section E, check the box indicating how you would like to have a replacement card delivered to you. If the shipment is by overnight delivery, include your department's account number to which the delivery cost will be charged.
7. Sign and date the form.
8. Forward the completed form to the procurement card manager.
9. If you locate your original purchasing card at a later date, cut it in half and send it to the procurement card manager.

2.3 Report Missing Procurement Card Information (Procurement Card Manager)

1. Upon receipt of the completed Missing Procurement Card form from the employee, review it for accuracy and forward it to the bank.
2. File the form in the lost cards file. On a monthly basis, transfer the information from all newly received missing procurement card forms to a lost cards tracking spreadsheet.
3. Review the spreadsheet to determine if some employees are losing a disproportionate number of procurement cards. If so, discuss the situation with the employee's manager to determine if procurement card privileges should be revoked.

Exhibit 2.18   Missing Procurement Card Form

Missing Procurement Card Form

[Company Name]

| A | **Your Contact Information:** |

Name: _____   Address Line 1: _____

Phone Number: _____   Address Line 2: _____

Fax Number: _____

| B | **Loss Information:** |

☐ Card was stolen.

☐ Card was lost.

☐ Other (describe): _____

| C | **Procurement Card Number:** |

☐☐☐☐ - ☐☐☐☐ - ☐☐☐☐ - ☐☐☐☐

☐ I do not have a record of the procurement card number.

| D | **Bank Notification Information:** |

Name of person contacted at bank:

_____

Date of contact: _____   Time of contact: _____

| E | **Card Replacement Information:** |

☐ Send me a replacement card by regular mail.

☐ Send me a replacement card by overnight delivery.

My FedEx account number is: _____

| F | Card Holder |

Signature: _____   Date: _____

Form PUR-197

Exhibit 2.19   Moved or Terminated Card User Notification Procedure

---

Policy/Procedure Statement   Retrieval No.:   PCM-08

Subject: Moved or Terminated Card User

1.   **PURPOSE AND SCOPE**

This procedure is used by company employees to determine the correct procedures for handling purchasing cards if their users either change departments or leave the company.

2.   **PROCEDURES**

2.1   Handling of Purchasing Card for Departing Employee (Employee)

1. If the card user moves to a different location or leaves the company, notify the procurement card manager and the department manager of the effective date of this event.

2. Collect all receipts related to purchases made since the last account statement, sorted by date of purchase, and turn them over to the department manager.

3. Cut up the card and properly dispose of it.

2.2   Processing of Final Account Statement (Department Manager)

1. The department manager is responsible for the reconciliation of the final account statement for the departed employee's purchasing card. The department manager should reconcile the statement as per the "Monthly Statement Reconciliation" procedure.

2. The department manager initials the reconciled expense packet before forwarding it to the procurement card manager and also should prominently note on the form the departure date of the employee.

---

procedure covers disposition of the card itself as well as the processing of the final statement of account.

2–5 Use Electronic Payments

There is a relatively small body of controls in use for electronic payments between business partners, because these payments typically have been between related parties or parties having done business with each other in significant volume over a long period of time. This familiarity has been substituted for control points. Nonetheless, given the large amounts of money involved and the rapidly expanding use of electronic payments, this is an area in need of the most stringent possible controls. A reasonable set of controls over the standard electronic payment process is noted in Exhibit 2.20, with additional supporting controls noted later in this section.

The controls shown in the flowchart are described in the bullet points that follow, in sequence from the top of the flowchart to the bottom.

- *Restrict access to master vendor file*. For those electronic payments being made automatically by the accounting software, it is important to keep tight control over changes to the vendor master file, since someone could access the file and alter the bank account information to which payments are being sent.
- *Require signed approval document for manually initiated electronic payments*. In a high-volume payment environment, nearly all electronic payments are routed through the accounting software, which handles the payments automatically. However, since a manually initiated payment falls outside the controls already imposed on the regular accounts payable process, the addition of an approval document is mandatory, preferably requiring multiple approval signatures.
- *Verify ACH debit filter with bank*. If the business arrangement with a supplier is for the supplier to initiate an ACH (Automated Clearing House) debit from the company's account, rather than the company initiating the transfer to the supplier, then the company should verify that it has authorized the bank to allow a specific supplier to debit an account.
- *Require password access to payment software*. It is necessary not only to enforce tightly limited access to the software used to initiate electronic

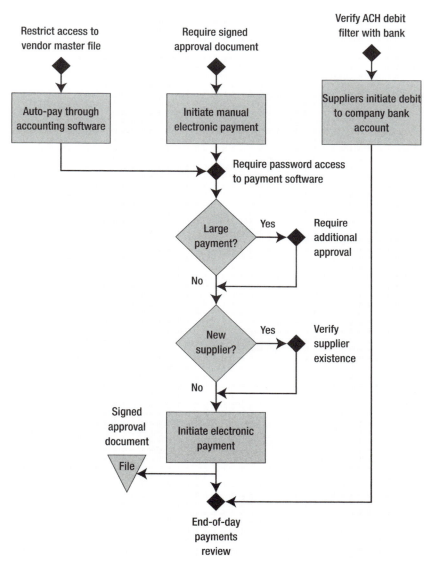

Exhibit 2.20   System of Controls for Wire Transfers

payments, but also to ensure that passwords are replaced on a frequent basis. This is a critical control, and should be rigorously enforced.

- *Require additional approvals.* Additional approvals are useful in some electronic payment situations. Certainly a very large payment is grounds for an additional approval step, as would also be the case for a large check payment. Another approval should be required whenever a new supplier is set up for electronic payment, since this is an excellent spot to detect the initiation of payments to a shell company. The additional approval could be linked to the generation of a credit report on the supplier, to verify its existence as a valid business entity. The highest level of control over electronic payments would be to require dual approvals for all such payments, though this may prove too onerous for ongoing business operations.

- *Require an end-of-day payments review.* A standard detection control should be to have a third party who is unrelated to the electronic payments process review all payments made at the end of each day. This review should encompass a comparison of authorizing documents to the actual amounts paid, as well as verification that payments are made to the correct supplier accounts.

The preceding set of controls relate only to the process of issuing an electronic payment to a supplier or allowing a supplier to debit the company's bank account, and do not address such problems as unauthorized account debits and the sheer size of potentially incorrect or fraudulent payments. The next controls address these additional issues.

- *Impose an outright debit block on all company accounts.* If the company does not wish to incur any risk of having a third party initiate a debit transaction against one of its bank accounts, it can impose a blanket debit block on those accounts, thereby preventing debit transactions from posting to a company account. A result of this control is that all electronic payments must be initiated solely by the company, not its trading partners.

- *Request a daily cumulative limit for authorized trading partner debits.* Even if a company has installed ACH debit filters that authorize only certain suppliers to initiate an ACH debit, there is still a risk that the employees of an authorized supplier could fraudulently initiate a very large ACH debit. To mitigate this risk, the company's bank can impose a daily cumulative limit on those suppliers who are allowed to initiate account debits.

- *Request notification of duplicate debits.* If a supplier initiates a debit transaction that is identical to one posted in the past day or two, there is an increased risk that this could be a duplicate charge. To reduce the risk of this problem going undetected, have the bank notify the company whenever a duplicate debit is posted or (even better) prior to posting.

- *Use a separate bank account as the source of electronic payments.* Because there is a risk of making extremely large fraudulent electronic payments, a useful control is to use a separate bank account as the source of electronic payments, with cash levels kept only high enough to fund those electronic payments made during the normal course of business, based on historical patterns. If an extremely large electronic payment is due to be made, this should initiate additional perusal of the transaction before additional cash is shifted to the account from which the payment will be made. To achieve a greater level of control, the person responsible for shifting funds into the electronic payments account should not be the same person who initiates or approves electronic payments.

2–6 Use Evaluated Receipt Settlement

Evaluated receipt settlement is an alternative approach to the traditional accounts payable process. Under evaluated receipt settlement, a company pays its suppliers based on receipt data rather than the supplier invoice. By doing so, the supplier invoice is eliminated from the three-way matching process, while the receiving staff is allowed to match receipts against online purchase orders. The result is no matching process at all, with the computer system automatically making payments based on the quantities received and the per-unit prices specified in the initiating purchase order. This is a much more efficient process than three-way matching, since all manual processing steps can be completely eliminated from the accounts payable process.

The evaluated receipts settlement approach is used primarily for purchases related to the cost of goods sold, since it requires training of suppliers to submit a specific set of information on packing slips that occasional suppliers may be less willing to do. Consequently, the normal three-way matching process is still likely to be retained for incidental, maintenance and repair, and capital purchases, so the control issues here should be considered additions to the standard computerized accounts payable system, not a replacement of them.

The key procurement card controls are enumerated in Exhibit 2.21, where controls are summarized next to the small black diamonds. The process flow begins with the issuance of a purchase order to a supplier, who uses it as authorization to make a delivery to the company, along with a packing slip containing the purchase order number, packing slip number, quantity delivered, and unit of measure. Once the delivery is received, the company's computer system verifies that the reported packing slip number is not a duplicate, that the referenced purchase order number exists and covers the delivered quantity, and that the reported unit of measure matches the one used in the purchase order. This is intended to be a highly automated process, so manual intervention in any of these control points is discouraged. Instead, the MRP system automatically issues the purchase order, supplier packing slip information is bar coded for simplified scanning into the receiving system, and all subsequent controls are handled automatically by the computer system. The only exception is a possibility of manual intervention if there is a conflict between the units of measure used by the two business partners.

The controls noted in the flowchart are described in the next bullet points, in sequence from the top of the flowchart to the bottom.

- *Mandatory purchase order authorization.* The purchase order lies at the core of the evaluated receipts settlement process, since it initiates each transaction and represents the only purchase authorization in the entire process. Issuing purchase orders is best left to the purchasing software for routine materials purchases, with manually generated purchase orders needed only for acquisitions falling outside of the MRP system.

- *Automatic rejection of duplicate packing slip numbers.* If the receiving staff has already recorded a packing slip number and then receives another delivery with the same packing slip number, this is a strong indicator that the supplier has mistakenly issued a duplicate delivery, which should be rejected. However, the rejected delivery could be for a needed

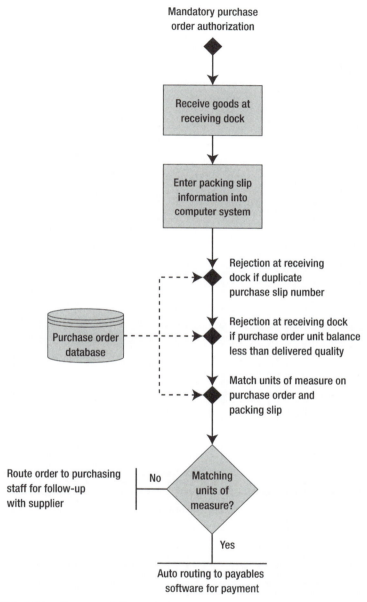

Exhibit 2.21   System of Controls for Evaluated Receipts Settlement

item, so this control can be modified to require a call from the receiving staff directly to the supplier's shipping department to clear up the problem. This control is handled automatically by the computer system.

- *Automatic rejection if purchase order unit balance is less than delivered quantity.* The receiving staff should reject a delivery if the authorized quantity is less than the delivered quantity. However, this rejection is subject to the percentage variation in delivered quantities, as specified in the master item number file. For example, if the delivered quantity is 9 percent higher than the authorized limit and the predetermined delivery variance is 10 percent for this item, then the computer system will accept the delivery. Also, depending on the circumstances, the receiving staff may be authorized to break down any deliveries to extract the maximum authorized quantity and return the remainder to the supplier. This control is handled automatically by the computer system.

- *Automated comparison of packing slip units of measure to purchase order units of measure.* There are rare situations when the supplier specifies a different unit of measure on its packing slip from what was specified in the purchase order, which can result in payment disputes. This usually is caused by a supplier error in creating the packing slip, so it is customary to accept the delivery but to route the problem to the purchasing staff, who notify the supplier of the problem. The receiving staff may also be assigned this chore. This comparison task is handled automatically by the computer system.

The preceding set of controls relate only to the step-by-step process of evaluating the packing slip that accompanies a delivery, and does not address such issues as control over the purchase order system, manual reviews of delivered quantities, how to handle supplier invoices, and so on. The next controls address these additional issues.

- *Restrict access to the purchase order database.* The evaluated receipts settlement process is driven entirely by issued purchase orders, so it is critical to maintain a high level of control over access to the purchase order database. Controls should include password-only access, frequent password changes, and a procedure to cancel system access if a purchasing person leaves the company.

- *Audit purchase orders issued by the MRP system.* The evaluated receipts system relies heavily on the ability of the MRP system to accurately and reliably issue purchase orders without human intervention. Though a possible control over the risk of incorrect orders is to have the purchasing staff manually monitor all purchase orders generated by the MRP system, this imposes inefficiency on a system that is supposed to be fully automated. An alternative is to have the system flag the purchasing staff if orders are generated for excessively high dollar values or quantities. A third alternative is to have the internal audit staff periodically examine issued purchase orders to see if errors in the supporting production schedule, bills of material, and inventory records are causing incorrect purchase orders to be issued.

- *Audit all manually issued purchase orders.* The primary control over evaluated receipts settlement is tight control over who is allowed to issue purchase orders, but what if even the authorized purchasing staff is tempted to commit fraud by entering manual purchase orders into the system? A reasonable control is to schedule periodic internal audits that look for improper orders being placed by the purchasing staff. These audits can focus on orders being placed for unusual quantities, items not normally purchased, and orders placed outside of business hours (all indicators of problematic orders).

- *Report on suppliers not sending packing slips in bar-coded format.* It is not an outright control weakness if suppliers issue handwritten packing slips. However, the receiving staff must enter this packing slip information into the computer system by hand, which introduces the risk of incorrect data entry (especially since the receiving staff is not typically trained in this function). Consequently, it makes sense to track which suppliers are not using bar-coded packing slips and to contact them regularly to encourage them to do so.

- *Audit supplier reporting of quantities shipped.* Because of the high level of automation used in an evaluated receipts settlement system, the assumption is that the corporate industrial engineering staff has already approved suppliers to send shipments without any need for a review of quantities shipped. However, there is always a risk that delivered quantities do not match the quantities listed on the packing slip, so the internal audit staff should periodically compare actual delivered quantities to reported quantities and inform the engineering department of significant discrepancies.

- *Issue updates to suppliers regarding changes in reporting requirements.* The evaluated receipts settlement process is a difficult one to set up, because the payment process is radically different from what suppliers are accustomed to seeing. Consequently, any subsequent changes to the process require a very high level of communication with the supplier base to ensure that suppliers can issue the information to the company that is needed to ensure that they are paid correctly and on time.

- *Automatically reject all supplier invoices referencing a purchase order number.* Even if every part of the evaluated receipts settlement process operates properly, what if a supplier mistakenly mails the company an invoice when it is no longer supposed to do so? Few companies are willing to throw away *all* incoming invoices, on the grounds that not all items received are ordered with a purchase order. Consequently, there must be a system for sorting through the remaining invoices arriving in the payables department to see which ones should be paid through the old payables system. The easiest approach is to immediately reject all supplier invoices that reference a purchase order number, since the deliveries addressed by these invoices obviously should have been paid through the evaluated receipts settlement system. Another approach is noted in the next bullet point.

- *Enter an evaluated receipts flag in the vendor master file for all designated suppliers.* As just noted in the last bullet point, companies sometimes still receive invoices from suppliers, even though the payables system does not require them anymore. To keep the payables staff from double paying based on these invoices, it is very useful to create a flag in the vendor master file that indicates which suppliers are paid solely through the evaluated receipts settlement system. If this flag is turned on, then any invoices received from these suppliers will be automatically rejected by the computer system.

In general, the evaluated receipts settlement process is designed to be a highly efficient one that can strip massive quantities of labor from the accounts payable process. However, if control points that require manual intervention are added to the process flow, the high level of process efficiency will be lessened, making the entire process less cost-effective. Consequently, the best controls are those that can be completed automatically by the computer system, with occasional audits to ensure that information accuracy is sufficiently high to keep significant losses from occurring.

2–7 Automate Repetitive Payments

Usually a small subset of payments is in exactly the same amount each month, and the payables department typically handles these payments by setting them up in the accounting software as recurring payments that require no three-way matching. Examples of such payments are rent, copier leases, and garnishments.

There are two problems with the automation of recurring payments. First, the computer system may continue issuing payments even after the underlying obligation has disappeared. Second, some payments may have escalation clauses that call for changes in the recurring payment, which the accounting staff may miss if it is relying on the computer system to make payments. A few simple controls can alleviate these problems.

- *Set up payment termination dates in the accounting software.* Most accounts payable systems allow users to set a termination date on a set of recurring payments. If this is not the case, then create a list of payment termination dates and include it in the month-end closing procedure, so the accounting staff is forced to review it once a month.

- *Create a payment escalation schedule.* If a recurring payment has a scheduled payment change at some point in the future, include this information in a central list of payment escalations and in the month-end closing procedure. This forces the accounting staff to review the escalation schedule every month.

- *Terminate payments in the accounting software on escalation dates.* Another way to remind the accounting staff to update recurring payments is to initially set up recurring payments in the accounting software to terminate as of their escalation dates. This forces the accounting staff to review the underlying documentation and reset the recurring payment schedule in the accounting software. However, this control can backfire if the accounting system does not issue a warning that a payment has been automatically terminated; if this goes unnoticed, the company will probably miss the next payment entirely.

Summary

This chapter began with a review of the standard controls used in a completely paper-based accounts payable system. Many of these controls have found their way into the computerized accounting systems that are also described in this chapter, probably because the accountants responsible for payer-based systems were the same ones who converted their systems to a computerized format, and they simply copied the same controls over to the new systems. As a result, many of today's computerized accounts payable systems contain unnecessary controls that interfere with the orderly and efficient flow of payables transactions. Examining older computerized systems with the objective of eliminating some of these older controls would certainly be worthwhile.

The chapter also noted a variety of changes in controls resulting from the use of key best practices in the accounts payable area: electronic payments, procurement cards, evaluated receipts, and so on. Installing any of these best practices requires significant changes to the accounts payable control structure. Though the most elaborate control structure was presented for the use of procurement cards, there is not really a major danger of financial loss in this area, since it is relatively easy to limit losses by imposing maximum expenditure levels on procurement cards. The use of electronic payments does present the risk of major financial losses (extending even to corporate bankruptcy), so it requires the most extensive and rigorously applied set of controls.

Chapter 3

Controls for Order Entry, Credit, and Shipment Best Practices

Overview

The process of creating a customer order, approving credit, picking it from stock, shipping it to the customer, and issuing an invoice is too lengthy to handle in a single chapter, so it is dealt with in three places. Controls over the order entry and shipment functions are noted in this chapter; a variety of inventory-related systems are described in Chapter 4; and the billing process is addressed in Chapter 5.

In this chapter, we address the usual baseline controls used for paper-based and computerized order entry, credit, and shipment systems, while also covering special controls needed for the receipt of electronic orders, drop-shipped orders, and shipments to customers who use evaluated receipt systems. The chapter concludes with a set of corporate-wide policies related to order entry, credit, and shipping practices.

3–1 Basic Order Entry, Credit, and Shipment Controls

It is increasingly unlikely that companies will use entirely paper-based order entry and shipment systems, but some smaller ones still use this approach. The flowchart in Exhibit 3.1 shows the basic process flow for these organizations, with the minimum set of controls needed to ensure that it operates properly. In essence, the order entry person converts a customer's purchase order into a sales order that is used as the foundation document for credit approval, shipment, and billing. The main reasons for controls in

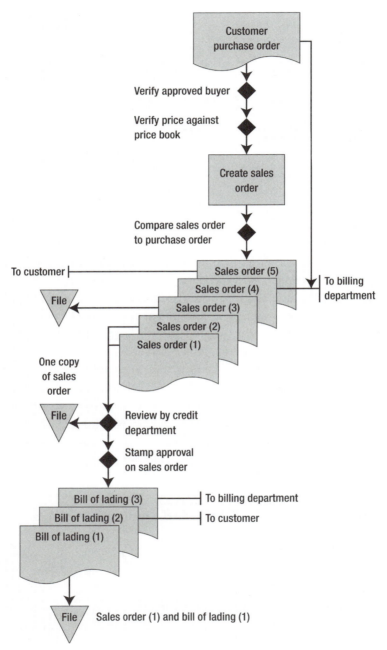

Exhibit 3.1 Basic Controls for Paper-Based Order Entry/Credit/Shipment

this process are to ensure that the initial purchase order is correctly translated into the sales order and that the order meets with the corporate credit-granting guidelines. The small black diamonds on the flowchart indicate the location of key control points in the process, with descriptions next to the diamonds.

The controls noted in the flowchart are described at greater length next, in sequence from the top of the flowchart to the bottom:

- *Verify approved buyer.* Even if the order entry staff receives an ostensibly complete purchase order document from a customer, it is possible that the person who completed and signed the purchase order is not authorized to do so by the customer's management team. This control is not frequently used, since the chances of a control problem are relatively slight in most cases. However, it may be useful when the size of the order being placed is extremely large.

- *Verify price against price book.* It is quite common for a customer to issue a purchase order for a unit price that differs from the official corporate price book. Consequently, a very useful control is to verify all purchase order line items against the corporate price book and to contact the customer regarding any discrepancies. It is also possible that the purchase order will not authorize any billing for freight or insurance costs, which may call for further communication with the customer.

- *Compare sales order to purchase order.* Once the order entry staff has completed the sales order, it may be necessary to have a second party compare the sales order to the purchase order to ensure that the information on both documents is identical. This control is more useful when the order entry staff is relatively untrained, the dollar value of items ordered is extremely high, or when customers are promised a high degree of accuracy in the fulfillment of orders placed.

- *Review by credit department.* If the order entry staff simply creates a sales order and forwards it to the warehouse for delivery, then there is a high risk that customers will default on their payments. This is an especially large problem where the gross margin on products sold is quite low, so the company will sustain a substantial loss if a customer does not pay. Accordingly, a mandatory control is to send all sales orders to the credit department for approval before any shipment is made. It is customary to bypass the credit approval process for small orders, repair and maintenance orders, and when customers have established credit lines with the company.

- *Stamp approval on sales order.* It is possible for sales orders to be fraudulently routed around the credit department and sent to the warehouse, so an approval stamp to be used on each sales order should be created. This approval stamp should include space for the signature of the credit manager and for the date when the approval was granted. The warehouse manager should not ship from any sales order that does not contain this signed approval stamp.

The order entry procedure shown in Exhibit 3.2 incorporates the control points already noted in Exhibit 3.1. This procedure contains a number of additional processing steps not shown in the flowchart.

Though the preceding controls are the basic ones needed for a paper-only order entry and shipping system, the next controls can be used to bolster the level of control over the process.

- *Verify credit limit at time of order placement.* The control point noted earlier that requires a mandatory review of all orders by the credit department can be supplemented by this control, which allows the order entry staff to verify the remaining amount of credit available under a customer's preestablished credit limit. This approach eliminates the queue time for some orders that would otherwise sit on the desk of a credit department employee. However, it also requires the ongoing tracking of available credit by the order entry staff, which can be quite difficult in a paper-based environment.

- *Prenumber sales order forms.* Only prenumbered sales order documents should be used. By doing so, the company can track which sales order numbers did not reach the billing department, which may indicate that a delivery was not invoiced.

- *Lock up unused sales order forms.* It is possible for someone to enter an order to a shell company on an unused sales order form, fraudulently stamp it as approved by the credit department, and route it to the warehouse as authorization for a delivery. Though this scenario is unlikely (since the credit authorization stamp must also be obtained), it may be useful to store all unused sales order forms in a locked file cabinet.

Exhibit 3.2 Procedure for Paper-Based Order Entry/Credit/Shipment

---

Policy/Procedure Statement   Retrieval No.:   ORD-01

Subject: Order Entry/Credit/Shipping for a Paper-Based System

1.   PURPOSE AND SCOPE

This procedure is used by the order entry, credit, and shipping departments to process customer orders in a paper-based environment.

2.   PROCEDURES

2.1   Verify Approved Buyer (Order Entry Clerk)

1. Upon receipt of the purchase order, compare the name of the purchasing agent on the purchase order to the approved purchasing agent name in the customer file. If the name is different, contact the customer and verify that the purchasing agent is authorized to issue the purchase order.

2. If the purchasing agent is authorized to issue purchase orders, stamp the purchase order as approved and continue with the next procedure step.

3. If the purchasing agent is not approved, send a copy of the purchase order to the manager of the customer's purchasing department. In addition, write the name of the unapproved purchasing agent on the department's master list of unapproved buyers. Finally, perforate the purchase order with a Void stamp and file it in the customer file.

2.2   Verify Price Against Price Book (Order Entry Clerk)

1. Match the prices listed on the customer purchase order to the prices listed in the corporate price book, taking into account all volume price breaks and special deals.

2. If there are any variances between the two sets of prices, contact the customer and request a replacement purchase order. File the existing purchase order until the replacement order arrives. At that time, perforate the old purchase order with a Void stamp, write the number of the replacement purchase order on it, and file it in the customer file.

2.3   Create Sales Order (Order Entry Clerk)

1. Unlock the storage cabinet containing blank sales orders and take the topmost sales order from the cabinet.

2. Transfer all information from the purchase order to the sales order, and add to it the company part number for each item ordered.

3. Compare the completed sales order to the purchase order, and revise the sales order for any missing or incorrect information.

4. Send one copy of the sales order to the customer, one to the billing department, and one to file. Send the remaining two copies to the credit department.

(continues)

Exhibit 3.2   *(Continued)*

2.4 Review Credit (Credit Clerk)

1. If the purchase order is from a new customer, send a credit application. Upon receipt of the application, circle all incomplete items and pay particular attention to why they were not completed. Verify with each customer reference the maximum and average amounts of credit granted and used as well as any issues with slow payment. Order a credit report on the customer. If the credit report indicates that payments are being made more than 15 days past due, deny any line of credit. If payments are being made more quickly, then grant a line of credit in the amount of ___ percent of the customer's net worth. Then continue with the order approval as outlined in the next step.

2. If the purchase order is from an existing customer, verify if the amount of the order is within the customer's existing line of credit, taking into account all other unshipped approved orders and shipped orders for which payment has not yet been received. If there is sufficient credit available, remove the approval stamp from locked storage, stamp the sales order as approved, initial the stamp, and forward one copy of the sales order to the shipping department. Return the approval stamp to locked storage. Retain the second copy of the sales order for file.

2.5 Release Goods for Shipment, Prepare Bill of Lading (Shipping Clerk)

1. Verify that the sales order has been stamped as approved by the credit department. If not, return it to the credit department.

2. Copy the information on the sales order onto a picking ticket, and release the picking ticket to the warehouse staff.

3. Upon receipt of the picked items, compare the sales order to the picked items to verify that all items match the sales order.

4. If some items are not in stock, complete a three-part Backorder Request form for the missing items. Send one copy to the order entry staff for follow-up with the customer, one to the purchasing department for ordering of the missing items, and retain one copy along with a photocopy of the sales order.

5. For all items in stock, prepare a three-part bill of lading. Ship the items with one bill of lading copy attached. Send another copy to the billing department as proof of delivery. Finally, staple the sales order to the final copy of the bill of lading and file it.

6. Complete the daily shipping log and verify that all bills of lading for that day match the log. Send a copy of the log to the billing department.

- *Lock up the credit approval stamp.* For the same reasons just noted for the fraudulent use of a sales order form, the credit approval stamp should be stored in a locked file cabinet when not in use.

- *Investigate product returns.* When products are returned by customers, it is possible that an error in the order entry or shipment processes caused the return. To investigate this potential problem, compare the return documents to the customer purchase order and sales order.

- *Compare quantity ordered to amount shipped.* The standard fulfillment approach is for a warehouse staff person to use a copy of the sales order as a picking document when pulling items from the warehouse for delivery. Once picked, this control requires a second person to verify that the quantity, unit of measure, and product picked match the sales order.

The types of controls shown here for the order entry and shipping processes make it clear that a great many handoffs occur in the overall process, which not only delays order processing, but also introduces the risk that paperwork will be lost before a product is shipped. For example, the initial order must be reviewed by a supervisor, sent to the credit department, sent to the warehouse for picking, and then reviewed prior to actually being shipped. In the next section, we will see that a computerized order entry and shipment system greatly compresses the time required to complete these processes while reducing the risk of information being lost.

3–2 Controls for a Computerized Order Entry, Credit, and Shipment Environment

The order entry, credit, and shipment process flow most familiar to readers is the one shown in Exhibit 3.3. This process flow takes advantage of the basic features of a computerized accounting system, including the minimum set of controls needed to ensure that it operates properly. In comparison to the paper-based system, please note that the sales order has been completely eliminated and replaced with a computer record that is routed through the company using a work flow management system. Also, the process flow now includes extra controls that take advantage of the ability of the computer system to automatically verify such information as on-hand inventory balances and product pricing. The only paperwork generated by this process

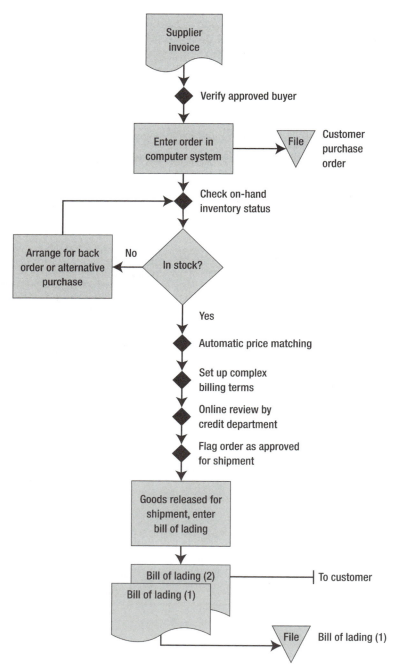

Exhibit 3.3   Controls for a Computerized Order Entry/Credit/Shipment
Environment

is the bill of lading, which is required for shipment. The small black diamonds on the flowchart indicate the location of key control points in the process, with descriptions next to the diamonds.

The controls noted in the flowchart are described at greater length next, in sequence from the top of the flowchart to the bottom.

- *Verify approved buyer.* Even if the order entry staff receives an ostensibly complete purchase order document from a customer, it is possible that the person who completed and signed the purchase order is not authorized to do so by the customer's management team. This control is not frequently used, since the chances of a control problem are relatively slight in most cases. However, it may be useful when the size of the order being placed is extremely large.

- *Check on-hand inventory status.* If the order entry computer system is linked to the current inventory balance, then the system should warn the order entry staff if there is not a sufficient quantity in stock to fulfill an order and should predict the standard lead time required to obtain additional inventory. This is a control over the company's ability to ship within its standard shipping period. A more advanced level of automation results in the computer system presenting the order entry staff with similar products that are currently in stock, which the staff can present to customers as alternative purchases.

- *Automatic price matching.* One of the best control improvements that a computer system brings to the order entry process is the ability to automatically set up product prices based on the standard corporate price book. If the information in the price book varies from the price listed on the purchase order, then the order entry staff must either obtain a supervisory override to use the alternative price or discuss the situation with the customer.

- *Set up complex billing terms.* If a sale requires unusually complex billing and payment terms, the best place to set up this information is during the initial order entry point, so the information will be available to all users of the order entry database. Ideally, the computer system will initiate invoice creation based on these payment terms automatically.

- *Online review by credit department.* If the order entry system has work flow management, then any orders entered by the order entry staff will be routed to the credit department as soon as the orders are entered. This control not only speeds up the credit review process, but also ensures that every order entered will be routed to the credit department. This control typically is modified so that orders falling below a minimum threshold are automatically approved.

• *Flag order as approved for shipment.* Once reviewed, the credit department can issue an online approval of a customer order, which the computer system then routes to the shipping department for fulfillment. The beauty of this control is that the shipping staff never sees the customer order until it has been approved, so there is minimal risk of an unapproved order inadvertently being shipped.

The order entry procedure shown in Exhibit 3.4 incorporates the control points already noted in Exhibit 3.3. This procedure contains a number of additional processing steps not shown in the flowchart.

Exhibit 3.4   Procedure for Computerized Order Entry/Credit/Shipment

Policy/Procedure Statement   Retrieval No.:   ORD-02
Subject: Order Entry/Credit/Shipment for a Computerized System

1.   PURPOSE AND SCOPE

This procedure is used by the order entry, credit, and shipping departments to process customer orders in a computerized environment.

2.   PROCEDURES

2.1   Verify Approved Buyer (Order Entry Clerk)

1. Upon receipt of the purchase order, access the vendor master file and verify the name of the purchasing agent on the purchase order. If the name is different, contact the customer and verify that the purchasing agent is authorized to issue the purchase order. If so, enter the purchasing agent's name in the vendor master file.

2. If the purchasing agent is authorized to issue purchase orders, stamp the purchase order as approved and continue with the next procedure step.

3. If the purchasing agent is not approved, e-mail a scanned image of the purchase order to the manager of the customer's purchasing department as well as to the company's internal audit department. Finally, perforate the purchase order with a Void stamp and file it in the customer file.

2.2   Enter Order in Computer System (Order Entry Clerk)

1. Access the order entry screen in the computer system and use it to enter all required information from the customer purchase order.

Exhibit 3.4 *(Continued)*

---

2. If the computer system's validation routine flags purchase order information as being potentially inaccurate, contact the customer to verify information. If the validation routine continues to reject entered information, then obtain a supervisory override. Validation problems are especially likely to occur for product pricing, shipment dates, sales taxes, and shipping charges.

3. Verify the on-hand status of inventory being ordered. If the projected delivery date is farther than ___ days in the future, notify the customer of the situation and ask if an alternative product would be acceptable, using the Related Products screen to access this information.

4. If the purchase order contains nonstandard billing terms, contact the order entry manager for approval. If granted, enter the nonstandard billing terms. If not granted, contact the customer regarding other billing options.

2.3 Conduct Online Credit Review (Credit Clerk)

1. If the automated credit decision shunts a customer order to the credit department and the order is from a first-time customer, e-mail the customer a link to an online credit application form. Once completed, e-mail a request to all customer references for the maximum and average amounts of credit granted and used as well as any issues with slow payment. Also access an online Business Information Report (BIR) from Dun & Bradstreet. If the BIR indicates that payments are being made more than 15 days past due, deny any line of credit. If payments are being made more quickly, then grant a line of credit in the amount of ___ percent of the customer's net worth. Access the customer master file and enter the maximum credit line in the Credit Limit field. Then continue with the order approval as outlined in the next step.

2. If the purchase order is from an existing customer, verify if the amount of the order is within the customer's existing line of credit, taking into account all other unshipped approved orders and shipped orders for which payment has not yet been received. If there is sufficient credit available, flag the order in the computer system as approved for credit.

2.4 Release Goods for Shipment, Prepare Bill of Lading (Shipping Clerk)

1. Print the daily shipping report to determine which customer orders have been approved for credit.

2. For each order on the daily shipping report, print a picking ticket and issue it to the warehouse staff for item picking.

3. Upon receipt of the picked items, compare the picking ticket to the picked items to verify that all items match the picking ticket.

4. For each customer order, enter all picked items in the computer system's shipment screen. When completed, print the multipart bill of lading.

5. Attach one copy of the bill of lading to the delivery, and file the remaining copy.

Though the preceding controls are the basic ones needed for a paper-only order entry and shipping system, the next controls can also be used to bolster the level of control over the process.

- *Maintain a complete audit trail.* The delivery of goods to a customer is, from the viewpoint of someone committing fraud, an avenue for obtaining goods from the company for free. There exists a variety of approaches for committing fraud. Though it is always to best to use preventive controls to ensure that fraud never occurs, the computer system should certainly record a complete audit trail for every transaction, so that auditors can investigate who entered what information and when. This detective control is vital for tracking down how a fraud was committed or how a control breach inadvertently occurred.

- *Audit orders below the credit review threshold.* The credit department does not usually have the resources to review small credit requests and so prefers to grant them automatically. This policy can be taken advantage of, if customers order in very small quantities and have no intention of paying. To see if this is a significant problem, the internal audit team can sample bad debts on receivables below the credit review threshold.

- *Automatically review credit for smaller orders.* Some higher-end accounting systems can use a rules-based system to automatically review and grant credit for smaller orders, thereby leaving more time for the credit staff to review larger orders. While primarily intended to be an efficiency improvement, this extra level of automation acts as a control as well, since it focuses the credit staff's time on large orders where there is the largest potential for loss.

- *Send customers a link to an online credit application form.* When customers apply for credit through a paper-based application, they may ignore entries in some fields and cross out text in other areas, both of which make the credit decision process more difficult. An alternative is to create an electronic credit application that incorporates validation checks, so that all fields must be entered prior to submission. This approach also keeps customers from crossing out application text they do not like, but it has the disadvantage of only allowing the use of a digital signature, which may not hold up in court. The resulting information can be routed by the computer system directly to the credit staff, resulting in more expeditious treatment of credit applications.

- *Password-protect the order entry system.* It is possible for someone to fraudulently access the order entry computer system and enter orders below the threshold where the credit department is required to review orders, resulting in shipments to shell companies owned by the perpetrators. To avoid this problem, access to the order entry system should be guarded with password protection, with the system regularly requiring replacement passwords.

- *Use validation checks.* Many of the better order entry systems allow for the maintenance of data entry validation checks, so information that is outside of a predetermined parameter range will be immediately rejected by the system. Validations typically apply to addresses, zip codes, delivery dates, and part or product numbers that do not exist. This control can also apply to the entry of shipping information.

This section focused on the general process flow and related controls used on a base-level order entry and shipping system. The next few sections describe how the system of controls is altered to accommodate various best practices.

3–3 Integrate Credit Management into Order Entry

Credit management is a difficult process to integrate into the order entry process flow in an automated manner. At best, systems can be designed to automatically approve modest changes in credit levels, grant credit at very low levels to new customers, or hand off credit issues to employees when order sizes or submitted financial information falls into the manual override conditions designated by the accounting software. Consequently, the integrated credit management system noted in Exhibit 3.5 provides a combination of limited automated credit reviews, combined with some manual credit analysis steps. A number of controls have been removed from the basic process flow shown earlier in Exhibit 3.3 in order to focus on credit-specific controls.

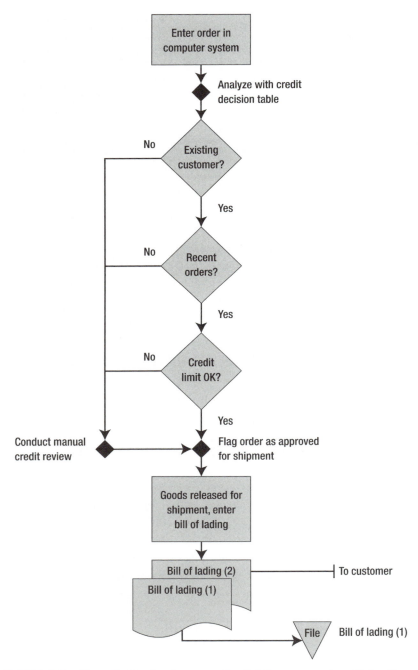

Exhibit 3.5   Controls Used to Integrate Credit Management into Order Entry

There is really only one major credit control noted in the flowchart, though it is spread over a number of decision points. An explanation of the control follows.

- *Analyze with credit decision table.* The beauty of having a computerized order entry system is that a credit decision table can be added to it, so that incoming orders are automatically evaluated based on fixed criteria and either approved on the spot or shunted to a staff person for a more in-depth evaluation. Thus, this is really an efficiency improvement over the standard approach of requiring a person to examine all incoming orders for creditworthiness. The flowchart in Exhibit 3.5 shows a typical set of credit decisions for the computer system to examine.
- If the order is from an existing customer, it passes to the next decision question; otherwise, it is routed to the credit staff for review.
- If the order from an existing customer is a recent one, it passes to the next decision question; otherwise, orders from customers who have not placed orders recently are routed to the credit staff for review.
- If the order from an existing customer with recent order history is within its existing credit limit, the order is flagged as approved for shipment; otherwise, it is routed to the credit staff for review.

The flowchart in Exhibit 3.5 is not translated into a procedure, since the bulk of it shows automated controls, and the manual credit review process was described earlier in the procedure in Exhibit 3.2.

In addition to the sole credit control listed in Exhibit 3.5, many additional controls can be added, depending on a company's risk of incurring credit losses. They are as follows.

- *Create a credit policy.* A serious control problem arises when there is no formal definition of how to calculate a credit limit, what information is required of customers in order to determine the credit limit, the standard terms of sale, and the collections methodology to be followed. The typical result is widely varying credit levels being granted, inconsistent billing terms, and a poorly managed collection strategy. All of these problems are mitigated through the formulation and consistent application of a credit policy. A sample policy is included at the end of this chapter in Section 3–7, "Order Entry, Credit, and Shipment Policies."

- *Conduct mandatory periodic credit policy reviews.* Any credit policy is based on a company's financial situation, its product margins and strategic direction, and the general economic conditions at the time when the policy was created. All of these factors can change, making the credit policy less relevant over time. For example, if a company's strategy is to expand market share with a loose credit policy, this could give rise to extremely high bad debts if the economy suddenly worsens. Consequently, a good control over the credit policy is to require a formal review at fixed intervals, with documentation of the results of the review.

- *Conduct regular staff training in credit procedures.* In order to ensure that customer credit–granting issues are dealt with in a reliable and consistent manner, the credit staff must receive training for the corporate credit policy and all related procedures. This is an extremely important step, since many of the controls noted in this section are manual ones that require adherence to a standard credit-granting approach in order to be successful.

- *Arrange for automatic notification of credit rating changes.* The initial credit application and review process can give a company a reasonable picture of a customer's financial situation, but this picture will begin to diverge from the customer's actual financial situation immediately. Credit monitoring services, such as Dun & Bradstreet, will issue an e-mail notification to the company whenever a targeted customer's credit rating changes. For this monitoring control to be successful, there should be a procedure in place for updating the company's list of customers to be reported on by the third-party rating agency as well as a person designated to follow up on all reported changes.

- *Require a credit application for orders above a baseline level.* The credit application yields detailed information about a customer's ownership and finances, and so provides key information regarding how much credit to grant. Accordingly, a good control is to require a credit application from new customers if their order is of a sufficiently large size or if a series of small orders cumulatively exceeds a baseline level.

- *Require a new credit application if customers have not placed orders recently.* If a customer has been granted a credit limit but has not placed an order recently, it may be prudent to require the customer to complete a new credit application to reevaluate the size of its credit limit. However, this places a burden on both the customer and the credit department, so the review typically is restricted to those customers not having placed orders in a long time and for whom the new order is an especially large one.

- *Investigate unanswered questions on the credit application.* When a customer does not answer a question on the standard company credit report, this is a potential warning sign that the customer does not want to impart information to the company. A standard control should be to require the credit staff to follow up in detail on all unanswered credit application questions. This control should be specifically included in the credit application procedure.

- *Verify the existence of a new customer.* If a customer is a new one, there is a chance that it is a shell company being used for fraudulent deliveries from the company. To guard against this, the computer system should flag all newly created customers for which a new order has just been received. This should trigger an investigation by the credit staff to verify the existence of the new company, usually through a credit report or online inquiry through the state secretary of state's office.

- *Review the credit levels of the top 20 percent of customers each year.* The primary risk of incurring a significant bad debt from a customer lies with the top 20 percent of customers by revenue, since they typically account for 80 percent of all corporate revenue. To keep a proper level of control over this subset of customers, it is reasonable to conduct a review of their credit levels each year, including an analysis of payment trends, order volumes, credit reports, and possibly site visits.

- *Review the credit levels of all customers issuing NSF checks.* If a customer pays with a check that is returned due to not sufficient funds (NSF), this is a clear indicator of future bad debt trouble and should trigger a control point whereby the customer's credit is immediately put on hold and its credit limit is subjected to an evaluation.

- *Review the credit levels of customers who skip payments.* If a customer skips a large payment in favor of paying a smaller amount that is due somewhat later, this can be a deliberate ploy to give the appearance of being approximately current with payments while actually delaying the bulk of payments beyond terms. Consequently, detecting this problem provides an early warning regarding potential bad debt situations.

Unfortunately, detecting skipped payments is difficult to automate and is most easily detected by the cash application staff.

- *Review the credit levels of customers who stop taking early payment discounts.* When a customer has a history of taking early payment discounts, it is a safe bet that the abrupt termination of those early payments signals a reduction in the customer's ability to pay. Consequently, a cost-effective control is to create a report listing customers who no longer take early payment discounts, and to include it on the credit department's schedule of reports to be printed at regular intervals. If a customer appears on the report, there should be a procedure in place to route the report to a credit analyst for further review.

- *Generate a report showing the last credit review date.* Since a customer's financial situation changes regularly, it is useful to conduct follow-up credit reviews to ensure that the current credit level coincides with the customer's ability to pay. Accordingly, the credit review procedure should require the credit staff to update the last credit review date field in the customer master file. In addition, the staff should regularly run a report listing the last review date for each customer, which it should use as the foundation for scheduling additional credit reviews.

- *Generate a report showing credit levels exceeded.* If a company's credit-granting systems are working properly, it should be impossible for a customer to be shipped more goods than its credit limit allows. By running a standard report that flags all customers who have exceeded their credit limits, the management team can determine if there are breakdowns in the credit granting process. This is a good detective control.

Everything about the credit department involves the mitigation of risk, so this section listed a great many controls, all targeted at ways to ensure that bad debt losses are minimized. Few of them can be integrated into a computerized system, instead requiring the close integration of numerous manual control points. Given the large volume of controls noted here, you should consider implementing the appropriate *minimum* mix of controls to ensure that risk levels are reduced to an appropriate level, without seriously increasing the workload of the credit staff.

3–4 Receive Electronic Orders

It is increasingly common for companies to allow customers to place orders through electronic forms over the Internet, while other firms have created interfaces into their order entry modules that allow electronic data interchange (EDI) messages to be entered without manual intervention. It is necessary to create a set of automated controls for these inputs, so that you can enjoy the benefits of automated order entry without any manual intervention that would slow down the process flow. The basic controls for receiving electronic orders are shown in Exhibit 3.6.

The controls noted in the flowchart are described at greater length next, in sequence from the top of the flowchart to the bottom.

- *Verify credit card.* If the customer is paying through an electronic form on the Internet, it is likely that the order is being paid for with a credit card. If so, the computer system should verify the amount of credit left on the card and notify the customer if it is insufficient to process the order.

- *Automated credit review.* When an electronic order arrives via an EDI transmission, this typically means that the order is from a long-term business partner who does a high volume of business with the company, so there is a large credit line already in place. Consequently, the computer system should allow these transactions to proceed unless the most recent order exceeds the total amount of the credit limit—in which case the system should flag the order for a manual review by the credit staff.

- *Flag order as approved for shipment.* Once either credit card verification or the automated credit review is completed, the system automatically flags the order as being approved for shipment. This control is not really needed anymore, but since the flag is likely to still be present in the computer system (and used for manually entered orders), there needs to be a mechanism for flagging automatically approved orders.

- *Communicate order status to customer.* When the human interface is removed from the order entry process, it is possible that the electronic systems will fail and not enter the order into the company's computer systems at all. Consequently, the system should issue a confirmation

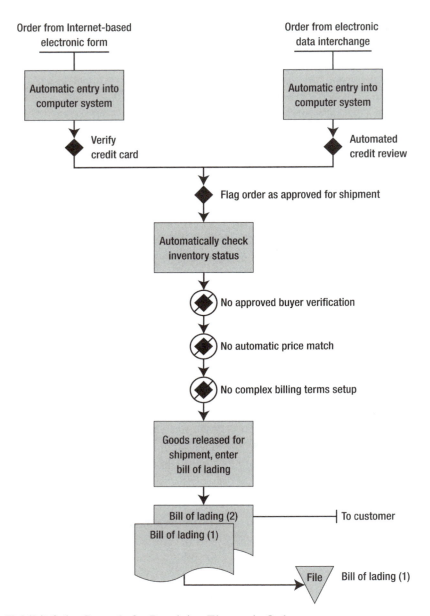

Exhibit 3.6   Controls for Receiving Electronic Orders

message to the customer, stating that the order has been received and perhaps noting an expected delivery date as well. If the customer does not receive this confirming message, its own control systems may flag the order as not having been received by the company, thereby triggering a follow-up call from its purchasing department to the company's order entry staff.

- *No control point for verification of approved buyer.* There is no longer a control point to verify that the buyer placing the order is approved by the customer to place orders. This is a manual control that would interfere with the automated nature of an electronic order. Further, if the electronic order comes from an EDI message, then the customer is probably a trading partner of long standing, for whom there is no question about who is approved to place orders. Also, if the electronic order was placed over the Internet, then the buyer probably paid in advance with a credit card, so there is no issue about the customer not paying on the grounds of having an invalid buyer.

- *No control point for automatic price match.* Price matching is not needed when orders are automatically received, for two reasons. First, a customer paying with a credit card through an electronic form has already been presented with the correct price and agreed to pay it. Second, a customer placing an order with an EDI transmission has previously sent in a master purchase order to which the company has agreed. Thus, no additional price matching is required.

- *No control for setting up complex billing terms.* When a customer places an electronic order, it is typically done within a tightly defined set of ordering parameters that leaves no room for complex billing terms. Thus, there is no need for a control point to enter special billing terms at the order entry point.

A key issue related to the receipt of electronic orders is the number of control points that are no longer required. By introducing a great deal of automation to the front end of the order entry process, there is no need for time-consuming manual controls later in the process. Also, no procedure was listed for the receipt of electronic orders, since the process is designed to be handled entirely by the computer system. No manual intervention is needed, unless exception conditions arise.

3–5 Drop-Ship Ordered Items

In some situations, a company does not keep a product in stock for delivery to customers. Instead, it routes customer orders directly to its supplier, who in turn ships the goods directly to the customer. As a result, the company never handles the related inventory at all, which reduces its working capital requirements. However, additional controls are needed to ensure that customer orders are sent to and received by the supplier. It is also necessary to ensure that notification of delivery is received from the supplier in a timely manner, so the company can issue an invoice to the customer. The additional controls are shown in Exhibit 3.7. In the exhibit, other controls re-

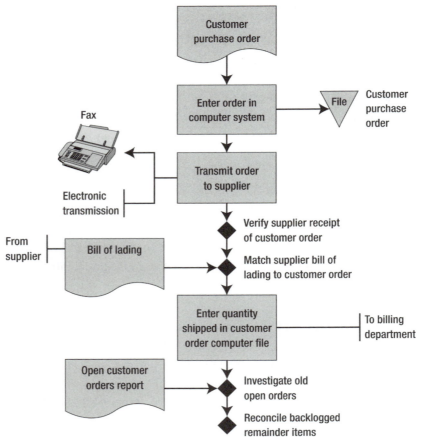

Exhibit 3.7   Controls for Drop Shipment Deliveries

lated to the general process flow have been removed in order to make room for those controls used only for drop-shipped orders.

The controls noted in the flowchart are described at greater length next, in sequence from the top of the flowchart to the bottom.

- *Verify supplier receipt of customer order.* The area of greatest risk in the process flow is simply ensuring that the supplier has received a copy of the customer order, which can be confirmed in a number of ways: through an automatic electronic receipt message if EDI is used or through a simple e-mail, fax, or phone call.

- *Match supplier bill of lading to customer order.* The company needs a method for determining what has shipped, so it can create customer invoices. When the supplier creates a bill of lading for its own records and that of the customer, it should create an additional copy for the company, which is then matched to the open customer order and sent to the billing staff for invoice creation.

- *Investigate old open orders.* By default, the preceding matching process leaves all the unmatched orders on file, which the order entry staff uses to create a report of all old open orders. With this report, it follows up with the supplier to determine when remaining orders are expected to be shipped.

- *Reconcile backlogged remainder items.* Once a customer order is largely completed, there may be a small number of items remaining on backlog. If so, the order entry staff should regularly follow up on these items to see if the supplier is still able to ship them or if the customer wants them. Proper attention to these items keeps small portions of orders from lingering in the computer system as open items and ensures that the maximum amount of each order is billed.

The drop-shipping procedure shown in Exhibit 3.8 incorporates the control points already noted in Exhibit 3.7. This procedure contains a number of additional processing steps not shown in the flowchart.

In essence, controls in a drop shipment situation revolve around the tracking of the order that has been transferred to the supplier. This is important not only to ensure that shipments are made to customers in a timely manner, but also to ensure that customers are billed immediately after their orders are shipped.

Exhibit 3.8   Procedure for Drop Shipment Deliveries

Policy/Procedure Statement   Retrieval No.:   ORD-04

Subject: Drop Shipment Deliveries

1. PURPOSE AND SCOPE

This procedure is used by the order entry department to handle drop shipment deliveries in a computerized environment.

2. PROCEDURES

2.1 Enter and Transmit Order (Order Entry Clerk)

1. Enter the customer order in the order entry system.

2. Print one copy of the sales order document.

3. Fax the sales order document to the supplier, and call to confirm receipt of the sales order and the supplier's best estimate of when the order will be shipped. If electronic data interchange (EDI) is available, verify receipt of a confirming transmission from the supplier.

2.2 Match Supplier Bill of Lading to Customer Order (Order Entry Clerk)

1. Upon receipt of a bill of lading copy from the supplier, access the customer order file and enter all items for which delivery has been completed.

2. Once all shipment quantities are entered, save the file and access the Backlog screen for that order to see if any items remain on back order. If so, contact the supplier and verify the most likely delivery date for those items.

3. If the projected delivery date exceeds __ days, contact the customer and see if an alternative product will be acceptable. If so, cancel the backlogged items, send a cancelled backlog report to the supplier, and create a new sales order file for the replacement goods. Print this new sales order and send it to the appropriate supplier.

2.3 Reconcile Backlogged Remainder Items (Order Entry Clerk)

1. On a daily basis, print the Open Customer Orders report, and review with suppliers any unshipped items for which the projected delivery date exceeds ___ days.

2. If projected delivery dates exceed ___ days, notify the customer service manager.

3. If ordered items are no longer available for delivery, cancel the relevant order line items and notify both the supplier and customer of this action.

3–6 Controls for Shipments to Evaluated Receipt Customers

The evaluated receipts process was first discussed in Chapter 2 as an advanced approach for planned purchases within the accounts payable system. This system involves issuing a purchase order number for each authorized delivery by a supplier, which the supplier affixes to its physical order to the company; the company's receiving staff then matches the received purchase order number against a database of open purchase orders, and the accounting software pays the supplier based on the purchase order—no supplier invoice is required. It is possible that customers will have their own evaluated receipts systems, in which case a company's order entry and shipping systems must be configured with the proper controls to deal with these customer systems.

Customers with evaluated receipts systems always place orders with purchase orders, since the purchase order number is the key number used by them to approve incoming shipments. Consequently, the evaluated receipts process flow shown in Exhibit 3.9 is designed to handle both paper-based and electronic purchase orders. As part of the order entry process, the key control is to ensure that the evaluated receipts flag is turned on in the customer master file, since this triggers the creation of an evaluated receipts tag that is sent to the customer with the delivery and also warns the billing department not to send an invoice to the customer. The credit analysis process is also simplified, since any customer placing orders under an evaluated receipts system is probably a long-term business partner with an established credit line.

The controls noted in the flowchart are described at greater length next, in sequence from the top of the flowchart to the bottom.

- *Set evaluated receipts flag.* If a customer issues a purchase order in which it notifies the company that it is now using an evaluated receipts system, then the order entry staff should set the evaluated receipts flag in the customer master file to indicate this change in status. By doing so, the accounting system will now notify the shipping department that it must print a shipping tag for attachment to the delivered goods. These tags always list the authorizing purchase order number, and frequently the company's supplier number as used by the customer, as well as the item number and quantity being delivered. Furthermore, this information

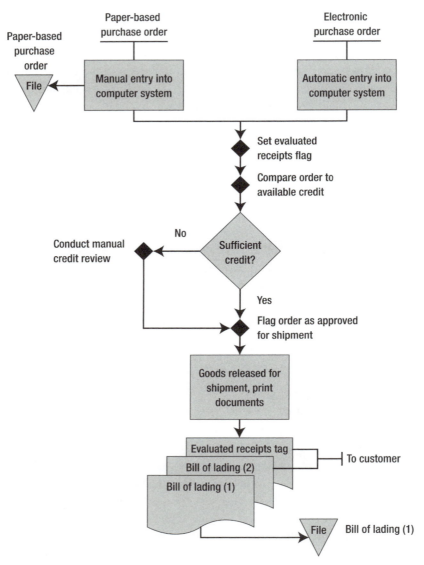

Exhibit 3.9   Controls for Shipments to Evaluated Receipt Customers

may be required in a bar-coded format as specified by the customer. This flag should also either keep an invoice from being printed (since the customer no longer pays from the invoice) or else add an identifying mark to the invoice, so the billing staff will not mail the invoice to the customer.

- *Compare order to available credit.* Orders for evaluated receipts are generally received from long-term business partners with whom a company has long since established a line of credit. Consequently, there is rarely a need for elaborate credit reviews with such orders. (If a credit review appears necessary, then the early discussion of credit controls in Section 3–3 will handily address that eventuality.) Thus, the minimal control point needed for this process is to have the computer system compare the dollar amount of the latest purchase order to the amount of available credit and to route the order to a credit staff person if the credit limit has been exceeded.

- *Conduct manual credit review.* This control is unlikely to be used, since it is triggered only if a customer's credit level is exceeded, which is unlikely if the customer is a long-tem business partner.

- *Flag order as approved for shipment.* As is the case for all computerized shipment systems, all orders must be flagged by the credit department as being approved for shipment. In this case, most evaluated receipts orders are likely to be approved automatically by the system, which automatically sets the approval flag.

The evaluated receipts procedure shown in Exhibit 3.10 incorporates the control points already noted in Exhibit 3.9, with the exception of credit processing and inventory picking activities that were described earlier in Exhibit 3.4.

The preceding controls are designed for daily evaluated receipts transactions. The additional controls that follow are intended to spot problems with the integrity of the overall process flow, and are needed only on an occasional basis.

- *Audit application of evaluated receipts orders to order entry system.* The internal audit staff should verify that incoming purchase orders are properly entered into the order entry system, particularly in regard to

Exhibit 3.10 Procedure for Shipments to Evaluated Receipts Customers

Policy/Procedure Statement   Retrieval No.:   ORD-05

Subject: Evaluated Receipts Deliveries

1. PURPOSE AND SCOPE

This procedure is used by the order entry and shipping departments to handle deliveries to customers who use evaluated receipts systems.

2. PROCEDURES

2.1 Set Evaluated Receipts Flag (Order Entry Clerk)

1. If the customer purchase order is not received electronically and indicates that the customer uses an evaluated receipts system, turn on the evaluated receipts flag in the customer master file. If turned on, indicate in the customer master file which of the following fields should be included in the evaluated receipts tag that is attached to the customer delivery:

   - Purchase order number
   - Supplier name
   - Supplier number
   - Item number
   - Item quantity
   - Evaluated receipts tag number
   - Bar code printing

2. If there is no evaluated receipts flag in the customer master file, complete the Evaluated Receipts form, indicating which items should be included on the evaluated receipts tag (as noted above), and forward it to the shipping department.

2.2 Print Shipping Documents (Shipping Clerk)

1. Upon completion of a delivery, print two copies of the bill of lading and one bar-coded evaluated receipts tag. Affix the evaluated receipts tag to one copy of the bill of lading and attach the packet to the shipment. Store the other billing of lading document in a file.

2. If there is no evaluated receipts flag in the customer master file, review the file of completed Evaluated Receipts forms to ascertain if a shipment is to a customer with an evaluated receipts system. If so, manually prepare an evaluated receipts tag based on the completed pick list and the customer purchase order number as listed in the customer order record. Affix the evaluated receipts tag to one copy of the bill of lading and attach the packet to the shipment. Store the other bill of lading document in a file.

how the evaluated receipts flag is set in the customer master file and how information is set up to be printed on the evaluated receipts tag that accompanies the delivery to the customer. This control may include matching the exact requirements specified by each customer for the contents of the evaluated receipts tag to the information on an actual tag at the shipping dock.

- *Audit billing procedure to ensure that invoices are not issued.* The internal audit staff should verify that all customers using evaluated receipts systems are not sent invoices. The simplest approach is to extract from the master customer file all those customer records with an activated evaluated receipts flag and compare this list to the sales journal to see if invoices were printed.

- *Review customer complaints for issues related to evaluated receipts.* The management team should regularly review the customer complaints log to see if there are any issues with evaluated receipts tags not being in the proper format or invoices incorrectly being sent to customers who do not want them.

Evaluated receipts is an advanced payables concept that is not likely to be adopted by the majority of businesses, so the controls noted here are likely to impact only a small proportion of all orders passing through the order entry, credit, and shipment processes. Nonetheless, ensuring that they function properly can have a significant impact on a company's ability to be paid in a timely manner by customers who use this system.

3–7 Order Entry, Credit, and Shipment Policies

A number of policies are related to the order entry, credit, and shipment areas can assist in the enforcement of controls. The next list itemizes four order entry policies that are intended to avoid fraudulent orders, ensure proper pricing, and avoid the acceptance of special customer terms. There are also three policies related to credit management, the most important of which is the overall corporate credit policy. The credit policy covers a great deal of territory, from the overall mission of the credit department to the collection methodology to be used and the standard terms of sale to be offered to customers. The intent of having such a policy is to provide some structure to what can be a chaotic process. Finally, there is a policy restricting the company from shipping any order that has not been released by the credit department. The policies follow.

1. *Customer existence must be verified for all orders exceeding $___ from new customers.* This policy is intended to root out any customers who have been fraudulently set up as shell companies with the intent of taking delivery of goods from the company with no intention of paying. The order threshold is built into the policy in order to avoid spending more money to investigate customer existence than the company will earn as profit from the transaction.

2. *All prices on manually received customer orders shall be reconciled prior to order processing.* This policy is designed to spot discrepancies between the prices at which customers order goods and the official company price. Customers must give their approval to revised prices (if any) before the company will process the order; otherwise, there is a significant risk of a dispute with customers that will likely delay payment.

3. *Extended rights of return shall not be allowed.* This policy limits the ability of the sales staff to engage in "channel stuffing," since it cannot offer special rights of return to customers in exchange for early sales. The policy keeps a company from gyrating between large swings in sales caused by channel stuffing.

4. *Special sale discounts shall not be allowed without senior management approval.* This policy prevents large bursts in sales caused by special price discounts that can stuff a company's distribution channels, causing rapid sales declines in subsequent periods.

5. *Credit policy.* The corporate credit policy follows.
   - *Mission.* The credit department shall offer credit to all customers except those for whom the risk of loss is probable.

   - *Goals.* The department goals are to operate with no more than one collections person per 1,000 customers, while attaining a bad debt percentage no higher than 2 percent of sales and annual days sales outstanding of no higher than 42 days.

   - *Responsibility.* The credit manager has final authority over the granting of credit and the assignment of credit hold status.

- ○ *Credit-level assignment.* All customers shall be granted a minimum credit level of $500 without any formal credit review. Any customers applying for a credit limit over this amount must submit financial statements and credit references, which shall be used with the company's credit scoring system to arrive at a credit line.
- ○ *Collections methodology.* The standard collection methodology shall be an e-mail message including a PDF file containing the invoice image, which shall be sent five days after the invoice due date. The second step is a fax containing the same information, which shall be issued seven days after the invoice due date. The third step is a phone call to the customer, to be sent nine days after the invoice due date. If an invoice larger than $1,000 is unpaid once it is 15 days past the invoice due date, all customer credit shall be halted. All invoices not yet paid shall be turned over to a collection agency once they are 60 days past due.
- ○ *Terms of sale.* The company's standard terms of sale are 2/10 net 30. All other terms of sale must be approved in advance by the credit manager.

6. *All customer orders exceeding the credit limit must be held until approved by the credit manager.* This policy is designed to keep the sales staff from ramming through large orders without the knowledge of the credit staff, thereby giving the credit department time to weigh the incremental increase in risk associated with making the shipment.

7. *The credit manager must approve all increases in customer credit limits.* This policy provides some control over the credit granting process, so there is reduced risk that lower-level staff will issue significant credit increases without the knowledge of management.

8. *No shipments are allowed without prior approval by the credit department.* This policy is targeted at one of the key control failures in many companies—shipping goods to customers without credit. Rigid enforcement of this policy is key to driving down credit losses.

The policies just described work best if adopted as a group. For example, the shipping policy requiring credit approval prior to shipment is the key driver behind the enforcement of the other credit policies, since anyone wanting a shipment to be released must first comply with the credit policies.

Summary

Though seven variations on the order entry/credit/shipment process controls flow were profiled in this chapter, a small number of key control points are common to nearly all situations: the assurance that both parties agree to pricing and related terms and the iron-clad denial of shipment until credit approval is made. Nearly all other controls are related to the credit approval process, which is the central risk area in this process flow.

Chapter 4

Controls for Inventory Management Best Practices

Overview

An enormous number of advanced systems are involved in the procurement, handling, and shipment of inventory, all of which require different types of controls. In this chapter, we discuss control systems for a wide range of system complexities, ranging from paper-based inventory acquisition systems, through bar-coded tracking systems, cross docking, pick-to-light systems, and zone picking, and on to controls for manufacturing resources planning and just-in-time systems. As usual, the number of controls that *could* be installed may appear to be oppressively large, and could certainly interfere with the efficient running of inventory-related activities. Consequently, always be mindful of the need to install only those controls that are truly necessary to the mitigation of significant risks.

4–1 Controls for Basic Inventory Acquisition

This section describes controls over the acquisition of inventory where there is no computerization of the process. Section 4–9, "Controls for Manufacturing Resources Planning," presents a more advanced application in which purchase orders are generated automatically by the computer system.

The basic acquisition process centers on the purchase order authorization, as shown in Exhibit 4.1. The warehouse issues a prenumbered purchase requisition when inventory levels run low, which is the primary authorization for the creation of a multipart purchase order. One copy of the purchase order goes back to the warehouse, where it is compared to a copy of the

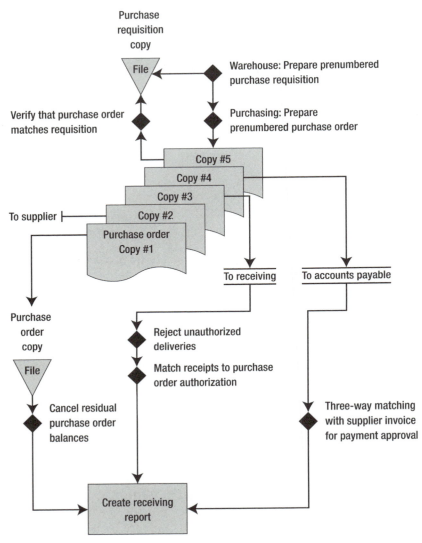

Exhibit 4.1   Controls for Basic Inventory Acquisition

purchase requisition to verify completeness; another copy goes to the supplier, while a third copy goes to the accounts payable department for eventual matching to the supplier invoice. A fourth copy is sent to the receiving department, where it is used to accept incoming deliveries, while a fifth copy is retained in the purchasing department. In short, various copies of the purchase order drive orders to suppliers, receiving, and payment.

The controls noted in the flowchart are described at greater length next, in sequence from the top of the flowchart to the bottom.

- *Warehouse: Prepare a prenumbered purchase requisition.* In the absence of a formal inventory management system, the only people who know which inventory items are running low are the warehouse staff. They must notify the purchasing department to issue purchase orders for inventory replenishments. To ensure that these requisitions are made in an orderly manner, only prenumbered requisition forms should be used, and preferably they should be issued only by a limited number of warehouse staff. By limiting their use, it is less likely that multiple people will issue a requisition for the same inventory item.

- *Purchasing: Prepare a prenumbered purchase order.* The primary control over inventory in a basic inventory management system is through the purchasing function, which controls the spigot of inventory flowing into the warehouse. This control can be eliminated for small-dollar purchases for fittings and fasteners, which are typically purchased as soon as on-hand quantities reach marked reorder points in their storage bins (visual reorder system). Since the purchase order is the primary control over inventory purchases, you can avoid fake purchase orders by using prenumbered forms that are stored in a locked cabinet.

- *Verify that purchase order matches requisition.* Once the warehouse staff receives its copy of the purchase order, it should compare the purchase order to the initiating requisition to ensure that the correct items were ordered. Any incorrect purchase order information should be brought to the attention of the purchasing staff at once.

- *Reject unauthorized deliveries.* To enforce the use of purchase orders for all inventory purchases, the receiving staff should be instructed to reject all deliveries for which there is no accompanying purchase order number.

- *Match receipts to purchase order authorization.* Once an order is received, the warehouse staff should enter the receiving information into a receiving report and send the receiving report to the accounts payable department for later matching to the supplier invoice and purchase order. It should also send a copy of the report to the purchasing department for further analysis.

- *Cancel residual purchase order balances.* Upon receipt of the receiving report from the receiving department, the purchasing staff compares it to the file of open invoices to determine which orders have not yet been received and which purchase orders with residual amounts outstanding can now be cancelled. Otherwise, additional deliveries may arrive well after the date when they were originally needed.

- *Three-way matching with supplier invoice for payment approval.* Upon receipt of the receiving report, the accounts payable staff matches it to the supplier invoice and authorizing purchase order to determine if the quantity appearing on the supplier invoice matches the amount received and that the price listed on the supplier invoice matches the price listed on the purchase order. The department pays suppliers based on the results of this matching process.

The next controls are supplemental to the primary controls just noted for the inventory acquisition process.

- *Segregate the purchasing and receiving functions.* Anyone ordering supplies should not be allowed to receive it, since that person could eliminate all traces of the initiating order and make off with the inventory. This is normally considered a primary control, but it does not fit into the actual transaction flow noted earlier in Exhibit 4.1 and so is listed here as a supplemental control.

- *Require supervisory approval of purchase orders.* If the purchasing staff has a low level of experience, it may be necessary to require supervisory approval of all purchase orders before they are issued, in order to spot mistakes. This approval may also be useful for larger purchasing commitments.

- *Inform suppliers that verbal purchase orders are not accepted.* Suppliers will ship deliveries on the basis of verbal authorizations, which circumvents the use of formal purchase orders. To prevent this, periodically issue reminder notices to all suppliers that deliveries based on verbal purchase orders will be rejected at the receiving dock.

- *Inform suppliers of who can approve purchase orders.* If there is a significant perceived risk that purchase orders can be forged, then tell suppliers which purchasing personnel are authorized to approve purchase orders and update this notice whenever the authorization list changes. This control is not heavily used, especially for large purchasing departments where the authorization list constantly changes or where there are many suppliers to notify. Usually the risk of purchase order forgery is not perceived to be that large.

4–2 Controls for Basic Inventory Storage and Movement

This section describes controls for only the most basic inventory management system, where there is no perpetual inventory tracking system in place, no computerization of the inventory database, and no formal planning system, such as manufacturing resources planning (MRP II) or just-in-time (JIT). Controls for perpetual inventory tracking systems are covered in Section 4–7. MRP II is addressed in Section 4–9 and JIT in Section 4–10.

When there is no perpetual inventory tracking system in place, the key control tasks of the warehouse staff fall into four categories:

1. *Guard the gates.* The warehouse staff must ensure that access to inventory is restricted, in order to reduce theft and unauthorized use of inventory. This also means that warehouse staff must accept only properly requisitioned inventory and must conduct a standard receiving review before accepting any inventory.
2. *Orderly storage.* All on-hand inventories must be properly organized, so it can be easily accessed, counted, and requisitioned.
3. *Accurate picking.* The production department depends on the warehouse for accurate picking of all items needed for the production process, as is also the case for picking of finished goods for delivery to customers.
4. *Timely and accurate requisitioning.* When there is no computer system or perpetual card file to indicate when inventory levels are too low, the warehouse staff must use visual reordering systems and frequent inventory inspections to produce timely requisitions for additional stock.

Exhibit 4.2 expands on the general control categories just noted. In the general category of "guarding the gates," controls include rejecting unauthorized deliveries as well as inspecting, identifying, and recording all receipts. The orderly storage goal entails the segregation of customer-owned inventory and the assignment of inventory to specific locations. To achieve

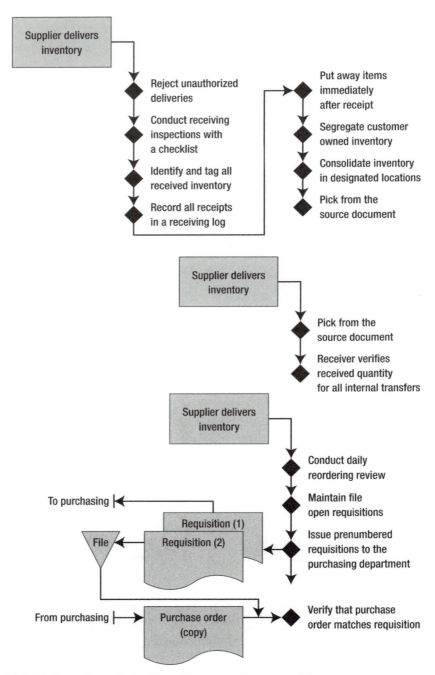

Exhibit 4.2   Controls for Basic Inventory Storage and Movement

the accurate picking goal calls for the use of a source document for picking, while the requisitioning target requires the use of prenumbered requisitions and document matching. A number of supplemental controls also bolster the control targets.

The controls noted in the flowchart are described at greater length next, in sequence from the top of the flowchart to the bottom. Also, a few controls from the last section (concerning requisitions and receiving) are repeated in order to form a complete picture of all required controls.

- *Reject unauthorized deliveries.* To enforce the use of purchase orders for all inventory purchases, the receiving staff should be instructed to reject all deliveries for which there is no accompanying purchase order number.

- *Conduct receiving inspections with a checklist.* The receiving staff is responsible for inspecting all delivered items. If staff members perform only a perfunctory inspection, then the company is at risk of having accepted goods with a variety of problems. To ensure that a complete inspection is made, create a receiving checklist describing specific inspection points, such as timeliness of the delivery, quality, quantity, and the presence of an authorizing purchase order number. Require the receiving staff to initial each item on the receiving checklist and then file it with the daily receiving report.

- *Identify and tag all received inventory.* Many inventory items are difficult to identify once they have been removed from their shipping containers, so it is imperative to properly identify and tag all received items prior to storage.

- *Record all receipts in a receiving log.* A primitive control over receiving records is to maintain a file of bills of lading, sorted by date. A more organized approach is to record receiving information in a receiving log, so that users can more quickly research when items were received as well as quantities and descriptions received. The receiving log is a standard tool used by the accounts payable staff to complete its month-end cutoff calculations. A sample receiving log is shown in Exhibit 4.4.

- *Put away items immediately after receipt.* It is difficult for the warehouse staff to determine whether more inventory should be requisitioned if the inventory is sitting in the receiving area rather than in its designated location. Consequently, a standard part of the receiving procedure should be to put away items as soon after receipt as possible.

- *Segregate customer-owned inventory.* In situations where customers send inventory to a company for inclusion in a finished product, there is a significant risk that the company will inadvertently include the customer-owned inventory in its own inventory valuations. To avoid this problem, route all such incoming inventory into a physically separate storage area.

- *Consolidate inventory in designated locations.* When there is no computerized inventory tracking system, it is very easy to put away the same inventory items in multiple locations and lose track of where they are located, resulting in stockout conditions even though the inventory is still somewhere in the warehouse. A major control is to preassign inventory to specific locations and always store it there (with a designated overflow location when there is too much stock on hand).

- *Pick from the source document.* There is a risk that copying information from a customer order document to a picking document may result in data entry errors that will yield picks of either incorrect inventory items or quantities. To avoid this, structure the customer order document so that it can be used as a picking sheet, and use a copy of the order as the picking document.

- *Receiver verifies received quantity for all internal transfers.* There are many internal transfers of inventory, typically shifting goods from the warehouse to the production department and back again. There is a risk that inventory will be stolen or lost at any point during these transfers, so a standard control should require all receiving employees to count the inventory received and match it to the transfer document that states the quantity being transferred. Once accepted, the person who received the goods is now responsible for the on-hand quantity.

- *Conduct daily reordering review.* When there is no perpetual inventory system, the only way to ensure that sufficient quantities are on hand for expected production levels is to conduct a daily review of the inventory and place requisitions if inventory items have fallen below predetermined reorder points.

- *Maintain file of open requisitions.* If the warehouse is large enough, there may be a great many items on order at any one time, so the warehouse staff should maintain an open requisitions file to track what items have already been ordered and which require new requisitions. A good additional control is to tape a copy of any open requisitions to the locations of items that are currently on order, so that employees reviewing inventory levels can easily determine if a requisition has already been placed. (If this is done, a procedure must be in place to *remove* the requisition copies once inventory arrives from the supplier.)

- *Issue prenumbered requisitions to the purchasing department.* The warehouse should issue only prenumbered requisitions to the purchasing department. By doing so, the warehouse staff can maintain a log of requisition numbers used and thereby determine if any requisitions have been lost in transit to the purchasing department.

- *Verify that purchase order matches requisition.* Once the warehouse staff receives its copy of the purchase order, it should compare the purchase order to the initiating requisition to ensure that the correct items were ordered. Any incorrect purchase order information should be brought to the attention of the purchasing staff at once.

The preceding primary controls are required to ensure that the warehouse maintains a basic level of control over inventory. In addition, the next two supplemental controls are useful for reducing the level of theft from the warehouse, while the third and fourth controls make it easier to determine when inventory should be reordered, and the fifth reduces the chance that inventory will be inadvertently requisitioned multiple times.

1. *Restrict warehouse access.* Without access restrictions, the company warehouse is like a large store with no prices—just take all you want. This does not necessarily mean that employees are taking items from stock for personal use, but they may be removing items for production purposes, which leads to a cluttered production floor. Also, this leaves the purchasing staff with the almost impossible chore of trying to determine what is in stock and what needs to be bought for immediate manufacturing needs. Consequently, a mandatory control over inventory is to fence it in and closely restrict access to it.

2. *Do not publicize warehouse locations.* To prevent inventory theft, do not post warehouse and manufacturing facility locations on a company Web site.

3. *Install a visual reordering system.* The warehouse staff can produce requisitions for more inventory with greater accuracy and reliability when there is a visual reordering system in place. For example, a line can be painted partway down the side of a storage bin; once the on-hand inventory drops below the line, the warehouse staff knows it must issue a requisition for more inventory.

4. *Regularly update visual reorder points.* Even if a visual reorder system is in place, it is likely that reorder quantities and supplier lead times will change over time, which may lead to either stockout conditions or excessive on-hand balances. To avoid either situation, schedule periodic reviews of the visual reorder points and modify them as necessary.

5. *Assign requisition responsibility to one person.* If more than one person conducts the daily review of inventory reorder points, it is quite likely that several requisitions will be placed for the same inventory, resulting in excess quantities on hand. To avoid this, either assign responsibility for completing requisitions to one person or clearly assign responsibility for specific areas of the warehouse to different employees.

The receiving procedure described in Exhibit 4.3 expands on the receiving controls already described, while providing additional detail about the receiving process.

When customer-owned inventory is delivered, it requires special handling to ensure that it is not subsequently counted as part of the company-owned inventory and valued as such, which would artificially inflate company profits. The procedure shown in Exhibit 4.5 describes how to address this issue.

Besides receiving, the central activity of the warehouse staff is picking items from stock. The procedure shown in Exhibit 4.6 describes the process, while incorporating the controls noted earlier in this section.

4–3 Controls for Inventory Valuation

Though most of the controls in this chapter are concerned with recording the correct inventory quantities, it is equally important to ensure that the valuation of inventory also is being calculated correctly. This section contains procedures for the lower of cost or market calculation and the period-end inventory valuation as well as controls intended to stop a variety of

Exhibit 4.3   Receiving Procedure

Policy/Procedure Statement	Retrieval No.: INV-01

Subject: Receiving Inspection

1.   PURPOSE AND SCOPE

This procedure is used by the receiving department to inspect and log in incoming deliveries.

2.   PROCEDURES

2.1   Inspect Incoming Goods (Receiving Staff)

1. When the delivery arrives, compare the shipment to the description on the bill of lading and the authorizing purchase order. If there are significant discrepancies, reject the shipment.
2. If there is no purchase order, reject the delivery.
3. Using the standard receiving checklist, inspect the delivery for quality, quantity, and delivery timing. Initial each inspection point on the receiving checklist to indicate that it has been completed, and note any issues on the checklist.
4. Sign a copy of the bill of lading to accept the delivery.

2.2   Identify and Tag All Received Inventory (Receiving Staff)

Using the purchase order and item master file report, determine the correct part number for each received item. Label each item or the carton in which it is stored with the item number. If there is uncertainty about which part number to use, contact the purchasing department for assistance. No inventory items may be sent to storage without first having been identified and tagged.

2.2   Log in Received Items (Receiving Staff)

1. Enter the receipt in the daily receiving log, noting the date and time of receipt, supplier name, shipper name, and description and quantity of goods received. An example of the receiving log is shown in Exhibit 4.4.
2. Make a photocopy of the bill of lading and forward it to the accounting department.
3. Store the original bill of lading by date.

Note: If items are received during a physical inventory count, clearly mark them as not being available for counting and segregate them. Also, do not enter the transaction in the corporate accounting system until after the count has been completed.

Exhibit 4.4   Receiving Log

Receipt Date	Supplier Name	Shipper Name	Item	Quantity Received
9/10/06	Acme Acorn Co.	Yellow Transport	Pistachio nuts	3 barrels
9/10/06	Acme Acorn Co.	Smith Shipping	Pine nuts	2 barrels
9/10/06	Durango Nut Co.	Able Trucking	Pinecones	98 pounds

Exhibit 4.5   Inbound Customer-Owned Inventory Handling Procedure

Policy/Procedure Statement   Retrieval No.:   INV-02

Subject: Inbound Customer-Owned Inventory Handling

1.   PURPOSE AND SCOPE

This procedure is used by the warehouse staff to track consignment inventory owned by third parties but stored at the company.

2.   PROCEDURES

2.1 Label Consignment Inventory (Warehouse Staff)

1. Upon receipt of consigned inventory, contact the purchasing department to obtain authorization to receive the inventory.
2. Prominently label the inventory with a colored tag, clearly denoting its status.
3. Assign a part number to the inventory using a unique part number that significantly differs from the normal part numbering scheme.

2.2 Store Consignment Inventory (Warehouse Staff)

Store the item in a part of the warehouse set aside for consigned inventory.

2.3 Update Status of Consignment Inventory (Cost Accountant)

Include the consigned inventory in a review by the materials review board, which should regularly determine the status of this inventory and arrange for its return if there are no prospects for its use in the near future.

valuation errors from occurring. The next seven controls should be considered primary controls over the month-end valuation process.

1. *Review the bill of materials and labor routing change log.* Alterations to the bill of materials or labor routing files can have a significant impact on the inventory valuation. To guard against unauthorized changes to these records, enable the transaction change log of the software (if

Exhibit 4.6 Stock Picking Procedure

Policy/Procedure Statement	Retrieval No.: INV-03

Subject: Picking Items from Stock

1. PURPOSE AND SCOPE

This procedure is used by the warehouse staff to ensure that all picking transactions are properly logged into the inventory database.

2. PROCEDURES

2.1 Pick Items from Stock (Warehouse Staff)

1. The materials management department issues a pick list to the warehouse for each new job to be produced. Alternatively, the order entry staff forwards a photocopy of a customer order to the warehouse.

2. Upon receipt of either the pick list or customer order, the warehouse staff sets up a pallet or bin in which to store the requested items.

3. The warehouse staff collects the requested items from the warehouse, checking off each completed part number on the list or customer order.

4. The warehouse staff delivers the filled pallet or bin to the production floor. The production staff verifies the quantity of all transferred items before accepting the delivery.

5. If the completed pick is being sent directly to the customer, then the warehouse staff photocopies the customer order for inclusion with the order, retains another copy filed by date, and sends the remaining copy to the billing department.

2.2 Handle Returned Items (Warehouse Staff)

1. If any parts remain after the production job is complete, the warehouse staff accepts them at the warehouse gate and stores them in the bins reserved for those items.

2. If any parts are returned in a damaged condition, the warehouse staff stores them in the review area where the materials review board can access them easily.

---

such a feature exists) and incorporate a review of the change log into the month-end valuation calculation procedure.

2. *Compare unextended product costs to those for prior periods.* Product costs of all types can change for a variety of reasons. An easy way to spot these changes is to create and regularly review a report that compares the unextended cost of each product to its cost in a prior period. Any significant changes can then be traced back to the underlying

costing information to see exactly what caused each change. The main problem with this control is that many less expensive accounting systems do not retain historical inventory records. If this is the case, the information should be exported to an electronic spreadsheet or separate database once a month, where historical records can be kept. An example of a cost changes report is shown in Exhibit 4.7.

3. *Review sorted list of extended product costs in declining dollar order.* This report is more commonly available than the historical tracking report noted in the last bullet point, but contains less information. The report lists the extended cost of all inventory on hand for each inventory item, sorted in declining order of cost. By scanning the report, you can readily spot items that have unusually large or small valuations. However, finding these items requires some knowledge of what costs were in previous periods. Also, a lengthy inventory list makes it difficult to efficiently locate costing problems. Thus, this report is inferior to the unextended historical cost comparison report from a control perspective.

4. *Review variances from standard cost.* When the materials management department creates a standard cost for an item, it is usually intended to be a very close approximation of the current market price for that item. Consequently, an excellent control is to run a monthly report comparing the standard cost and most recent price paid for all items, with only those items appearing on the report for which a significant dollar variance has occurred. This variance can indicate the presence of such pur-

Exhibit 4.7   Cost Changes Report

Part Description	Beginning Unit Cost	Cost Changes	Ending Unit Costs	Remarks
Power unit	820.00	+30.00	850.00	Price increase
Fabric	142.60		142.60	
Paint	127.54	−22.54	105.00	Modified paint type
Instruments	93.14	−1.14	92.00	New altimeter
Exhaust stock	34.17		34.17	
Rubber grommet	19.06	−.06	19.00	New material
Aluminum forging	32.14	−2.00	30.14	Substitute forging
Cushion	14.70		14.70	
Total	**1,283.35**	**4.26**	**1,287.61**	

chasing problems as supplier kickbacks or special-order purchases that result in higher prices.

5. *Investigate entries made to the inventory or cost of goods sold accounts.* Because the inventory and cost of goods sold accounts are so large, it is more common for employees attempting to hide fraudulent transactions to dump them into these accounts. Accordingly, part of the standard month-end closing procedure should include the printing and analysis of a report listing only the manual journal entries made to these two accounts. This is also a good audit procedure for the internal auditing department to complete from time to time.

6. *Review inventory layering calculations.* Most inventory layering systems are maintained automatically through a computer system and cannot be altered. In these cases, there is no need to verify the layering calculations. However, if the layering information is maintained manually, you should schedule periodic reviews of the underlying calculations to ensure proper cost layering. This usually involves tracing costs back to specific supplier invoices. However, you should also trace supplier invoices forward to the layering calculations, since it is quite possible that invoices have been excluded from the calculations. Also, verify consistency in the allocation of freight and sales tax costs to inventory items in the layering calculations.

7. *Verify the calculation and allocation of overhead cost pools.* Overhead costs usually are assigned to inventory as the result of a manually derived summarization and allocation of overhead costs. This can be a lengthy calculation, subject to error. The best control over this process is a standard procedure that clearly defines which costs to include in the pools and precisely how these costs are to be allocated. In addition, regularly review the types of costs included in the calculations, verify that the correct proportions of these costs are included, and ensure that the costs are being correctly allocated to inventory. A further control is to track the total amount of overhead accumulated in each reporting period; any sudden change in the amount may indicate an error in the overhead cost summarization.

There is no flowchart of the preceding controls, since there is no specific order in which they must be used. A procedure for conducting a period-end inventory valuation, which includes the preceding primary controls, is shown in Exhibit 4.8.

Exhibit 4.8   Period-End Inventory Valuation Procedure

Policy/Procedure Statement   Retrieval No.:   INV-04

Subject: Period-End Inventory Valuation

1.   PURPOSE AND SCOPE

This procedure is used by the cost accountant to ensure that the inventory valuation created by a computerized accounting system is accurate as well as to update it with the latest overhead costs.

2.   PROCEDURES

2.1   Review Change Log (Cost Accountant)

Following the end of the accounting period, print out and review the computer change log for all bills of material and labor routings. Review them with the materials manager and production engineer to ensure their accuracy. Revise any changes made in error.

2.2   Review Cost Variances (Cost Accountant)

1. Go to the warehouse and manually compare the period-end counts recorded on the inventory report for the most expensive items in the warehouse to what is in the warehouse storage racks. If there are any variances, adjust them for any transactions that occurred between the end of the period and the date of the review. If there are still variances, adjust for them in the inventory database.

2. Print a report that sorts the inventory in declining extended dollar order and review it for reasonableness. Be sure to review not only the most expensive items on the list but also the least expensive, since this where costing errors are most likely to be found. Adjust for any issues found.

3. Print the cost changes report and investigate any significant cost changes. Adjust for any issues found.

4. Print a report showing only items for which purchases were made during the preceding month and for which the purchase cost varied from the standard cost. Investigate the reason for significant pricing changes. If a pricing change appears to be permanent, obtain the controller's approval to adjust standard cost records to the new prices.

2.3   Review General Ledger Entries (Cost Accountant)

1. Print a report showing only manual entries made to the cost of goods sold and inventory accounts for the reporting period. Investigate *all* manual entries made for appropriateness and adjust as necessary. Be sure to include in the review all inventory and cost of goods sold accounts.

2. Obtain a list of all supplier invoices received within the past month that contained inventory costs. Complete the following steps:

    a. Trace the unit prices on a sample of the invoices into the inventory layering calculations. Verify that sales tax and shipping charges are being added to or excluded from the layered costs, in accordance with company policy.

Exhibit 4.8 *(Continued)*

b. Trace the unit prices listed on a sample of layered information from the past month back to the supplier invoices. Verify that sales tax and shipping charges are being added to or excluded from the layered costs, in accordance with company policy.

c. If there are any errors resulting from this investigation, notify the data entry manager of the problem, to initiate a more general review of the entered supplier invoices.

3. Review all entries in the general ledger during the reporting period for costs added to the cost pool, verifying that only approved costs have been included. Only the following expenses may be included in the overhead allocation calculations, and should be allocated based on machine hours unless otherwise noted in parentheses next to each one:

- Depreciation of factory equipment (allocate by individual asset)
- Factory administration expenses
- Indirect labor and production supervisory wages
- Indirect materials and supplies
- Maintenance on factory equipment
- Officer salaries related to production
- Production employees' benefits (allocate by labor cost)
- Quality control and inspection
- Rent on the production facility and equipment (allocate by square footage)
- Repair expenses
- Rework labor, scrap, and spoilage (allocate by units of production)
- Taxes related to production assets (allocate by individual asset)
- Uncapitalized tools and equipment
- Utilities

4. Verify that the overhead allocation calculation conforms to the standard allocation used in previous reporting periods or that it matches any changes approved by management.

5. Verify that the journal entry for overhead allocation matches the standard journal entry listed in the accounting procedures manual.

2.4 Compare to Prior Period Results (Cost Accountant)

Print out the inventory valuation report and compare its results by major category to those of the previous reporting period, in terms of both dollars and proportions. Investigate any major differences.

The next three controls are supplemental to the primary ones already noted, mostly because they fall outside the normal month-end inventory valuation procedure. Instead, they can be completed at any time, with a frequency level dictated by the level of planned risk mitigation. The fourth control is an access control to prevent employees from modifying key computer records. The controls follow.

1. *Audit inventory material costs.* Inventory costs usually are assigned either through a standard costing procedure or as part of some inventory layering concept, such as last in, first out (LIFO) or first in, first out (FIFO). In the case of standard costs, you should regularly compare them to the actual cost of materials purchased to see if any standard costs should be updated to bring them more in line with actual costs incurred. If it is company policy to update standard costs only at lengthy intervals, then verify that the variance between actual and standard costs is being written off to the cost of goods sold.

    If inventory layering is used to store inventory costs, then periodically audit the costs in the most recently used layers, tracing inventory costs back to specific supplier invoices.

2. *Audit production setup cost calculations.* If production setup costs are included in inventory unit costs, there is a possibility of substantial costing errors if the assumed number of units produced in a production run is incorrect. For example, if the cost of a production setup is $1,000 and the production run is 1,000 units, then the setup cost should be $1 per unit. However, if someone wanted to artificially increase the inventory valuation in order to increase profits, the assumed production run size could be reduced. In the example, if the production run assumption were dropped to 100 units, the cost per unit would increase tenfold to $10. A reasonable control over this problem is to regularly review setup cost calculations. An early warning indicator of this problem is to run a report comparing setup costs over time for each product to see if there are any sudden changes in costs. Also, access to the computer file storing this information should be strictly limited.

3. *Review inventory for obsolete items.* The single largest cause of inventory valuation errors is the presence of large amounts of obsolete inventory. To avoid this problem, periodically print a report that lists which inventory items have *not* been used recently, including the extended cost of these items. A more accurate variation is to print a report

itemizing all inventory items for which there are no current production requirements (possible only if a material requirements planning system is in place). Alternatively, create a report that compares the amount of inventory on hand to annual historical usage of each item. With this information in hand, you should then schedule regular meetings with the materials manager to determine what inventory items should be scrapped, sold off, or returned to suppliers. This concept is addressed more extensively in Section 4–5.

4. *Control updates to bill of material and labor routing costs.* The key sources of costing information are the bill of materials and labor routing records for each product. A few easy modifications to these records can substantially alter inventory costs. To prevent such changes from occurring, always impose strict security access over these records. If the accounting software has a change tracking feature that stores data about who made changes and what changes were made, be sure to use this feature. Periodically print a report (if available) detailing all changes made to the records, and review it for evidence of unauthorized access.

Because there are so many elements involved in inventory that can lead to an incorrect inventory valuation, it is best to use all of the preceding controls as part of a comprehensive system of valuation controls. Given the level of risk mitigation involved, there is a greater payoff in using all of the controls than in eliminating a few.

An additional inventory valuation activity is to conduct a periodic lower of cost or market (LCM) valuation, which is outlined in Exhibit 4.9. The next two controls are sufficient for ensuring that an LCM analysis is completed on a regular basis.

1. *Follow a schedule of lower of cost or market reviews.* The primary difficulty with LCM reviews is that they are not done at all. Adding them to the financial closing procedure, at least on a quarterly basis, will ensure that they are completed regularly.

2. *Follow a standard procedure for lower of cost or market reviews.* It is not uncommon for an LCM review to be very informal—perhaps a brief discussion with the purchasing staff once a year regarding pricing levels for a few major items. This approach does not ensure that all valuation problems will be uncovered. A better approach is to formulate a standard LCM procedure to be followed, such as the one shown in Exhibit 4.9.

Exhibit 4.9   Lower of Cost or Market Inventory Valuation Procedure

Policy/Procedure Statement   Retrieval No.:   INV-05

Subject: Lower of Cost or Market Inventory Valuation

1.   PURPOSE AND SCOPE

This procedure is used by the cost accountant to periodically adjust the inventory valuation for those items whose market value has dropped below their recorded cost.

2.   PROCEDURES

2.1   Prepare Inventory Valuation Report (Cost Accountant)

1. Export the extended inventory valuation report to an electronic spreadsheet. Sort it by declining extended dollar cost, and delete the 80% of inventory items that do not comprise the top 20% of inventory valuation. Sort the remaining 20% of inventory items by either part number or item description. Print the report.

2. Send a copy of the report to the materials manager, with instructions to compare unit costs for each item on the list to market prices, and mutually agree on a due date for completion of the review.

2.2   Adjust Inventory Valuations (Materials Manager and Cost Accountant)

1. When the materials management staff has completed its review, meet with the materials manager to go over its results and discuss any major valuation adjustments.

2. Have the materials management staff enter the revised valuation of selected items in the inventory database whose cost exceeds their market value.

2.3   Adjust Accounting Records (Cost Accountant)

1. Have the accounting staff expense the value of the write down in the accounting records.

2. Write a memo detailing the results of the lower of cost or market calculation. Attach one copy to the journal entry used to document the valuation, and issue another copy to the materials manager.

4–4 Controls for Goods in Transit

The default approach to handling goods in transit is that they are not the company's property prior to arriving at the receiving dock or after leaving via the shipping dock. However, this is not always correct, since shipping terms can specify that the company is responsible for the goods for all or some portion of their in-transit interval. If so, there is a risk of damage to inventory owned by the company for which many companies provide no controls at all. The next primary controls will assist in mitigating risk in this area.

- *Specify standard shipment terms on purchase orders.* It is in the interests of the company to include standard shipment terms on its purchase orders that shift the responsibility for in-transit inventory to the supplier or third-party delivery service. Any variation from the standard terms should require special approval by the purchasing manager as well as notification of the corporate insurance staff, who may need to arrange special insurance coverage for the delivery.
- *Mandate a review of shipment terms required by customers.* It is entirely possible that customer purchasing departments will attempt to shift shipment responsibility to the company, so the order entry staff should be required to review the shipment terms listed on incoming customer orders and to notify the corporate insurance staff of any special terms.

The next ancillary controls will help management gain assurance that the primary controls are installed and being used properly.

- *Audit shipment terms.* The internal audit team should schedule a periodic review of shipment terms mandated by customers, to see if the order entry staff detected these terms and warned the corporate insurance staff in a timely manner of in-transit inventory ownership issues requiring insurance coverage.
- *Audit the receiving dock.* A significant problem from a record-keeping perspective is that the receiving staff may not have time to enter a newly received delivery into the corporate computer system, so the accounting and purchasing staffs have no idea that the items have been received. Accordingly, a periodic audit should compare items sitting in the receiving area to the inventory database to see if they have been recorded and to match the purchase order numbers listed on received items to the database of outstanding purchase orders.

4–5 Controls for Obsolete Inventory Determination and Handling

There is inevitably a certain amount of inventory that will not be used, due to excessive purchasing of raw materials beyond a company's needs, customers not buying certain items, or assembly requirements no longer calling for particular parts. The most common approach is inattention: letting obsolete inventory pile up until external auditors force the company to devalue and dispose of it, resulting in large and unexpected losses. A proper obsolete inventory recognition system with accompanying controls results in a much more organized approach.

The primary risks associated with obsolete inventory are that the inventory will not be promptly recognized as obsolete, that inventory will be improperly designated as obsolete, that dispositioned inventory will be accidentally reordered, and that disposition of such items will be for substantially less money than originally estimated. The next controls deal with these risks.

- *Regularly complete an obsolete inventory review.* The best way to ensure that obsolescence is recognized promptly is to conduct a regularly scheduled obsolescence review of the entire inventory, typically using an obsolescence report such as the one shown in Exhibit 4.11, which lists items for which there appear to be excessive quantities on hand. This review should be conducted by the Materials Review Board (MRB), which is comprised of representatives from the warehouse, purchasing, sales, and production scheduling departments (thereby ensuring a broad range of opinions regarding the need to eliminate something from stock).

- *Draw down impacted inventory before implementing engineering change orders.* Whenever the engineering department issues a change order for a product, there is a risk that the new product configuration will no longer require in-stock raw materials for which there is no other use, rendering the materials obsolete. Accordingly, a standard part of the change order issuance procedure should be an examination of on-hand inventory balances, so that existing stocks can be drawn down prior to the change order going into effect.

- *Implement reorder flag shut-off procedure for inventory being elimi-nated.* There is nothing more frustrating than to deliberately reduce the quantity of a particular item in stock, only to have the reduced quantity trigger an automatic reorder transaction by the computer system, re-sulting in more stock on hand. To prevent this, there should be an in-ventory reduction procedure that includes a requirement to turn off the inventory reorder flag in the item master file.

- *Move obsolete inventory to segregated area.* It is much easier to review and leave as-is obsolete inventory if it is congregated in a single area rather than scattered throughout the warehouse.

- *Match obsolescence authorization to tagged obsolete inventory.* It is pos-sible that warehouse employees will deliberately tag inventory as being obsolete, so they can remove it from the warehouse or acquire it at a low price from the company. To avoid this problem, periodically compare the meeting notes from the MRB (see the obsolete inventory review pro-cedure in Exhibit 4.10) to tagged obsolete inventory, to ensure that only authorized items are tagged. Any other items marked as obsolete should immediately be brought to the attention of the warehouse manager and internal audit manager as being a possible case of fraud.

- *Record cash receipts from obsolete inventory dispositions in a separate account.* Part of the obsolete inventory review procedure is to revise the recorded cost of obsolete inventory downward to its estimated dis-position value. To determine if this disposition value actually was achieved, it is best to record the cash receipt in a separate general ledger account, with supporting detail, so that receipts can be reconciled to initial estimated values more easily.

Several policies designed to reduce the amount of inventory subject to obsolescence are noted in Section 4–11, "Inventory Policies."

4–6 Controls for a Basic Perpetual Inventory Tracking System

Perhaps the single most important control over the amount and location of inventory on hand is the use of a perpetual inventory system. Under this ap-proach, inventory records are updated constantly with purchases arriving

Exhibit 4.10   Obsolete Inventory Review Procedure

Policy/Procedure Statement   Retrieval No.:   INV-06

Subject: Obsolete Inventory Review

1.   PURPOSE AND SCOPE

This procedure is used by the materials review board (MRB) to determine which inventory items are to be considered obsolete, their proper valuation, and how each item is to be dispositioned.

2.   PROCEDURES

2.1   Prepare for MRB Meeting (Cost Accountant)

1. Schedule a meeting of the MRB, to meet in the warehouse.
2. Prior to the meeting, print enough copies of the Inventory Obsolescence Review Report (see Exhibit 4.11) for all members of the committee.

2.2   Review Potentially Obsolete Inventory (MRB)

1. Review all items on the report for which there appear to be excessive quantities on hand.
2. Determine the proper disposal of each item judged to be obsolete, including possible returns to suppliers, donations, inclusion in existing products, or scrap.
3. Have the warehouse staff flag each item as obsolete in the inventory database.

2.3   Determine Obsolescence Values (Purchasing and Cost Accountant)

1. Print the obsolete inventory report and send it to the purchasing department, with instructions for them to note on the report the estimated disposal value of each item.
2. Upon receipt of the disposal values from the purchasing department, enter the values in the item master file.
3. Reprint the revised obsolete inventory report and use it to write down the value of the inventory to its disposal value in the general ledger.

2.4   Issue Meeting Memo (Cost Accountant)

Issue a memo to the MRB, summarizing the results of its actions. Append a copy of the final obsolete inventory report to the memo prior to distribution.

Exhibit 4.11 Inventory Obsolescence Review Report

Description	Item No.	Location	Quantity on Hand	Last-Year Usage	Planned Usage	Extended Cost
Subwoofer case	0421	A-04–C	872	520	180	$9,053
Speaker case	1098	A-06-D	148	240	120	1,020
Subwoofer	3421	D-12-A	293	14	0	24,724
Circuit board	3600	B-01-A	500	5,090	1,580	2,500
Speaker, bass	4280	C-10-C	621	2,480	578	49,200
Speaker bracket	5391	C-10-C	14	0	0	92
Wall bracket	5080	B-03-B	400	0	120	2,800
Gold connection	6233	C-04–A	3,025	8,042	5,900	9,725
Tweeter	7552	C-05-B	725	6,740	2,040	5,630

from suppliers, sales to customers, picked items being sent to the production area, and so on. In its simplest form, no computers are used, and inventory updates are maintained in a card catalog. The materials handling staff is not allowed to record transactions directly in the card file (in order to segregate the handling and recording functions), instead completing prenumbered move tickets that are then entered in the card file by a warehouse clerk. The controls in this section are geared toward information storage in a card file; the controls in the next section are designed for a more advanced perpetual system involving a computer database.

The four counting and variance analysis controls at the bottom of the flowchart in Exhibit 4.12 would normally be considered supplemental controls for most other transaction flows. However, since the perpetual inventory card file will inevitably become more inaccurate over time, they are considered primary controls in this context. The controls noted in the flowchart are described at greater length next, in sequence from the top of the flowchart to the bottom.

- *Record inventory transactions on move tickets.* When the warehouse staff moves inventory and records each move in the perpetual inventory card file, the opportunity exists for staff members to remove inventory from the warehouse and alter the card file to mask the theft. To avoid this, the materials handling staff can document moves on a standard move ticket and give it to a warehouse clerk, who records the

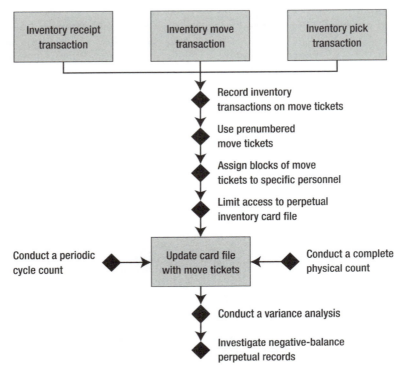

Exhibit 4.12   Controls for a Basic Perpetual Inventory Tracking System

transaction in the card file. Since this approach requires a considerable amount of extra labor, an alternative is to assign responsibility for record accuracy for specific locations within the warehouse to the materials handlers and then allow them to maintain their portions of the card file.

- *Use prenumbered move tickets.* If move tickets are used to document inventory transactions, consider prenumbering them and investigating all missing move tickets at the end of each shift. This will ensure that all transactions are entered in the card file.

- *Assign blocks of move tickets to specific personnel.* To obtain a tighter level of control over move tickets, record the range of move ticket numbers assigned to each warehouse person, so that responsibility for specific missing move tickets can be assigned to individual employees. This procedure should contribute to a reduction in the proportion of missing move tickets.

- *Limit access to perpetual inventory card file.* Even if warehouse employees are not allowed to update inventory records, they still may be able to do so by gaining illicit access to the card file and making alterations after the fact, which may cover up their theft of inventory. Accordingly, always restrict access to the card file.

- *Conduct a complete physical count.* Despite the best record keeping, perpetual records will become less accurate over time, due to the gradual accumulation of errors. To increase record accuracy, conduct a periodic physical count and reconcile the results to the perpetual records. The physical count procedure is shown in Exhibit 4.13.

- *Conduct a periodic cycle count.* An excellent alternative to the full-blown physical inventory count just described is to implement an on-going program of cycle counts, where small sections of the storage area are counted each day. The cycle counting procedure is shown in Section 4–7, in Exhibit 4.17. It is listed in that section, which addresses computerized perpetual tracking systems, because cycle counts are much easier to conduct in a computerized environment.

- *Conduct a variance analysis.* Whenever either a physical or a cycle count uncovers a variance between the actual and book quantity, it is mandatory that the variance be fully investigated and the underlying cause be corrected. Otherwise, the reason for the error will continue to cause errors in the future.

- *Investigate negative-balance perpetual records.* A record in the perpetual inventory card file contains a running balance of the current on-hand inventory quantity, usually in the far-right column. If this number ever reaches a negative balance, always investigate to determine what transaction or counting error caused the problem, and take steps to ensure that it does not happen again.

4–7 Controls for a Computerized Perpetual Inventory Tracking System

The perpetual inventory tracking system noted in the last section still exists in many companies but is considered primitive in comparison to a system founded on a computer database. Under this approach, warehouse employees typically enter all transactions "on the fly," using radio frequency bar

Exhibit 4.13   Physical Count Procedure

Physical Count Procedure

1. PURPOSE AND SCOPE

This procedure is used by the warehouse staff to conduct a thorough physical count of all inventory in the facility.

2. PROCEDURES

2.1 Activities One Week Prior to Count (Count Supervisor)

1. Contact the printing company and order a sufficient number of sequentially numbered count tags. (See Exhibit 4.14.) The first tag number should always be "1000." The tags should include fields for the product number, description, quantity count, location, and the counter's signature.
2. Review the inventory and mark all items lacking a part number with a brightly colored piece of paper. Inform the warehouse manager that these items must be marked with a proper part number immediately.
3. Clearly mark the quantity on all sealed packages.
4. Count all partial packages, seal them, and mark the quantity on the tape.
5. Prepare "Do Not Inventory" tags and use them to mark all items that should not be included in the physical inventory count.
6. Issue a list of count team members, with a notice regarding where and when they should appear for the inventory count.

2.2 Activities One Day Prior to Count (Count Supervisor)

1. Remind all participants that they are expected to be counting the next day.
2. Notify the warehouse manager that all items received during the two days of physical counts must be segregated and marked with "Do Not Inventory" tags.
3. Notify the manager that no shipments are allowed for the duration of the physical count.
4. Notify the warehouse manager that all shipments for which the paperwork has not been sent to accounting by that evening will be included in the inventory count on the following day.
5. Notify the warehouse manager that all shipping and receiving documentation from the day before the count must be forwarded to the accounting department that day, for immediate data entry. Likewise, any pick information must be forwarded at the same time.
6. Notify all outside storage locations to fax in their inventory counts.

2.3 Activities During the Count (Count Supervisor)

1. Enter all transactions from the previous day.
2. Assemble the count teams. Issue counting instructions to them, as well as blocks of tags, for which they must sign. Give each team a map of the warehouse with a section highlighted on it that the team is responsible for counting. Those teams with forklift experience will be assigned to count the top racks; those without this experience will be assigned the lower racks.

Exhibit 4.13 *(Continued)*

3. Call all outside storage warehouses and ask them to fax in their counts of company-owned inventory.

4. The count supervisor assigns additional count areas to those teams that finish counting their areas first.

5. The tag coordinator assigns blocks of tags to those count teams that run out of tags, tracks the receipt of tags, and follows up on missing tags. All tags should be accounted for by the end of the day.

6. The data entry person enters the information on the tags into a spreadsheet, summarizes the quantities for each item, and pencils the totals into the cycle count report that was run earlier in the day.

7. The count supervisor reviews any unusual variances with the count teams to ensure that the correct amounts were entered.

8. Review the test count with an auditor, if necessary. Give the auditor a complete printout of all tags as well as the cycle counting spreadsheet, showing all variances.

The following job descriptions apply to the inventory counting procedure.

- The *count supervisor* is responsible for supervising the count, which includes assigning count teams to specific areas and ensuring that all areas have been counted and tagged. This person also waits until all count tags have been compared to the quantities listed in the computer and then checks the counts on any items that appear to be incorrect.

- The *tag coordinator* is responsible for tracking the blocks of count tags that have been issued as well as for accounting for all tags that have been returned. When distributing tags, this person should mark down the beginning and ending numbers of each block of tags on a tracking sheet and obtain the signature of the person who receives the tags. When the tags are returned, this person must put them in numerical order and verify that all tags are accounted for. Once the verification is complete, the tag coordinator checks off the tags on the tracking sheet as having been received. Once returned tags have been properly accounted for, this person forwards them to the extension calculation clerk.

- The *extension calculation clerk* is responsible for summarizing the amounts on the tags (if there are multiple quantities listed) to arrive at a total quantity count on each tag. This person also compares the part numbers and descriptions on each tag to see if there are any potential identification problems. This person forwards all completed tags to the data entry person.

- The *data entry person* is responsible for entering the information on all count tags into the computer spreadsheet. When doing so, this person must enter *all* the information on each tag into a spreadsheet. Once a group of tags has been entered, the data entry person must stamp them as having been entered, clip them together, and store them separately. Once all tags are entered in the spreadsheet, this person sorts the data by part number. Next the data entry person prints out the spreadsheet and summarizes the quantities by part number, and transfers the total quantities by part number to the cycle count report. Any significant variances between the counted and cycle count quantities should be brought to the attention of the count supervisor for review.

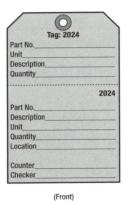
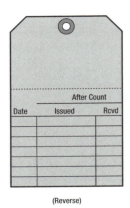

(Front)   (Reverse)

Exhibit 4.14   Inventory Tag Form

code scanners as they move inventory around the warehouse. Since this approach eliminates some segregation of duties, with materials handlers both moving assets and recording the transactions, it is best to require cycle counting in order to continually verify the record-keeping accuracy of the materials handlers. The system of controls for such a system is shown in Exhibit 4.15. Additional controls specific to bar code scanners are listed in Section 4–8, "Controls for Advanced Warehouse Systems."

As shown in the exhibit, materials handlers record inventory transactions in the computer system as soon as they complete a transaction. A key control is requiring the staff to complete all transaction backlogs, which allows cycle counters to conduct counts using the most accurate set of computer records and then perform variance analyses to correct any problems. In addition, the computer system can be used to flag customer-owned inventory, rather than having to manually segregate it. Finally, the right side of the exhibit shows the one common inadequacy in computerized tracking systems: there is no simple way to record scrap and rework transactions, since these usually occur on the production floor, and the production staff has no experience with data entry. Instead, a traditional system of prenumbered forms and specialized data entry staff is used to ensure that these transactions are correctly recorded. Given the extra level of paperwork involved, these transactions tend to take longer to record.

The controls noted in the flowchart are described at greater length next, in sequence from the top of the flowchart to the bottom.

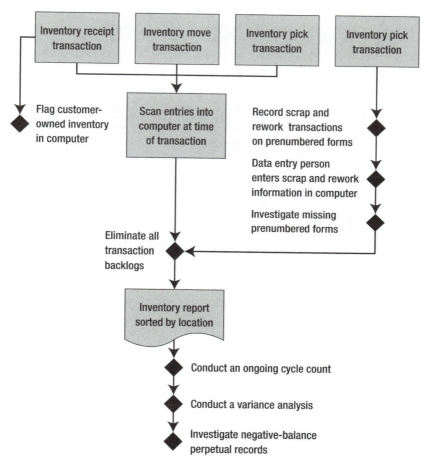

Exhibit 4.15 Controls for a Computerized Perpetual Inventory Tracking System

- *Flag customer-owned inventory in computer.* In situations where customers send inventory to a company for inclusion in a finished product, there is a significant risk that the company will inadvertently include the customer-owned inventory in its own inventory valuations. When inventory records are maintained in a computer system, the easiest way to handle this inventory is to flag it in the computer record as being customer-owned, which assigns it a zero cost. By flagging such inventory, there is no need to physically segregate it.

- *Record scrap and rework transactions on prenumbered forms.* A startling amount of materials and associated direct labor can be lost through the scrapping of production or its occasional rework. This tends to be a difficult item to control, since scrap and rework can occur at many points in the production process. Nonetheless, the manufacturing staff should be well trained in the use of transaction forms, such as the sample form shown in Exhibit 4.16, that record these actions, so that the inventory records will remain accurate.

- *Data entry person enters scrap and rework information in computer.* Since the production staff typically has no experience with data entry, it is better to send all completed scrap and rework forms to the warehouse clerk, who enters the information. This tends to result in significantly lower data entry errors.

Exhibit 4.16   Scrap/Rework Transaction Form

Date: _____

Item Number: _____

Description: _____

Scrapped	**Sent to Rework**
Quantity Scrapped: _____	Quantity to Rework: _____
Reason: _____	Reason: _____
_____	_____
_____	_____
Signature: _____	Signature: _____

- *Investigate missing prenumbered forms.* Any missing scrap or rework form could represent a valid transaction that has not been included in the computer database. Accordingly, the data entry person should use the computer to print a list of missing form numbers and conduct a search for the documents.

- *Eliminate all transaction backlogs.* A major ongoing difficulty for any inventory handling operation is when inventory-related transactions (e.g., receipts, putaways, picks, etc.) are not recorded as soon as they occur. When this happens, anyone counting the inventory will arrive at a total inventory quantity that varies from what the current record states and will post an adjusting entry to alter the supposedly incorrect record balance to match what was just counted. Then, when the late transaction entry is made, the record balance will differ from the physical quantity on hand. One control over this problem is to ensure that there is never a backlog of unrecorded transactions.

- *Conduct an ongoing cycle count.* Because the materials handlers not only move inventory but also record their own transactions, it is mandatory to conduct an ongoing cycle counting program to ensure that they have entered transactions correctly. The cycle counting procedure is shown in Exhibit 4.17.

- *Conduct a variance analysis.* Whenever either a physical or cycle count uncovers a variance between the actual and book quantity, it is mandatory that the variance be fully investigated and the underlying cause be corrected. Otherwise, the reason for the error will continue to cause errors in the future.

- *Investigate negative-balance perpetual records.* A record in the perpetual inventory card file contains a running balance of the current on-hand inventory quantity, usually in the far-right column. If this number ever reaches a negative balance, always investigate to determine what transaction or counting error caused the problem and take steps to ensure that it does not happen again.

The next control is supplemental to the controls embedded in the primary transaction flow but is useful for eliminating fraud through the illicit modification of inventory records.

Exhibit 4.17   Cycle Counting Procedure

Policy/Procedure Statement	Retrieval No.: INV-08

Subject: Cycle Counting Procedure

1.   PURPOSE AND SCOPE

This procedure is used by the cycle-counting staff and warehouse clerk to conduct ongoing daily cycle counts.

2.   PROCEDURES

2.1   Obtain Count Report (Cycle Counter)

Sort the inventory report by location, and print the location range designated for the daily cycle count. An example of the report, sorted by location code, is shown in Exhibit 4.18.

2.2   Count Inventory and Note Discrepancies (Cycle Counter)

1. Go to the first physical inventory location to be cycle-counted and compare the quantity, location, and part number of each inventory item to what is described for that location in the inventory report. Mark on the report any discrepancies in on-hand quantity, location, and description for each item.

2. Use the reverse process to ensure that the same information listed for all items on the report matches the items physically appearing in the warehouse location. Note any discrepancies on the report.

3. Verify that the noted discrepancies are not caused by recent inventory transactions that have not yet been logged into the computer system.

4. Forward the discrepancies to the warehouse clerk.

2.3   Adjust Inventory Records (Warehouse Clerk)

1. Correct the inventory database for all remaining errors noted.

2. Initial the discrepancies report. Photocopy it and send the copy to the cycle counter.

3. Calculate the inventory error rate and post it to the inventory accuracy report. (See Exhibit 4.19.)

4. File the original of the discrepancies report by date.

2.4   Adjust Inventory Records (Cycle Counter)

1. Call up a history of inventory transactions for each of the items for which errors were noted, and try to determine the cause of the underlying problem.

2. Investigate each issue and recommend corrective action to the warehouse manager.

Exhibit 4.18 Cycle Counting Report

Location	Item No.	Description	U/M	Quantity
A-10-C	Q1458	Switch, 120V, 20A	EA	_____
A-10-C	U1010	Bolt, Zinc, 3 × ¼	EA	_____
A-10-C	M1458	Screw, Stainless Steel, 2 × ⅜	EA	_____

Exhibit 4.19 Inventory Accuracy Report

Aisles	Responsible Person	2 Months Ago	Last Month	Week 1	Week 2	Week 3	Week 4
A–B	Fred P.	82%	86%	85%	84%	82%	87%
C–D	Alain Q.	70%	72%	74%	76%	78%	80%
E–F	Davis L.	61%	64%	67%	70%	73%	76%
G–H	Jeff R.	54%	58%	62%	66%	70%	74%
I–J	Alice R.	12%	17%	22%	27%	32%	37%
K–L	George W.	81%	80%	79%	78%	77%	76%
M–N	Robert T.	50%	60%	65%	70%	80%	90%

- *Control access to the inventory database.* The security levels assigned to the files containing inventory records should allow access to only a very small number of well-trained employees. By restricting access, the risk of inadvertent or deliberate changes to these valuable records will be minimized. The security system should also store the keystrokes and user access codes for anyone who has accessed these records, in case evidence is needed to prove that fraudulent activities have occurred.

4–8 Controls for Advanced Warehouse Systems

Additional technology and management concepts can be built on top of the basic computerized perpetual inventory tracking system described in the last section to improve the overall level of efficiency while also reducing the amount of manual transaction processing. However, since so many different systems are in use, they are not described here as a single integrated system. Instead, each one receives a separate description and set of associated controls. The systems are described next.

- *Bar code scanners.* Under this approach, the warehouse staff creates a bar-coded part number for each item as it enters the warehouse and attaches the bar code to the item. It also creates preset barcode labels for each warehouse location and posts them at each location. Anyone moving stock then scans the part number bar code and the bar code for the location to which it is being shifted and manually enters a quantity and transaction code to complete the transaction. This information typically is entered on a portable scanner that can be placed in a cradle to upload batched information to the central computer system or used in real time with a built-in radio to transmit and receive transaction information. Related controls are described next.

  ○ *Print part description on bar code labels.* A major risk with a bar-coded scanning system is that the bar code label contains an incorrect part number, which will then be scanned multiple times as the item to which it is attached moves through the warehouse. To make it easier to detect incorrect bar codes, always include the item description on the bar code label, which should print out just below the bar code.

  ○ *Laminate warehouse location tags.* The bar-coded tag identifying each bin location in the warehouse can be subject to a great deal of abrasion from forklifts and other materials-handling equipment, resulting in damaged bar codes that cannot be scanned. To avoid the risk of having the warehouse staff manually input the location information (with the attendant higher risk of data entry error) into their bar code scanners, laminate all location tags to increase their durability.

  ○ *Regularly review location tags.* Given the durability problems with location tags as described in the preceding control point, it is useful to conduct a regularly scheduled review of *all* location tags to determine which ones should be replaced. This is also a good way to determine if inventory is now being stored in locations where there is no identifying tag at all, so that tags can be created for those locations.

  ○ *Require specific character lengths for scanner data entry fields.* Entering an inventory movement transaction in a bar code scanning device will require several entries: for the item number, bin location, transaction code, and quantity being moved. If the scanner accepts character strings of any length in each of these fields, it is quite likely that the materials handling staff will enter scanned and keypunched information into the wrong fields. To avoid this, set up the scanner to allow specific maximum character strings in each field. For example, eight digits may be both the minimum and maximum character string for a location code, while ten digits is required for an item number, and nothing over four digits is allowed for quantities. As an additional control, always use different numbers of characters for location codes and item numbers, so they cannot be confused with each other.

○ *Require scanner uploads at all scheduled breaks*. If the materials handling staff is using batch-mode scanners that must upload their contents to the central computer, require the staff to put the scanners in their upload cradles whenever they have scheduled breaks. This prevents an excessive amount of information from being stored in the scanners while also keeping location-specific inventory counts more accurate.

○ *Assign picking and putaway responsibilities by aisle*. Since bar code scanning requires the materials handling staff to both move items and record transactions, it is possible that the staff will forget to conduct scanning transactions in the midst of other duties. To track down which employees are most likely to not be completing their scanning chores, assign picking and putaway responsibilities by aisle. By doing so, errors found through cycle counts can be traced more easily to specific employees.

• *Cross-dock inventory*. Under this approach, items arrive at the receiving dock and are moved immediately to a shipping dock for delivery elsewhere. This approach eliminates inventory moves into a storage rack as well as subsequent picking and movement back to the shipping dock. Related controls are described next.

○ *Use warehouse clerks for all data entry*. When the materials handling staff is responsible for recording both receiving and shipping transactions, as well as moving the physical goods, it is entirely likely that they will occasionally forget to record transactions. To avoid this problem, concentrate all transaction-recording tasks with warehouse clerks whose sole responsibility is to ensure that receiving and shipping transactions are properly recorded.

○ *Replace receiving data entry with advance shipping notices (ASN).* If suppliers can reliably send the company exact information about the precise contents of each truckload being shipped to the company, it is possible to use each ASN as a receiving document that is entered as a receipt as soon as the truckload arrives. This approach works only if suppliers can prove that they can be relied on to send an ASN for every shipment and to detail the contents of each truckload in the ASN correctly.

- *Pick-to-light systems.* Under this approach, light sensors are mounted on the front of each bin location in the warehouse (though usually only for small, easily picked items). Each sensor unit is linked to the computer system's picking module and contains a light that illuminates to indicate that picking is required for an order, a liquid crystal display (LCD) readout listing the number of items to be picked, and a button to press to indicate completion of the pick. When a stock picker enters an order number into the system, the bin sensors for those bins containing required picks will light up and their LCDs will show the number of units to pick. When a stock picker has completed picking from a bin, he or she presses the button, and the indicator light shuts off. Related controls are described next.

  ○ *Assign putaway responsibilities by location.* Even the best pick-to-light systems still will result in errors if the materials handling staff is putting goods away in the wrong locations, which causes the pick-to-light system to direct employees to pick the wrong items. To detect materials handlers who putaway in the wrong locations, always assign putaway responsibilities by location.

  ○ *Assign picking responsibilities by location.* Though the pick-to-light system is quite intuitive, some employees are better than others at using the system to accomplish accurate picks. Accordingly, always assign picking responsibilities by location and then use cycle counts to determine count inaccuracies by assigned picker locations.

- *Stage received goods for zone putaways.* This approach involves setting up several portable conveyors at a dock door, each one leading to a separate staging area representing a different putaway zone; the receiving staff then places items on the correct conveyor for a specific putaway zone. Related controls are listed next.

○ *Identify putaway zones by computer.* If a company has thousands of products in stock, it should not rely on the memory of the receiving staff to determine which conveyor to place incoming items on. This problem is exacerbated if the warehouse manager regularly optimizes warehouse locations, which makes it even more difficult to remember where products are stored. The result is inventory piling up in the wrong aisles, which delays their storage as well as their entry into the computer system. To avoid this problem, have the receiving staff enter each part number into the computer as it arrives, so that a nearby computer monitor automatically calls up the correct putaway zone, telling the user which conveyor to place the received item on.

○ *Record incorrect putaway zones for employee training.* If a company relies on employee knowledge of where products are to be stored, then all items sent to the wrong zones should be recorded, so that employees can receive rapid feedback regarding where the inventory was sent and where it should have gone.

• *Zone picking.* Under this approach, an entire day's picks are consolidated into a single master pick list, which is then sorted by warehouse location. Different pickers are then sent to specific sections of the warehouse with their portions of the master pick list, where they complete their share of the picks with much less travel time than would be the case if they were picking for all items on the list. All picked items are then consolidated in a central order breakdown area, where they are broken down to fulfill individual orders. Related controls are described next.

○ *Record picks at the central picking area.* Inventory pickers are much more efficient when they have no data entry responsibilities. Also, since zone picking results in all picked items being sent to a central order breakdown area, these two factors combine to make it highly efficient to have a designated data entry person record all picks in the order breakdown area.

○ *Have pickers specialize in limited picking areas.* Though zone picking is a very efficient process, its main difficulty is that no single employee is responsible for all items to be picked, which makes it difficult to determine who is responsible for missed or incorrect picks. Responsibility can be more closely traced by giving employees specific responsibility for selected areas of the warehouse. This also gives pickers greater knowledge of where products are located and what they look like, resulting in both faster and more accurate picking times.

4–9 Controls for Manufacturing Resources Planning

The MRP II system is an automated system for scheduling the purchase of materials and the production process. It takes as input the current on-hand and in-transit inventory record for each component of a product as well as the amount of labor required to build it and the bill of materials that lists the components of each item to be produced. Its output is a production and staffing schedule that takes into account all constraints and produces purchase orders for any required materials. Given the automated nature of the system, it is critical that all information entered into it be as accurate as possible. Consequently, virtually all controls associated with MRP are concerned with maintaining the highest possible degree of record accuracy. In the flowchart in Exhibit 4.20, the small black diamonds indicate the location of key control points in the process, with descriptions next to the diamonds.

The controls noted in the flowchart are described at greater length next, in sequence from the top of the flowchart to the bottom.

- *Maintain 95 percent inventory record accuracy.* For the MRP logic to function properly, not only must the inventory quantity be accurate, but the record of its location, unit of measure, part number, and description must be accurate. A generally accepted minimum level of record accuracy is 95 percent. If a lower level of accuracy is maintained, the MRP logic will yield incorrect results.
- *Maintain 95 percent labor routing record accuracy.* As was the case for inventory record accuracy, labor routing records must also be sufficiently accurate to result in accurate workload scheduling throughout the production process.
- *Maintain 98 percent bill of material record accuracy.* The bills of material are critical for determining the value of inventory as it moves through the work-in-process stages of production and eventually arrives in the finished goods area, since these bills itemize every possible com-

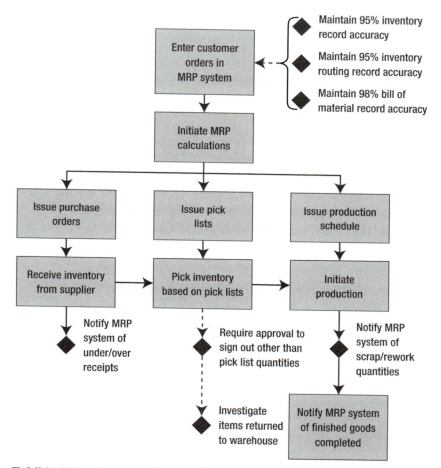

Exhibit 4.20 System of Controls for Material Requirements Planning

ponent that comprises each product. These records should be compared regularly to actual product components to verify that they are correct, and their accuracy should be tracked.

- *Notify MRP system of under/over receipts.* It is very likely that suppliers will not ship precisely the amount ordered, either because some portion of an order is rejected for quality reasons or simply due to slight miscounts in the quantities delivered. In either case, the MRP system will not function properly unless it is aware of the exact amount of usable inventory that has been received, which calls for notification by the receiving staff of receiving variances.

- *Require approval to sign out other than pick list quantities.* When the production staff asks for additional quantities of a component from the warehouse, this is a strong indicator that the bill of materials used to originally pick the goods is incorrect, probably listing too low a quantity. To correct the bill of materials, carefully document all excess issuances and forward them to the engineering department for examination.

- *Investigate items returned to warehouse.* When picked items are returned to the warehouse, this is a strong indicator that the bill of materials used to pick the goods is incorrect, probably listing too high a quantity. A good control is to assign the investigation of all returned items to the engineers who originally constructed the bill of materials, so they can determine the problem and correct the bill of materials record.

- *Notify MRP system of scrap/rework variances.* The production process inevitably yields a certain amount of scrap or products that must be reworked. If not reported back to the MRP system, it will assume that a certain quantity of finished goods have been completed when in fact additional production must be scheduled. Consequently, it is critical to enter scrap and rework quantities into the MRP system as soon as they occur.

The MRP II procedure shown in Exhibit 4.21 integrates many of the preceding controls into the operation of the MRP II system.

Though not listed as a primary control point in the MRP II controls flowchart, the next activity is required throughout the production planning process.

- *Immediately review all action/exception messages.* The MRP system will generate action/exception messages involving problems that will interfere with the production process. A monitoring system should be in place to track how rapidly the production planners respond to these messages.

The next supplemental controls assist in improving the record accuracy of the MRP II system.

Exhibit 4.21 MRP II Procedure

Policy/Procedure Statement   Retrieval No.:   INV-09

Subject: MRP II Operations Procedure

1.   PURPOSE AND SCOPE

This procedure is used by the order entry, production, and materials management staffs to correctly operate the MRP II system.

2.   PROCEDURES

2.1   Enter Customer Orders in MRP System (Order Entry Staff)

1. Upon receipt of a customer order, enter the order in the MRP II system.
2. If the order is for finished goods, inform the customer of the expected shipment date.
3. If the order requires production to be completed, inform the customer that he/she will be contacted shortly regarding the expected shipment date.

2.2   Adjust Production Schedule (Production Scheduler)

1. Review all newly entered customer orders, and slot them into the unfrozen portion of the production schedule.
2. Run the MRP II logic, and revise the production schedule based on the presence of warning messages for too little production capacity or inventory.
3. Continue revising the production schedule until all warning messages have been eliminated.

2.3   Review Work Center Utilization (Production Manager)

1. Review the projected workloads report, and verify that a sufficient amount of downtime has been scheduled for each work center for routine maintenance.
2. Review the production load on all bottleneck operations to be certain that they can handle the needed load. If not, arrange to shift production work elsewhere or adjust the production schedule and process the MRP II logic again.

2.4   Issue Purchase Orders (Materials Management Staff)

1. Review the list of proposed purchase orders issued by the MRP II system for raw materials requirements.
2. If the proposed quantity to be ordered appears excessive, verify the usage requirements, on-hand balance, and any changes to the unit of measure field in the item master record. Correct any errors and process the MRP II logic again.
3. If the purchase orders are acceptable, release them to suppliers and verify receipt.
4. Inform the order entry staff that they can contact customers regarding preliminary estimated shipping dates.

(continues)

Exhibit 4.21   *(Continued)*

2.5 Review Labor Schedule Requirements (Production Manager)

Review the labor requirements by work center report, and verify with the human resources department that a sufficient number of workers will be available to operate machinery. Arrange for overtime labor, and schedule specific staff to all shifts.

2.6 Receive Inventory (Materials Management Staff)

1. Upon receipt of inventory, call up the purchase order number in the computer at the receiving dock to determine the quantity ordered.

2. Inspect the received item for quality problems, and verify that the received quantity matches the ordered quantity.

3. Log the quantity of usable inventory received into the MRP II system.

4. Contact the supplier about all items not meeting quality standards, obtain an RMA number, and return these items to the supplier.

2.7 Pick and Issue Inventory (Materials Management Staff)

1. Print the pick list for all jobs scheduled for production during the next work shift.

2. Assign each pick list to a warehouse staff person, who picks items that are listed on the pick list from stock, and check off completed picks on the report.

3. Upon completion of a pick sequence, record the picked quantities in the MRP II system.

4. Notify the production scheduler and materials manager if there were not sufficient quantities on hand to pick all required items completely.

5. Store all picked items for a specific job in a separate bin, and attach the pick list to the bin. Highlight on the pick list all incomplete picks.

6. When needed, move the storage bin to the production area. In the MRP II system, log the picked items out of the warehouse and transfer them to the production location.

2.8 Record Additional Pick Transactions (Materials Management Staff)

1. If the production staff requests additional components for a job, record in the MRP II system the quantity requested and the job number. Also e-mail this information to the product engineering staff, for review of errors in the bill of materials.

2. If the production staff returns excess parts to the warehouse, record the returned quantities and related job number in the MRP II system. Also e-mail this information to the product engineering staff, for review of errors in the bill of materials.

2.9 Enter Scrap/Rework Transactions (Production Staff)

- Whenever scrap or rework occurs, put it into a scrap/rework bin, complete a two-part scrap/rework form that itemizes the component and quantity, attach one copy to the bin, and place the other copy in the workstation out box.

Exhibit 4.21 *(Continued)*

- At the end of each shift, collect all completed scrap/rework forms from the workstation out boxes and enter them in the MRP II system.

- At the end of each shift, tour the production area and collect all scrap that has not been placed in scrap/rework bins. Complete scrap/rework forms for these items, store them in bins, and record the forms in the MRP II system.

2.10 Enter Completed Production Transactions (Materials Management Staff)

1. Upon completion of the production process, return all finished goods to the warehouse for storage. At the warehouse gate, count and tag all inventory and record it in the MRP II system.

2. Store the finished goods in bins within the warehouse, and record the bin locations in the MRP II system.

3. At the end of each shift, tour the production area and collect all finished goods that have not been delivered to the warehouse. Verify with the production manager that these items can be designated as finished goods, and bring them to the warehouse for storage. At the warehouse gate, count and tag the finished goods inventory and record it in the MRP II system. Store the finished goods in bins within the warehouse, and record the bin locations in the MRP II system.

- *Review the production area for excess inventory.* The production staff may not want to spend the time returning excess inventory to the warehouse and instead may let it pile up on the shop floor. By conducting a periodic sweep of the production area for these items and returning them to the warehouse, the engineering staff will have evidence of possible bill of materials problems, which it should fix.

- *Restrict access to the inventory item master file.* The ordering subroutine within the MRP system can be severely disrupted if the unit of measure field within the inventory item master file is altered. To avoid this, always tightly restrict access to the inventory item master file.

- *Review excess usage report.* The MRP II system is designed to calculate how much material is needed for a specific job. By linking this information to actual materials usage data on each job, it is possible to calculate the amount of excess materials usage by job, as shown in Exhibit 4.22. This is a valuable control, since it can be used to improve ongoing operations and to increase the accuracy of the bill of materials.

Exhibit 4.22   Excess Material Usage Report

Material Used	Standard Usage (Units)	Actual Usage (Units)	Excess Usage (Units)	Unit Cost	Total Excess Cost	Comments
A	3,960	4,110	150	$4.75	$712.50	(a)
B	15,840	15,960	120	2.00	240.00	(b)
C	3,960	4,000	40	21.50	860.00	(c)
D	3,960	3,970	10	65.40	654.00	(d)
E	15,840	15,920	80	3.25	260.00	(e)
Total	—	—	—	—	$2,726.50	

(a) Parts defective
(b) Careless workmanship
(c) Power down
(d) Wrong speed drilling
(e) Maintenance technician dropped case

4–10 Controls for Just-in-Time Systems

A just-in-time system is comprised of a number of manufacturing techniques whose central goal is to produce only to specific customer orders, and in the shortest possible period of time. The next techniques are some of the ones used to reach this goal.

- Frequent supplier deliveries directly to production
- Reliance on fewer suppliers
- Material movements initiated by a kanban authorization from the downstream workstation
- Constant reduction of lot sizes, lead times, and equipment setup times
- Minimization of machine setup times

These manufacturing techniques are sometimes coupled with payments to suppliers that are based solely on the content of their components in finished goods produced by the company rather than by supplier invoices.

Given the small number of in-process controls required by a JIT system, no controls flowchart is provided. All of the next controls should be considered primary ones necessary to the ongoing functioning of a JIT system.

- *Certify the quality and delivery reliability of suppliers.* A common JIT technique is to allow suppliers to deliver directly to the production facility without any receiving function, so a critical control is to precertify the quality and delivery reliability of suppliers.

- *Create a supplier performance scoring system.* The preceding control is designed to measure the *initial* capability of a supplier to deliver high-quality goods in a reliable manner. However, there must also be a mechanism for ensuring that suppliers' ongoing performance remains at a high level. Thus, using a supplier performance scoring system that is based primarily on quality and delivery criteria is a necessary control.

- *Use standard containers to move, store, and count inventory.* A control problem in a JIT environment is the lack of any system for counting inventory once it is in the production process. One solution is to shut down the inflow of raw materials into the production process and let all work in process be completed before conducting a count. Another approach is to use standard containers to move, store, and count inventory. Using these containers makes it extremely easy to determine quantities on hand.

- *Inspect parts at downstream workstations.* Because JIT systems produce exactly enough goods to meet immediate customer needs, it can be devastating if parts are incorrectly made and this is not discovered until the end of the production process. Thus, a major control point is to require each workstation to inspect the work-in-process inventory provided to it by the immediately preceding workstation. This immediately highlights production problems and initiates the timely creation of replacement parts.

- *Do not work without an open kanban.* A kanban is an authorization to create a specific quantity of inventory. Once the specified amount is completed, the kanban is closed, and no further production work is authorized. If a workstation were to continue to create inventory without an open kanban, the potential exists for the creation of too much inventory, which may never be used. Thus, absolute enforcement of the kanban authorization rule is necessary to ensure that inventory levels are kept to a minimum.

4–11 Inventory Policies

A number of policies can be used to bolster the system of controls for inventory. The 20 policies in this section are broken down into subcategories for receiving, record accuracy, valuation, and obsolescence. The next three policies help ensure that incoming inventory is properly inspected, recorded, and stored.

1. *Incoming inventory shall be recorded after it has been received and inspected.* This policy ensures that the quantity and quality of incoming inventory has been verified prior to recording it in the inventory database, thereby avoiding later problems with having incorrect usable quantities on hand.
2. *Goods received on consignment shall be identified and stored separately from company-owned inventory.* This policy keeps a company from artificially inflating its inventory by the amount of incoming consignment inventory, which would otherwise increase reported profits.
3. *Consignment inventory shipped to reseller locations shall be clearly identified as such in both the shipping log and the inventory tracking system.* This policy keeps a company from inflating its sales through the recognition of shipments sent to resellers that are actually still owned by the company.

The next six policies are useful for improving inventory record accuracy by assigning responsibility for accuracy, mandating regular counts, requiring up-to-date record updates, and restricting access to both the inventory itself and the inventory database:

1. *The materials manager is responsible for inventory accuracy.* This policy centralizes control over inventory accuracy, thereby increasing the odds of it being kept at a high level.
2. *A complete physical inventory count shall be conducted at the end of each reporting period.* This policy ensures that an accurate record of the inventory is used as the basis for a cost of goods sold calculation. However, it is considered counterproductive if an effective cycle counting system is already in place.
3. *Cycle counters shall continually review inventory accuracy and identify related problems.* This policy is intended for perpetual inventory

systems, and results in a much higher level of inventory accuracy and attention to the underlying problems that cause inventory errors.

4. *No inventory transaction shall occur without being immediately recorded in the perpetual inventory database.* This policy keeps the inventory database accurate at all times, preventing errors from arising when employees adjust the database on the incorrect assumption that the current record is correct.

5. *No access to the inventory is allowed by unauthorized personnel.* This policy generally leads to the lockdown of the warehouse, yielding much greater control over the accurate recording of inventory issuance transactions.

6. *Only designated personnel shall have access to the inventory database and item master file.* This policy ensures not only that just trained employees adjust inventory records, but also that the responsibility for record accuracy can be traced to designated people.

The next seven policies improve the accuracy of the inventory valuation by enforcing regular updates to key costing databases, restricting access to that data, and promptly identifying such costs as lower of cost or market determinations, obsolescence, and scrap.

1. *Changes in production processes shall be immediately reflected in labor routings.* This policy ensures that the costs assigned to products through labor routings accurately reflect the actual production process, equipment usage, and production staffing.

2. *Changes in product components shall be immediately reflected in the associated bills of material.* This policy ensures that the costs assigned to a product through a bill of materials accurately reflects the current product configuration as designed by the engineering staff.

3. *Standard cost records shall be updated at least annually.* This policy ensures that standard costs used in inventory valuations do not stray too far from actual costs.

4. *Only designated personnel shall have access to the labor routing and bill of materials databases.* This policy ensures that untrained employees are kept away from the critical computer files needed to value inventory quantities.

5. *Lower of cost or market calculations shall be conducted at least annually.* This policy ensures that excessively high inventory costs are

stripped out of the inventory before they can become an excessively large proportion of it. This policy may be modified to require more frequent reviews, based on the variability of market rates for various inventory items.

6. *Formal inventory obsolescence reviews shall be conducted at least annually.* This policy requires an inventory review team to scan the inventory periodically for obsolete items, which not only removes the cost of such items from stock, but also gives management a chance to profitably dispose of older inventory items before they become worthless.

7. *Management shall actively seek out, identify, and dispose of scrap as soon as possible.* This policy requires the production team to remove scrap from the manufacturing process immediately, thereby keeping it from being recorded in the inventory records and artificially inflating profits.

Inventory obsolescence is caused in part by the purchase of excessive inventory quantities and change-over to new product configurations before using up available supplies. The next three policies address these issues.

1. *Purchasing quantities shall be based on specific production requirements.* The purchasing staff sometimes may feel tempted to buy a large quantity of some item at a bargain price, even though the amount purchased may represent sufficient inventory for an excessively long period of time. This policy requires the purchasing staff to make acquisitions based only on specific purchasing requirements.

2. *Minimum order quantities shall be used when cost-effective.* This policy requires the purchasing staff to acquire goods from suppliers who sell in the smallest possible minimum order quantities. By doing so, there is less inventory on hand and therefore less risk that some of the inventory will become obsolete.

3. *Engineering change orders shall be phased in to reduce inventory obsolescence.* This policy forces the engineering staff to consider the amount of on-hand inventory when determining the date when an engineering change order is to take effect, thereby reducing the amount of inventory that may be rendered obsolete by the change order.

Summary

Inventory controls can require a significant proportion of the materials handling staff's time if entirely manual systems are being used, since staff members must divide their time between moving inventory and documenting their actions for record-keeping purposes. The amount of time required for controls diminishes rapidly when bar coding is introduced, since materials handlers can scan transactions at the pick or putaway point, though this new approach does not segregate the record-keeping and asset-handling functions. The system requiring the fewest controls *during* the materials handling process is the just-in-time system, though new controls are needed to certify the capabilities of suppliers before they ever ship anything to the company. Thus, the system of controls for inventory varies considerably, based on the level of technology in place and the manufacturing system being used.

Chapter 5

Controls for Billing Best Practices

Overview

This chapter covers the billing portion of the customer order cycle. Chapter 3 addressed the other portions of the cycle: order entry, credit, and shipping. Controls for billing differ substantially for entirely paper-based systems and computerized systems and so are described separately in Sections 5–1 and 5–2. Section 5–3 covers controls for several of the more advanced billing best practices, including billings using evaluated receipts, electronic data interchange, and drop shipments.

5–1 Basic Billing Controls

It is uncommon to see billing systems that are entirely paper-based, since computerized billing systems are inexpensive to purchase and maintain. Nonetheless, paper-based billing systems still are sometimes found in smaller establishments where shipping or service volumes are so low that there is little need for a formal computer system.

The basic process flow for a paper-based billing system is shown in Exhibit 5.1. As the flowchart reveals, the process uses as input the customer order, bill of lading, and customer purchase order, which are forwarded from other departments, as noted in Chapter 3. Upon receipt, the billing clerk verifies that a credit approval stamp has been placed on the sales order. If not, the clerk notifies the credit department of the problem. If the stamp exists, the clerk uses a three-part prenumbered invoice form to prepare an invoice and has a second person review the invoice for errors. Once completed, one copy of the invoice is used to post the transaction to the accounts receivable ledger, while the second copy is used to post the transaction to the

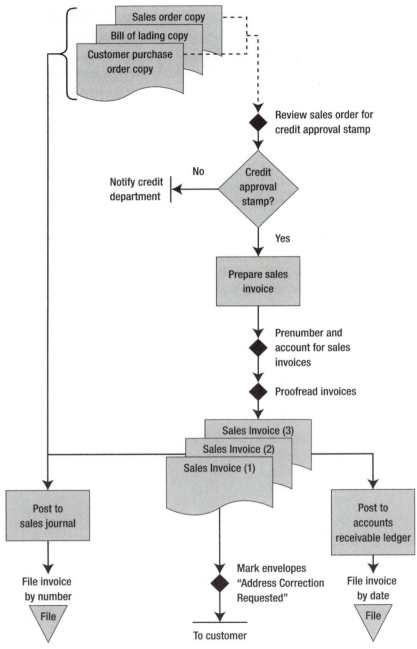

Exhibit 5.1 Basic Controls for Paper-Based Billing

sales journal. The remaining copy of the invoice is mailed in an envelope marked "Address Correction Requested," so the billing staff will know if the customer's address has changed.

The controls noted in the flowchart are described at greater length next, in sequence from the top of the flowchart to the bottom.

- *Review sales order for credit approval stamp.* As noted in Chapter 3, all customer orders should have been reviewed by the credit department and received an approval stamp prior to being forwarded to the billing department. Thus, this control should spot few missing credit approval stamps. Any such instances represent a control breach, so the credit department should be notified of the problem at once. This is only a detective control, since the billing clerk receives no paperwork until after a shipment is made.

- *Prenumber and account for sales invoices.* Invoices should always be created using prenumbered forms, so the billing staff can track the sequence of invoices more easily and will not issue the same invoice number to multiple customers.

- *Proofread invoices.* Some invoices are so complex, involving the entry of purchase order numbers, many line items, price discounts and other credits, that it is difficult to create an error-free invoice. Customers reject invoices with errors, thereby delaying the payment process. To correct this problem, assign a second person to be the invoice proofreader. This person has not created the invoice and so has an independent view of the situation and can provide a more objective view of invoice accuracy. However, due to the delay caused by proofreading, it may be unnecessary for small-dollar or simplified invoices.

- *Mark envelope "address correction requested."* The primary purpose of the invoice is to allow customers to pay on time. If the invoice is sent to the wrong address, then this goal is not being met. Since customers regularly move to new locations, the company needs a simple mechanism to track them. One such approach is to mark the words "Address Correction Requested" on each envelope mailed. If the customer has moved and filed a forwarding address with the U.S. Postal Service, the Postal Service will forward the mail to the new address and also notify the company of the new address. The company then can update the customer address file. The Postal Service charges a small fee for this notification service.

A procedure that itemizes the manual generation of an invoice is described in Exhibit 5.2. It includes all the preceding controls as well as a number of other steps needed for the billing process.

The next controls are supplemental to the primary controls just noted for the paper-based billing process.

- *Segregate duties for billing and collections.* The billing and collection functions should always be segregated. If they are segregated, it becomes much more difficult for a collections person to fraudulently access incoming customer payments and alter invoices and credit memos to hide the missing funds.

- *Verify contract terms prior to invoicing.* If invoices are being created based on the terms of long-standing contracts with customers, then a useful control is to verify contract terms prior to invoicing. This approach ensures that invoiced amounts match the terms set forth in the agreement and change on the stipulated trigger dates.

- *Monitor customer complaints about improper invoices.* If there are continuing problems with the accuracy of issued invoices, then a good control is to include an accounting manager's phone number on the standard invoice form and encourage customers to call if they have problems. Do not have customers call the person who created the invoice, since this person would be more likely to ignore or cover up the complaint.

- *Route all address changes to the billing staff.* Customer address changes can put a serious crimp in the cash collection process, since the Postal Service often takes two weeks to return mail sent to an old address. To prevent this, the company's mailroom staff should route all returned invoices directly to the accounting staff, which should assign a high priority to researching the correct address, updating the customer address file, and reissuing the invoice.

- *Reconcile goods shipped to goods billed.* There should be a continual comparison of billings to the shipping log. Doing this reduces the likelihood that a shipment is made without a corresponding invoice being issued.

Exhibit 5.2 Paper-Based Billing Procedure

Policy/Procedure Statement　　　　　　　　　　Retrieval No.:　BIL-01

Subject: Paper-Based Billing Procedure

1. PURPOSE AND SCOPE

This procedure is used by the billing clerk to create invoices in a paper-based environment.

2. PROCEDURES

2.1 Review Incoming Billing Documentation (Billing Clerk)

1. Match the sales order bill of lading and customer purchase order to ensure that all supporting paperwork is available.

2. If there is no sales order or customer purchase order, contact the order entry department. If there is no bill of lading, contact the shipping department.

3. If there is no credit approval stamp on the sales order, notify the credit department for billing instructions.

2.2 Create Invoice (Billing Clerk and Billing Clerk #2)

1. Unlock the document storage cabinet and remove a three-part prenumbered invoice from the top of the stack of prenumbered forms. Lock the cabinet.

2. Enter the invoice number on the invoice log-in sheet. If there is a gap in the numeric sequence since the last invoice was entered, notify the controller of the problem.

3. Create the invoice using the quantities noted on the bill of lading and the prices noted on the customer purchase order. Manually extend all prices and add freight and shipping charges.

4. Give the invoice to a second billing clerk, who proofreads the invoice, recalculates all extensions, and verifies that prices match the company price list for the indicated quantity levels. If there are errors, note them on the invoice and return it to the first billing clerk for correction.

2.3 Burst and Distribute Invoice (Billing Clerk)

1. Burst the invoice into its three component parts. Send the first copy to the customer, using an enveloped stamped with the phrase "Address Correction Requested."

2. Send the second and third copies to the general ledger accountant.

2.4 Record and File Invoice (General Ledger Clerk)

1. Using information on the second invoice copy, record the sale in the accounts receivable ledger. File the invoice by date.

2. Using information on the third invoice copy, record the sale in the sales journal. File the invoice by invoice number.

- *Identify shipments of product samples in the shipping log.* A product that is shipped with no intention of being billed is probably a product sample being sent to a prospective customer or marketing agency. These should be noted as product samples in the shipping log, and the internal audit staff should verify that each of them was properly authorized, preferably with a signed document.

- *Revise the invoice layout to prevent payment errors.* Companies regularly issue invoices that are too complex or cluttered to be readily understandable to recipients, leading to delayed or incorrect payments. The next improvements to the formatting of invoices represent an indirect control over the reliability of issued invoices.

  ○ *Add contact information.* If customers have a problem with an invoice, they want immediate access to the billing staff in order to make the correction. To make this as easy as possible for them, clearly state contact information in a box on the invoice, preferably in bold or colored print.

  ○ *Clearly state the payment due date.* Rather than state such abbreviated and arcane payment terms as "2/10 N 30" (take a 2 percent discount if paid within 10 days, or the net amount if paid within 30 days), state the exact date on which the payment is due and the amount of the payment due on that date. This avoids problems with recipients incorrectly interpreting the payment terms or paying based on their receipt date for the invoice rather than the invoice date.

  ○ *Remove unnecessary information.* The accounting staff likes to add information that is useful for it but that may be confusing and irrelevant to the customer, and which therefore may interfere with the timely payment of the invoice. Such information can include the name of the salesperson, the job number, and the document number. Whenever possible, remove all such unnecessary information from the invoice. The key factor in determining what information stays or is removed is that the primary purpose of the invoice is to allow customers to pay the correct amount on time—if it has no bearing on that goal, then it has no place on the invoice.

- *Review all journal entries to the receivables account.* The general ledger accounts for sales, and accounts receivable should include only entries summarizing activity in the accounts receivable ledger and sales journal. Any other entry posted to these accounts may represent an attempt to alter balance sheet or revenue amounts improperly, and so should be actively reviewed for appropriateness.

- *Analyze metrics.* A few metrics indicate the possible presence of improper billing situations. One is a comparison of inventory levels to revenues; if billings are made prior to shipment of the related goods, then the proportion of inventory to sales will increase (usually at the end of the month). Also, if channel stuffing (selling too many goods to distributors) is occurring, an indicator is an increased level of product returns after period-end as well as an increased number of days in accounts receivable outstanding.

- *Audit billings.* The internal audit staff should periodically review a sample of all invoices issued. The audit should focus on the matching of supplier purchase order information to the amounts actually billed as well as the presence of credit approval stamps and bills of lading.

5–2 Controls for a Computerized Billing Environment

When a computer is used to create invoices, the level of control needed over the process varies considerably, based on the level of computerized integration with preceding steps in the order entry and shipping cycle. If the steps leading up to the billing process involve either paper-based systems or computer systems that are not integrated with the billing process, then all the paperwork and related controls shown earlier for a paper-based billing system are still needed. If, however, there is complete integration with the order entry, credit, and shipping functions, then considerably fewer controls are needed in the billing process. Both scenarios are shown in Exhibit 5.3, along with the necessary primary control points.

Under Scenario A in the exhibit, the computerization of the billing process means little, because all inputs to the process are still on paper, requiring complete reentry of all information from the source documents and subsequent proofreading of the resulting invoice. The only advantage of using the computer is that it automatically creates a sequential invoice number on each invoice, so there is no need for prenumbered invoice forms. Scenario B takes much greater advantage of complete system integration, since all information previously entered in the computer system by the order entry staff can now be copied directly into the invoice.

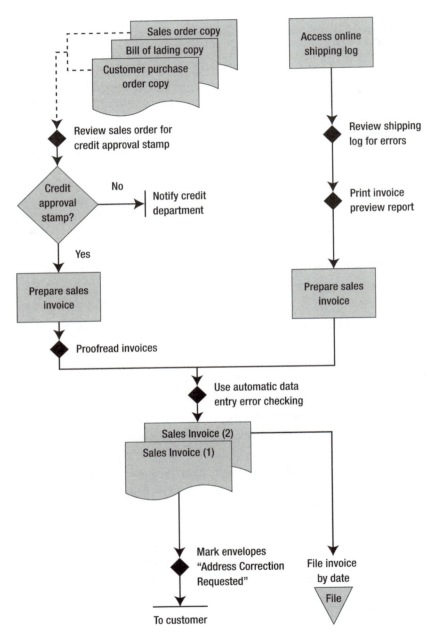

Exhibit 5.3   Basic Controls for Computerized Billing

The controls noted in the flowchart are described at greater length next, in sequence from the top of the flowchart to the bottom, though controls already described in Section 5–1 are not repeated here.

- *Review shipping log for errors.* In a fully integrated system, the billing clerk accesses the online shipping log each day to see what has been shipped and then automatically prints invoices in a single batch for all shipped items. A reasonable control is to have the billing person conduct a cursory review of the shipping log to ensure that all items noted should be invoiced.

- *Print invoice preview report.* Though the preceding control may be sufficient for verifying the quantity of goods shipped, it does not reveal pricing information. To access that information, print a preview report of all invoices and review it for accuracy prior to printing the actual invoices.

- *Use automated data entry error checking.* There are a number of common errors that the billing staff may create on an invoice, such as the wrong price, product, or service description and wrong customer name. All of these errors can lead to considerable additional time to research and correct, leading to late customer payments. In a computerized system, some automated data-checking methods can be used to reduce the frequency of these problems. For example, the zip code field can be linked to a file containing all cities and states, so that entering the zip code automatically calls up the city and state information. Similarly, the product number field can be linked to a file containing the product description, so that entry of the product number automatically accesses the description information. Also, prices of unusual length can be rejected automatically, or prices can be called up automatically from a file that is linked to a unique product number. There can also be required fields that must have a valid entry or else the invoice cannot be completed, such as the customer purchase order number field.

A procedure that itemizes the computerized generation of an invoice (combining elements of Scenarios A and B in the preceding flowchart) is described in Exhibit 5.2. It includes many of the preceding controls as well as a number of other steps needed for the billing process.

Exhibit 5.4   Computerized Billing Procedure

Policy/Procedure Statement	Retrieval No.: BIL-02

Subject: Prepare and Print Sales Invoices

1.   PURPOSE AND SCOPE

This procedure is used by the billing clerk to print and issue invoices to customers as well as to file the retained copy.

2.   PROCEDURES

2.1   Review Billing Information (Billing Clerk)

1. Access the daily shipping log in the computer system.
2. Review each shipment and flag it as ready for invoicing if it has a billable code.
3. Go to the invoice preview screen and call up the list of shipments that have been flagged for invoice printing.
4. Verify that each price matches the standard corporate price or contains an approval flag from the order entry staff.
5. If the shipping code is Prepaid, do not charge the customer for freight. If it is Prepay and Add, add the standard freight cost based on the cubic volume listed in the computer. If the shipping code is Customer Pickup, add no freight charge.
6. Verify that the correct sales tax code is being used.

2.2   Print Invoice Batch (Billing Clerk)

1. Go to the Billing option in the computer and select All Unprinted Invoices.
2. Turn on the printer and verify that the invoice stock is correctly positioned in it.
3. Using the Run Test option, print a sample invoice to ensure that the line settings are correct.
4. Using the Run Full Batch option, print all invoices in the batch.

2.3   Prepare and Send Invoices (Billing Clerk)

1. Burst the invoices, and put the pink copies in the To File bin and the white copies in the To Customer bin.
2. Stuff envelopes with the white invoice copies.
3. Stamp the envelopes with the "Address Correction Requested" stamp.
4. Affix postage to the envelopes and put them in the interoffice mail, marked for outside delivery.

2.4   File Invoice Copies (Billing Clerk)

File the pink invoice copies by customer.

The next controls are supplemental to the primary controls just noted for the computerized billing process.

- *Restrict access to the invoicing software.* The invoice generation software can also be used to create credit memos, which can be used to hide the theft of incoming cash from customers. Employees can also use the software to alter the due dates or payment terms of customer invoices. To prevent these problems, always use passwords to restrict access to the invoicing software.

- *Computer prevents invoice generation until shipment has occurred.* It is possible for the accounting staff to issue an invoice in order to recognize revenue, even if the related product delivery has not yet left the shipping dock. If a company has an enterprise resources planning (ERP) system, it is possible to configure the ERP system to not allow invoice generation until the shipment has occurred. This level of automated control is not available to most companies, since few have a sufficiently high level of system integration.

- *Review billing terms on all issued invoices.* A company's collection task is greatly magnified if the sales staff offers an excessive range of payment terms to customers. Though these terms should be spotted during the order entry procedure, it is also useful to periodically print a report that shows all special terms listed on invoices that fall outside the standard company payment terms.

- *Issue month-end statements.* The billing staff may alter customer invoices to meet the needs of various fraud schemes intended to hide their theft of cash. A good detective control over this risk is to have a person other than the normal billing clerk create and mail month-end account statements to customers. Since customers know which invoices should be open, and the amounts of those invoices, they may spot problems on the account statements and notify the company of the problem. Also, the contact name on the statements should be that of someone other than the billing clerk, so that complaints will not be received by the person engaged in fraudulent activities.

Several of the supplemental controls listed in Section 5–1 for a paper-based billing system are also relevant to a computerized system but have not been included here to avoid duplicate text. Thus, please review Section 5–1 for additional controls that may be of use.

5–3 Controls for Advanced Billing Systems

Additional technology and management concepts can be built on top of the basic computerized billing system described in Section 5–2 to improve the speed of billing delivery. However, since there are so many different systems in use, they are not described here as a single integrated system. Instead, each one receives a separate description and set of associated controls.

- *Enter invoices on supplier Web site.* Some customers have created Web sites on which they require suppliers to manually enter invoices. Controls are:
    - *Match confirmation sheet to invoice.* When Web site entry is required, the Web site typically creates a confirmation page showing what information was entered for the invoice. If available, print it, compare it to the invoice for accuracy, attach it to the invoice, and file both documents in the customer file.
    - *Create activity checklist for customer.* If few customers require Web entry, then create a customized checklist for each one, specifying how to enter an invoice in each site and requiring a sign-off by the person entering the invoice. This increases the likelihood that a correct entry will be made.
    - *Call the customer.* If the customer's Web site does not create a confirmation page, then it may be necessary to call the customer and ask if the invoice has appeared in its computer system.
- *Delivery person creates invoice.* In situations where the amount delivered is not finalized until the point of delivery, the person delivering the goods must create an invoice and hand it directly to the supplier. Controls are:
    - *Use a prenumbered invoice in duplicate.* When the delivery person creates an invoice at the customer location, be sure to use a prenumbered invoice form in duplicate. The delivery person gives one copy to the customer and brings the other copy back to the company, where it is given to the accounting department. The billing staff then

can enter the amount shown on the invoice in the computer system and also track the numerical sequence of invoices issued.

○ *Track invoice numbers issued to delivery staff.* To trace which invoices have been issued to the delivery staff, always track the invoice numbers issued. This keeps the delivery staff members from issuing on-site invoices to customers, collecting cash on the spot, and destroying their copy of the invoice to hide evidence of the theft.

○ *Match customers listed on delivery schedule to invoices received.* If the delivery staff is sent to a specific set of customers, always compare the invoices received from the delivery person to the customer list. If there is no invoice for a customer, then the delivery person has made no delivery, misplaced the invoice, or issued an invoice and stolen the related cash payment. If the delivery person claims that no delivery was made, confirm this fact with the customer.

• *Issue electronic data interchange (EDI) invoices.* When EDI is used, the company sends an electronic message to the customer, in which is embedded an invoice in a strictly defined format. An EDI invoice can be manually entered in EDI software before being sent or can be created and issued automatically by the computer system. Controls are:

○ *Verify that acknowledgment EDI has been received.* Once the customer receives an EDI invoice, it should send an acknowledgment of receipt EDI message back to the company. The company's computer system automatically can match sent and acknowledged EDI messages and report on missing acknowledgments. The same control can be conducted manually if the computer system cannot handle this chore automatically.

○ *Match EDI transmission document to invoice.* If the EDI message is keypunched manually into EDI software, then print a confirmation from the EDI software and compare it to the original invoice for data entry errors prior to transmitting the message.

○ *Send an EDI statement of account.* A standard EDI format for statements of account should be used as a backup means of ensuring that the customer has received information about all transmitted invoices.

• *Deliver with drop shipments.* Drop shipments occur when the company receives an order from a customer and has a supplier deliver the order directly to the customer, bypassing the company entirely. This requires a different billing notification system, since there is no internal shipment system to trigger creation of the invoice. Controls are:

- *Match open customer orders to supplier bills of lading.* Since drop shipping involves no internal record of a shipment, the billing trigger must be the supplier's bill of lading. Consequently, the control point is to match open and unbilled customer orders to bills of lading, and to follow up on any customer orders for which shipment documents have not been received from the supplier.

- *Deliver into an evaluated receipts system.* When a customer operates an evaluated receipts system, it pays based on the prices shown in its purchase order and the quantity delivered—it does not rely upon an invoice at all, and does not want one delivered. Controls are as follows:

  - *Match invoice to payment.* The standard control for evaluated receipts is still to have the computer system print an invoice, but to retain it and match the cash receipt to the invoice. The problem with this control is that there may be multiple payments being made in the same amount, making it difficult to match payments to invoices.

  - *Match payment to invoiced purchase order.* An improvement on the preceding control is to include the customer's purchase order number on each invoice and then match the supplier's cash receipts and the associated purchase order number to the purchase order number on the invoice.

- *Use automated revenue recognition software.* An automated revenue recognition system does not provide speedier billing delivery; instead, it ensures that revenue is recognized in the correct proportions in each accounting period, based on the various components of the billed revenue. Such software is itself a control, and includes these features:

  - Deferred revenues are scheduled at the time of order entry, including a recognition schedule for each item. If revenue is recognized based on a milestone, then the system pauses recognition until the milestone is confirmed.

  - Revenue for nondelivered contract components is recognized automatically based on established revenue recognition rules.

  - Revenue components (license fees, services, hardware, training, and maintenance) are split apart automatically and allocated to revenue based on established revenue recognition rules.

5–4 Controls for Credit Memos

Credit memos are an area in which fraud can occur, because the accounting staff could waylay incoming cash being paid by customers for outstanding invoices and then issue credit memos to cancel the related invoices. Use the next controls to keep this type of fraud from occurring.

- *Require prior supervisory approval for all credit memos issued.* A second party should approve all requests for credit memos prior to their being issued. By doing so, credit memos can be issued fraudulently only if collusion is present. This control can be negated for very small credits, on the grounds that the cost of the control exceeds the level of risk reduction it provides.

- *Segregate the credit memo request and recording functions.* A collections person usually requests that a credit memo be issued. Since the collections personnel may have access to cash or checks sent by customers, they should not be allowed to cover their tracks by issuing a credit memo. Instead, have a clerk independent of the collections function issue the credit memo.

- *Prenumber and account for credit memos.* If credit memos are issued without a computer system, then use prenumbered credit memo forms and account for all missing forms. By doing so, there is less risk that credit memos will be inadvertently or intentionally issued without being recorded in the accounting database.

- *Store unused credit memos in a secure area.* As a follow-up to the preceding control, always store prenumbered credit memos in a secure, locked location. By doing so, there is less risk that any credit memos will be removed. An enhanced control is also to maintain a list in a separate location of the numbered documents that have been removed from storage, so that the list and forms can be compared to determine if any additional forms have been taken.

- *Match credit memos to receiving documents.* If a person independent of the collections function matches the list of returned goods on the receiving log to issued credit memos, this will result in a shortened list of credit memos for which no goods have been returned. Some of the credit memos on this shortened list may have been fraudulently issued and are an excellent starting point for an audit (see the next control).

- *Audit credit memos and supporting documentation.* The internal audit staff should schedule periodic examinations of a sample of all issued credit memos, as well as the supporting documentation for each one and the security of any unused prenumbered credit memo forms. Audit tasks should include a review for the presence of an authorized approval signature and for a received item that matches the quantity indicated on the credit memo.

5–5 Billing Policies

The first two of the next four policies relate directly to the act of issuing an invoice or credit memo, while the third and fourth policies assist in adopting consistent revenue recognition practices that are tied to billings. The adoption of these policies assists in enforcing various control systems described in this chapter. The policies follow.

1. *All invoices must be issued within one day of shipment or completion of service delivery.* This policy is designed to accelerate cash flow by avoiding billing delays. It also impacts the speed of the month-end closing, since billing is typically a significant bottleneck in the closing process.
2. *Credit memos require prior supervisory approval.* This policy prevents employees in the collections area from fraudulently intercepting customer payments and then offsetting the related invoices with credit memos.
3. *The company shall not use bill and hold transactions.* Though bill and hold transactions are allowable under clearly defined and closely restricted circumstances, they are subject to abuse and so generally should be avoided. If used, the form shown in Exhibit 5.5 can be used to document customer approval of the method.
4. *A single revenue recognition method shall be used for all installment sales.* This policy keeps an accounting department from switching back and forth between the installment method and cost recovery method for recognizing this type of revenue, which would otherwise allow it to manipulate reported levels of profitability.

Exhibit 5.5   Acknowledgment of Bill and Hold Transaction Form

Acknowledgment of
Bill and Hold Transaction

Customer Name: _____

This document indicates your acknowledgment that a bill and hold transaction exists in regard to purchase order number _____, which you ordered from [company name]. Please indicate your acknowledgment of this transaction by initialing next to each of the following statements and signing at the bottom of the page. If you disagree with any of the statements, please indicate your concerns at the bottom of the page. Thank You!

_____ I agree that I ordered the items noted in the purchase order.
(initial)

_____ I agree that [company name] is storing the items noted in the
(initial)   purchase order on my behalf.

_____ I acknowledge that I have taken on all risks of ownership related
(initial)   to this purchase order.

_____ I agree that I requested the bill and hold transaction, and my
(initial)   reason for doing so is as follows:

_____

_____

_____ I agree that all performance issues related to this purchase order
(initial)   were completed no later than _____.

_____ I agree that the held goods will be delivered to me not later than
(initial)   _____.

I disagree with some or all of the statements on this page. My concerns are as follows:

_____

_____

_____

_____   _____
Signature   Date

_____   _____
Name (please print)   Title

Summary

In a paper-based environment or where shipping information is not electronically transmitted to the billing software, the billing process requires a considerable amount of data entry, and so controls are focused on error reduction. When billings are linked directly to the order entry and shipping databases, billing becomes a relatively simple and error-free operation. Thus, the level of controls required is directly based on the amount of computer integration with upstream operations.

Chapter 6

Controls for Cash-Handling Best Practices

Overview

Cash handling is an area that has attracted a great deal of control attention over the years, since it is one of the easiest areas from which to remove assets from a company. This fact has resulted in a baseline cash-handling system that requires the involvement of four people—mailroom clerk, cashier, receivables clerk, and accounting supervisor—in order to spread cash-handling responsibilities for cash receipts, recording transactions, deposits, and reconciliation among so many people that the risk of fraud is reduced. However, though risk is reduced, the large number of transaction movements among different people makes this a highly inefficient process. Even the baseline cash-handling process in a computerized environment is not much better, since all four people are still involved. Only when the lockbox best practice is used, thereby shifting actual cash receipts away from the company, can this process be made reasonably efficient while still retaining a maximum level of control.

A number of types of cash-handling systems are addressed in this chapter, including both paper-based and computerized systems for incoming checks, receipts delivered to a bank lockbox, checks cashed through a lockbox truncation system, cash receipts (as opposed to check receipts), credit card receipts, petty cash, and investments.

6–1 Basic Check-Handling Controls

Some small businesses still use an entirely paper-based cash-handling process, though the availability of such low-end accounting software as

Peachtree and QuickBooks makes it increasingly less likely. The flowchart in Exhibit 6.1 shows the basic process flow for these organizations, with the minimum set of controls needed to ensure that it operates properly. In essence, a variety of control points are used to ensure that checks cannot be fraudulently removed without detection. The small black diamonds on the flowchart indicate the location of key control points in the process, with descriptions next to the diamonds.

As outlined in Exhibit 6.1, the essential process flow is for check receipts to first be routed through the mailroom, where the mailroom staff creates a list of received checks that is used to ensure that all received checks are accounted for appropriately once they reach the accounting department. The checks then go to the cashier, who manually enters receipt information into the cash receipts journal and prepares a bank deposit. The receivables clerk uses the check remittance advices or copies of the checks to record receipts against specific customer accounts in the accounts receivables ledger. Finally, the accounting manager completes the month-end bank reconciliation.

The controls noted in the flowchart are described at greater length next, in sequence from the top of the flowchart to the bottom.

- *Mailroom prepares check prelist.* As soon as the mail arrives, the mailroom staff should open all envelopes and prepare a list of checks that itemizes from whom checks were received and the dollar total on each check. It then copies this check prelist, sending the original to the cashier and the copy to the accounts receivables clerk. A slight improvement in the control is to make an additional copy of the check prelist and retain it in a locked cabinet in the mailroom, thereby providing evidence of initial receipt in case both the cashier and receivables clerk are in collusion and have destroyed their copies.
- *Mailroom endorses checks "for deposit only."* By immediately stamping checks as "for deposit only" upon their arrival in the company, it becomes much more difficult for anyone in the accounting department to remove a check and cash it for personal use.
- *Cashier matches check prelist to cash receipts journal.* Once the cashier has recorded the amounts of all received checks in the cash receipts journal, he or she should compare the entries to the check prelist. By doing so, the cashier can locate any errors in the entry.

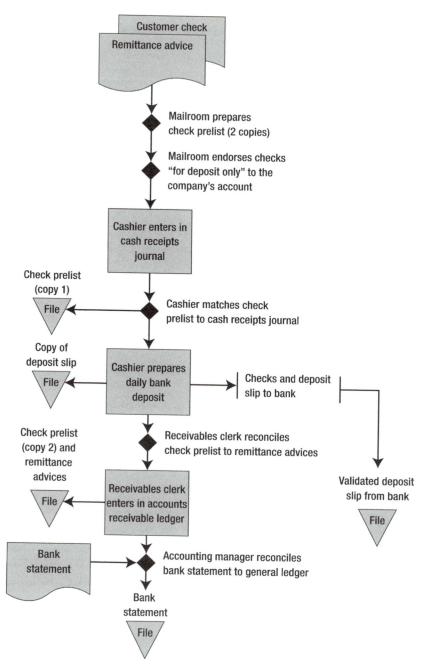

Exhibit 6.1 System of Controls for Paper-Based Check Receipts

- *Receivables clerk reconciles check prelist to remittance advices.* Though the first use of the check prelist (by the cashier) was intended to reduce data entry errors, this second review is intended to prevent fraud by having a different person conduct the review.

- *Accounting manager reconciles bank statement to general ledger.* Upon receipt of the monthly bank statement, the accounting manager should reconcile it to the accounting records; in a manual accounting environment, this calls for the use of subsidiary ledgers, such as the cash receipts journal, since detailed records usually are not recorded in the general ledger, only batch totals. This control provides an independent review of both cash receipts and payable checks processed, and detects the removal of cash after it has been entered in the accounting system (larceny). This task should be performed by the accounting manager rather than anyone in the cash-handling or recording processes.

A procedure listing the basic steps needed to receive and deposit cash in a paper-based environment is shown in Exhibit 6.2.

Exhibit 6.2   Procedure for Check Receipts in a Paper-Based Environment

---

Policy/Procedure Statement   Retrieval No.:   CASH-01

Subject: Receive, Record, and Deposit Checks (Paper Environment)

1. PURPOSE AND SCOPE

This procedure is used by the mailroom and various accounting staff to receive checks from a variety of sources and deposit them in the company bank account.

2. PROCEDURES

2.1 Receive Checks and Cash Through Mail (Mailroom Staff)

1. Enter today's date on a new copy of the Mailroom Remittance Sheet. (See Exhibit 6.3.)

2. Enter on the sheet for each check received the check number, customer name, the city and state from which the payment was sent, and the amount paid. If cash is received, enter this amount in the "Source if not check" column. Enter the grand total of all checks and cash received at the bottom of the sheet. Sign and date the sheet.

3. Make two photocopies of the sheet and store the original in a locked cabinet.

4. Insert all checks and cash received, along with one copy of the completed sheet, in a locking interoffice mail pouch and have it couriered to the cashier.

5. Send the second copy of the sheet to the receivables clerk.

Exhibit 6.2 *(Continued)*

2.2 Total and Record Cash (Cashier)

1. Open the interoffice mail pouch from the mailroom containing the daily checks and cash receipts.

2. Summarize all cash and checks received on an adding machine tape.

3. Enter all checks received on a deposit slip as well as cash receipts in a lump sum. Verify that the deposit slip total and the adding machine tape total are the same. If not, recount the cash and checks. File the copy of the deposit slip by date.

4. Enter the total of all cash and checks received in the cash receipts journal.

2.3 Prepare and Issue Deposit (Cashier)

1. Split all remittance advices from the checks, and copy all checks that have invoice numbers written on them. Verify that this packet of information matches the total that is to be sent to the bank in the deposit.

2. Send the completed deposit to the bank by courier.

3. Upon the return of the courier with the bank-validated deposit slip, staple it to the copy of the deposit slip that was retained earlier and file it by date.

2.4 Forward Information (Cashier)

Send the remittance advice packet to the accounts receivable staff.

2.5 Update the Accounts Receivable Ledger (Receivables Clerk)

1. Verify the total for all checks and cash listed on the mailroom remittance sheet, and adjust the total if it is different from the total already listed on the sheet by the mailroom staff. Investigate any differences.

2. Open the accounts receivable ledger and enter the following information for each cash receipt:

   • Date of receipt

   • Amount of receipt

   • Invoice number against which it is applied

3. Using an adding machine, total all receipts recorded for that day in the accounts receivable ledger and match the total to the mailroom remittance sheet. Investigate any differences.

The mailroom remittance sheet referenced in the preceding procedure is shown in Exhibit 6.3. This document is used to create an initial record of receipts as soon as they arrive in the mailroom.

Thus far, the discussion of check handling has concentrated solely on the primary process flow. In addition, the next ancillary controls are designed to provide some additional degree of control over the process.

Exhibit 6.3   Mailroom Remittance Sheet

Company Name

Receipts of [Month/Day/Year]

Check Number	Source if Not Check	Sender	City and State	Amount
1602		Rush Airplane Company	Scranton, PA	$ 126.12
	Cash	Rental Air Service	Stamford, CT	$ 19.50
2402		Automatic Service Company	Los Angeles, CA	$ 316.00
1613		Voe Parts Dealer	Toledo, OH	$ 2.90
9865		Brush Electric Company	Chicago, IL	$ 25.50
2915		Ajax Manufacturing Company	Cleveland, OH	$1,002.60
8512		Apex Machine Tool Co.	New York, NY	$ 18.60

Total Receipts	$1,511.22
Prepared by:	————
Date:	————

- *Have two people open the mail.* Smaller companies may have no mail-room staff and thus have no one available to create a check prelist. A common alternative is to have two people open the mail, though it is still necessary to create a check prelist or a photocopy of checks received if this control is to be truly effective.

- *Review restrictive endorsements before cashing checks.* A customer could insert a restrictive clause on a check payment that limits a company's ability to legally collect additional funds. Restrictive endorsements are rare, so most organizations do not conduct this review. However, if there is a reasonable probability of losses, then train the cashier to examine checks for restrictive endorsements and withhold them from the daily deposit until the company lawyer can review them.

- *Immediately review unapplied cash.* Unapplied cash is a rich opportunity for a fraud-minded employee. Anyone intent on removing funds from the company can apply unapplied cash to open customer receivables when payments arrive from those customers and then cash the check themselves. To avoid this problem, it is imperative to put the collections staff to work at once on any unapplied cash, so that cash can be applied legitimately to the correct receivables. Where possible, all cash should be applied within one day of receipt.

- *NSF checks are independently investigated.* If a customer issues a check that is returned due to not sufficient funds (NSF), this is strong evidence of a credit problem, and so should be immediately routed to the accounting manager for credit investigation as well as resubmission to the bank.

- *Restrict deposit withdrawals by branch offices.* If a company has multiple branch locations where cash is collected, there is a risk that someone at a branch location could deposit cash receipts at the bank and then improperly withdraw the funds. To prevent this, the only people allowed to withdraw cash from the depository account should be corporate office executives.

- *Require cash application staff to take vacations.* "Lapping" involves taking money paid by customer A, then using cash from customer B to pay customer A's account, and so on. This type of fraud tends to be difficult to maintain, requiring constant attention by the person perpetrating the fraud. Requiring employees to take their designated vacations often brings lapping situations to light while they are absent.

- *Employees cannot deposit checks and create supplier invoices.* Employees can deliberately double pay a supplier invoice, then intercept the supplier refund check and cash it. To avoid this, someone who does not deal with supplier invoices should handle depositing refund checks.

- *Use metrics analysis to detect skimming.* "Skimming" is the removal of cash prior to its entry into the accounting system, usually involving the removal of cash from a sale transaction and then destroying all evidence of the sale. If there is a significant amount of skimming, its presence can be indicated through several metrics: decreasing cash to total current assets, decreasing ratio of cash to credit card sales, and flat or declining sales with an increasing cost of sales.

In brief, a paper-based check-receiving process that includes a sufficient level of control is painfully inefficient, because it requires the participation of multiple employees in order to segregate duties properly. Many smaller companies concentrate all check-handling tasks with a single person rather than implementing a safer system. The result is a substantially increased risk of loss due to fraud.

6–2 Controls for a Computerized Check-Handling Environment

Unfortunately, the basic computerized check-handling system is not a considerable improvement over the inefficiencies inherent in a paper-based system. The primary improvement is in the consolidation of two posting tasks: Instead of updating the cash receipts journal and receivables ledger in two separate steps, both are now combined into a single online process. Otherwise, most controls remain the same, as shown in Exhibit 6.4. The situation improves after we add lockbox receipts and lockbox truncation to the basic computerized system, as noted later in this chapter, both of which improve the efficiency of the check-handling controls.

The controls noted in the flowchart are described at greater length next, in sequence from the top of the flowchart to the bottom.

- *Mailroom prepares check prelist (two copies).* This control is the same one used under a paper-based system. However, if the accounting software has the capability, the mailroom staff can create the list through an online electronic form rather than by writing it on paper.
- *Mailroom endorses checks "for deposit only" to the company's account.* Even in a computerized environment, it is still a good control to restrictively stamp checks as soon after receipt as possible.
- *Cashier matches check prelist to cash receipts journal.* Though the intent is the same as under a paper-based system, the matching process is done against a computer printout of the cash receipts journal.
- *Receivables clerk reconciles check prelist to remittance advices.* This control often is excluded in a computerized environment, because the receivables clerk is no longer involved in data entry—this person's role has devolved into a cross-examination of work done by the cashier. Nonetheless, it is still a useful control, since the cashier must realize that the receivables clerk is conducting an independent review of all steps in the cash receipts process.

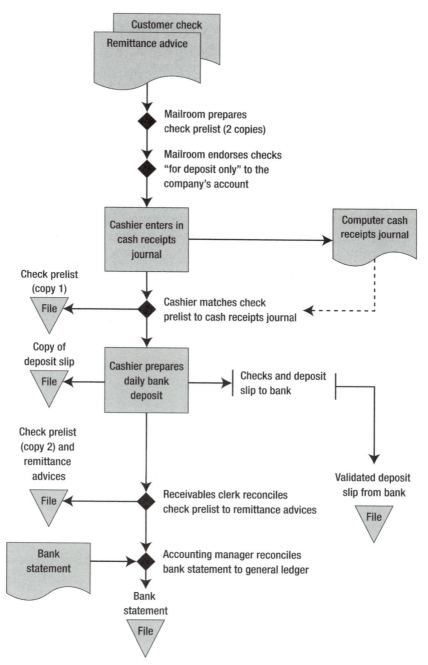

Exhibit 6.4   System of Controls for Computerized Check Receipts

- *Accounting manager reconciles bank statement to general ledger.* Upon receipt of the monthly bank statement, the accounting manager should reconcile it to the general ledger cash account, using the computerized bank reconciliation module in the accounting software. This control provides an independent review of both cash receipts and payable checks processed and detects the removal of cash after it has been entered in the accounting system (larceny). This task should be performed by the accounting manager rather than anyone in the cash-handling or recording processes.

The procedure shown in Exhibit 6.5 includes many of the same steps itemized for the paper-based check receipts process described in Exhibit 6.2. It provides altered procedural information where the computerized system modifies the processing steps.

The final control step noted at the bottom of the Exhibit 6.4 flowchart was a bank reconciliation by the accounting manager, which is essentially a final review of all cash receipts and disbursements for a one-month period. A sample bank reconciliation procedure is shown in Exhibit 6.6.

Exhibit 6.5 Procedure for Computerized Check Receipts

Policy/Procedure Statement   Retrieval No.: CASH-02

Subject: Receive, Record, and Deposit Checks (Computer Environment)

1. PURPOSE AND SCOPE

This procedure is used by the mailroom and various accounting staff to receive checks from a variety of sources and deposit them in the company bank account.

2. PROCEDURES

2.1 Receive Checks and Cash Through Mail (Mailroom Staff)

See Exhibit 6.2 for the detailed mailroom staff procedure. However, if the Mailroom Remittance Sheet has been converted into an electronic form, then enter cash receipts in the form and press Enter to route the completed form to the cashier. Verify through the work-flow management system that the cashier has opened the file.

Exhibit 6.5 *(Continued)*

2.2 Prepare and Issue Deposit (Cashier)

1. Open the interoffice mail pouch from the mailroom containing the daily checks and cash receipts.
2. Total all cash and checks received, and match the total to the total shown on the mailroom remittance sheet. Investigate any variances.
3. Enter all checks received on a deposit slip as well as cash receipts in a lump sum. Verify that the deposit slip total and the mailroom remittance sheet total are the same. If not, recount the cash and checks. File the copy of the deposit slip by date.
4. Split all remittance advices from the checks, and copy all checks that have invoice numbers written on them. Verify that this packet of information matches the total to be sent to the bank in the deposit.
5. Send the completed deposit to the bank by courier.
6. Upon the return of the courier with the bank-validated deposit slip, staple it to the copy of the deposit slip that was retained earlier and file it by date.

2.3 Update the Cash Receipts Journal (Cashier)

1. Open the cash receipts screen in the accounting software and set the receipt date to today's date.
2. For each customer payment, enter the customer number, individual check amount, and check number and date, and then TAB to the detail section of the screen. The list of all open invoices for each customer will appear. Click on each invoice being paid and enter any discounts taken. After identifying all invoices paid by each customer, click on the "Next Payment" button at the bottom of the screen. Continue in this fashion until all receipts have been entered.
3. Print the cash receipts journal for the entry date and match the total received to the total on the deposit slip copy. Investigate if there is a variance.

2.4 Forward Information (Cashier)

Send the remittance advice packet to the accounts receivable staff.

2.5 Reconcile Cash Receipts Information (Receivables Clerk)

1. Match the mailroom remittance sheet to the cash receipts journal and remittance advices. Investigate any variances.
2. Staple the cash receipts journal to the remittance advices and Mailroom Remittance Sheet.
3. If the reconciliation is complete and all variances have been investigated successfully, stamp the packet as approved and initial inside the stamp.
4. File the receipts packet in the applied cash filing cabinet.

Exhibit 6.6   Bank Reconciliation Procedure

Policy/Procedure Statement	Retrieval No.: CASH-03

Subject: Reconcile Bank Statement

1. PURPOSE AND SCOPE

This procedure helps the accounting manager compare his or her internal cash records to those of the bank and reconcile any differences between the two.

2. PROCEDURES

2.1 Reconcile the General Ledger Balance (Accounting Manager)

Once the month-end bank statement arrives, reconcile the general ledger to the bank balance with the following steps:

1. Go to the accounting computer system and access the bank reconciliation module.

2. Check off all issued checks listed in the bank reconciliation module that are listed as having cleared the bank on the bank statement. If any check amounts listed by the bank differ from the amounts listed in the module, make a journal entry to correct to the bank balance.

3. Check off all deposits listed in the bank reconciliation module that are listed as having been received by the bank on the bank statement. If any deposit amounts listed by the bank differ from the amounts listed in the module, make a journal entry to correct to the bank balance.

4. Make a separate journal entry for each special expense or revenue item on the bank statement, such as a monthly account processing fee.

5. Record in the accounting system any manual checks not previously recorded but that are listed on the bank statement as having cleared the bank.

6. If all items reconcile and the bank statement still does not match, the only remaining possible solution is that the beginning bank reconciliation was incorrect. If so, verify that the bank reconciliation for the preceding month was completed correctly.

7. When the reconciliation is complete, print the Bank Reconciliation (see Exhibit 6.7) and store it with the bank statement in a bank statement file for the current year, sorted by month.

8. Review all journal entries resulting from the bank reconciliation, determine which ones were the result of transaction errors, and meet with the accounting staff to determine remediation steps to keep these errors from occurring in the future.

Exhibit 6.7 Bank Reconciliation

Company Name

Bank: _____

Account No: _____

As of _____

	Balance 11/30/xx	Receipts	Disbursements	Balance 12/31/xx
Per bank	$ 126,312.50	$ 92,420.00	$ 85,119.00	$ 133,613.50
Add:				
Deposits in transit				
11/30 per book	$ 5,600.00	$ (5,600.00)		
12/31 per book		$ 12,500.00		$ 12,500.00
				$ 12,500.00
Deduct:				
Outstanding checks				
November (see list)	$ 4,320.00		$ (4,115.00)	$ 205.00
December (see list)			$ 6,110.00	$ 6,110.00
Other Items:				
Bank charges not recorded			–5.01	5.01
Per books	$ 127,592.50	$ 99,320.00	$ 87,108.99	$ 139,803.51

Prepared by _____

Date _____

When computers are used, there are a few ancillary controls not mentioned that can increase the level of control over check receipts. They are:

- *Impose password access to cash receipts software.* An employee could improperly shift cash receipts among a variety of customer accounts in order to conceal the fraudulent removal of cash. This can be avoided to some degree by the use of password control, though it is still possible for the cashier (who has password access) to conduct this type of fraud.

- *Request electronic payments from customers.* With the increased ease of use of Automated Clearing House (ACH) payments, it is not unreasonable to ask customers to remit electronic payments. In this process, payments are sent straight to the corporate bank account, so no one has an opportunity to abscond with the funds. Thus, most controls related to check receipts can be eliminated.

6–3 Controls for Lockbox Receipts

A lockbox is essentially a separate mailbox to which deposits are sent by customers. The company's bank opens all mail arriving at the lockbox, deposits all checks at once, copies the checks, and forwards all check copies and anything else contained in customer remittances to the company. The bank may also scan the checks and post them online for immediate viewing by the company. This approach has the advantage of accelerating the flow of cash into a company's bank account, since the lockbox system typically reduces the mail float customers enjoy by at least a day while also eliminating all of the transaction-processing time that a company would also need during its internal cash-processing steps.

The number of controls needed in a lockbox environment is considerably reduced, since there is no cash on the corporate premises. The reduced set of controls is shown in Exhibit 6.8. In this revised system, the cashier accesses check images over the Internet or obtains this information from the remittances advices forwarded to the company by the bank. In either case, the cashier logs the receipts into the cash receipts journal, while the receivables clerk verifies that all receipts were correctly logged in to the computer system.

The controls noted in the flowchart are described at greater length next, in sequence from the top of the flowchart to the bottom.

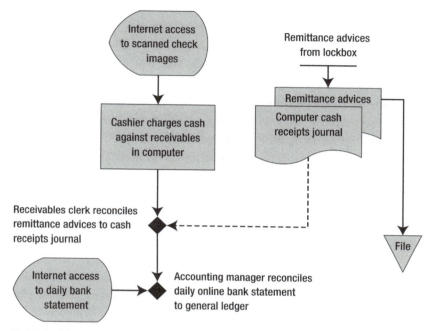

Exhibit 6.8 System of Controls for Lockbox Receipts

- *Receivables clerk reconciles remittance advices to cash receipts journal.*
  On a daily basis, the receivables clerk prints the cash receipts journal for
  the date associated with remittance advices and check copies forwarded
  by the bank, and matches them to a printout of the cash receipts journal.
  This control ensures that all cash receipts are entered in the computer and
  that receipts are charged to the correct customer accounts.

- *Accounting manager reconciles daily online bank statement to general
  ledger.* With online access to bank records, the accounting manager can
  conduct a daily review of the online bank statement, incrementally reconciling the bank account in the computer system. This control is an excellent detective method for quickly spotting any unusual transactions
  flowing through the cash account. A daily reconciliation is also useful for
  immediately recording any electronic payments and charging them to the
  correct customer account in a timely manner. This task should be performed by the accounting manager rather than anyone directly involved
  in the cash recording process. The same bank reconciliation procedure
  described earlier in Exhibit 6.6 can be used for this daily reconciliation.

Though not noted in the primary transaction flow for lockbox transactions, the next additional procedure is also useful for ensuring that all cash receipts are processed through the lockbox.

- *Mailroom staff sends all checks received by the company to the lockbox address.* Even with proper notification of all customers regarding a lockbox address, some will still send their payments to the company instead. In order to retain a simplified cash-handling system, it is best to have the mailroom staff immediately mail these payments to the lockbox address as soon as they are received.

A comparison of the controls required under a lockbox system to a basic cash receipts system makes it obvious that control systems can be greatly simplified if all cash is routed through a lockbox. However, customers are not always so accommodating in sending their payments to a lockbox—there are always a few who persist in sending payments straight to the company. Consequently, unless arrangements are made with the mailroom staff to mail these additional payments promptly to the lockbox address, it will be necessary to retain the traditional cash-handling controls.

6–4 Lockbox Truncation

Lockbox truncation is the process of converting a paper check into an electronic deposit. The basic process is to insert a check into a check reader, which scans the magnetic ink characters on the check into a vendor-supplied software package. The software sends this information to a third-party ACH processor, which typically clears payment in one or two days. This approach removes from the typical check-handling process the need for any daily bank deposit, though most other controls involved in the standard process flow noted earlier in Exhibit 6.3 are still required. The modified process flow is shown in Exhibit 6.9.

The principal control addition in the exhibit is that the cashier should verify that the lockbox truncation report printed by the lockbox truncation software matches the checks just entered into the system and then should initial the report to indicate that this control has been completed. This is a simple error-correction control. Also, since the truncation report replaces the deposit slip, the truncation report is filed instead of the validated deposit slip.

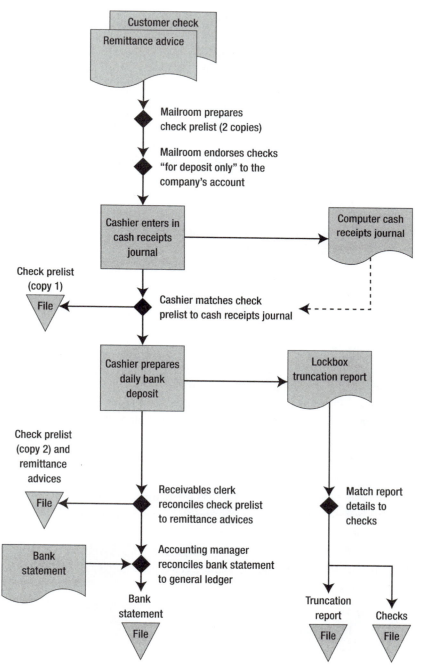

Exhibit 6.9 System of Controls for Lockbox Truncation

6–5 Basic Cash Receipts Controls

The preceding control systems were all designed primarily for the receipt of payments made by check. But what if the primary form of payment is cash? Unlike checks, cash is completely untraceable, and so is the preferred asset to steal. Thus, cash handling calls for tighter physical controls. The essential cash receipts process flow is for the initial cash receipt to be stored in a cash register, which is reconciled at the end of each shift; cash is removed at the end of each shift for deposit, after which the bank's validated deposit slip is reconciled to the company's original deposit slip. The basic controls are shown in Exhibit 6.10.

The controls noted in the flowchart are described at greater length next, in sequence from the top of the flowchart to the bottom.

- *Enter cash in cash register.* The primary role of the cash register is to record the amount of cash stored in it, either electronically or on a paper tape, while also providing a moderate level of security over the cash. If there is no cash register, as may be the case in very low-volume cash-handling situations, at least use prenumbered receipts to record the cash.

- *Give copy of receipt to customer.* When using a cash register, there is a risk that the cash register operator will remove cash and punch in a reduced cash receipt. To reduce this risk, always require cash register operators to give a copy of the receipt to the customer, since customers may review their receipts to ensure that the correct amount of cash was received. As an added inducement, many retail operations offer a free purchase to customers who do not receive a receipt.

- *Reconcile cash to cash receipts.* At the end of a cash handler's shift, a different person with no responsibility for cash handling should reconcile the cash in the cash register to the total of cash received as recorded on the register. Once completed, the person completing the reconciliation should sign and date it, so there is a record that a reconciliation indeed took place.

- *Transport cash in locked container.* To reduce the risk of unauthorized access to any cash being transported for deposit, always store it in a locked cash pouch. The most elaborate extension of this concept is to hire an armored truck to transport the cash, which is mandatory for larger quantities of cash.

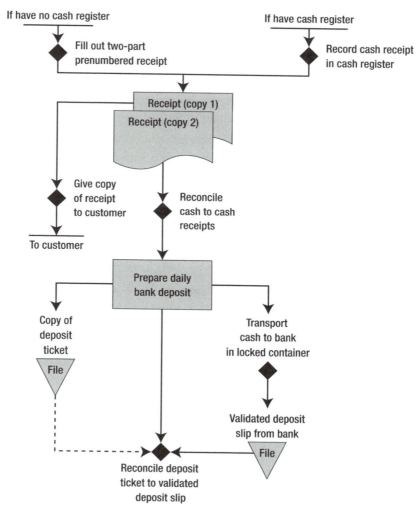

Exhibit 6.10   System of Controls for Cash Handling

- *Reconcile deposit ticket to validated deposit slip.* Once deposited, the bank will issue a validated receipt for the cash. Someone other than the person who made the deposit should compare the original deposit ticket to the validated receipt and investigate any differences. This control is needed to ensure that the person making the deposit does not remove cash during delivery to the bank.

In addition to the basic process flow just noted, the next controls are also useful for improving the security of the cash-handling operation.

- *Only one person has access to each cash register during a shift.* If multiple people can access a cash register, then it is impossible to assign responsibility for the illicit removal of cash from the register. Thus, it is better to restrict access to a single person.

- *Use video surveillance of cash register operators.* Though not usually used except in high-volume cash-handling situations, it is useful for cash handlers to know that their actions are being recorded by a video camera. The mere presence of such cameras, even if the resulting video is not being actively reviewed, can be a deterrent to fraud.

- *Move on-site cash to a safe for overnight storage.* Cash registers are easier to break in to than a safe, so move all cash into the safe during nonbusiness hours.

- *Change the safe combination periodically.* The risk that the combination to the safe will become public knowledge will grow over time, especially if anyone knowing the combination moves to another department or leaves the company. Accordingly, change the combination on a fixed schedule, and do so at once if anyone knowing the combination leaves the department.

- *Position the safe in a visible location.* A safe is easier to break in to if no one can see the perpetrator. However, if the safe is continually visible to anyone working in the department, it is much more difficult to remove cash from it without being seen.

- *Require supervisory approval of cash refunds.* One way to steal cash is to take money from the cash register and record a refund on the cash register tape. By requiring a supervisory password or key entry every time a refund is issued, the cash register operator has no opportunity to steal cash by this method. If there is a minimum level above which supervisory approval is needed for a refund, then review the cash register tape for an unusually large number of cash refunds just below the approval limit.

- *Monitor metrics associated with cash removal.* If employees are recording cash refunds on the cash register while pocketing the indicated refund amount, this means that inventory is not actually being returned by customers, as would normally be the case as part of a refund transaction. Thus, a rise in the level of inventory shrinkage is associated with this type of theft. It will also cause net sales to decrease as a proportion of gross sales. It is also possible to track the proportion of refunds to sales over time, preferably by individual cash register.

When actual cash payments are being handled, it is especially important to ensure that there is proper segregation of duties. Consequently, no one person should be responsible for more than one of these cash-related duties: receiving cash, recording cash payments, depositing cash, and reconciling cash. If the accounting department has too few employees to spread around this work, then consider using people from other departments for selected tasks.

6–6 Basic Credit Card Receipts Controls

When customers pay with credit cards, there is no need for many of the controls used for the handling of cash or checks, since payments are made into the corporate checking account. However, two other control problems arise with this payment method. First, there must be assurance that every credit card payment is coupled with a cash receipt transaction in the accounting system; otherwise, customer receivables balances will remain open even after they have paid, or vice versa. Second, there is a risk that customer credit card information will be fraudulently accessed, requiring strong security controls to prevent. The next control points will mitigate these risks.

- *Set up a separate bank account for incoming credit card payments.* Proper control over credit card transactions begins with a clear knowledge of exactly which credit card payments have resulted in cash actually reaching the company bank account. It is much easier to ascertain this information if all such payments are made into a separate bank account, so there is no risk of a variety of other transactions interfering with the available information.

- *Conduct a daily reconciliation of credit card receipt payments to cash receipt transactions.* In many accounting systems, there is no integration between the processing of a credit card transaction and the offsetting of the corresponding account receivable with the payment. Consequently, it is extremely important to itemize all credit card transactions at the end of each day and compare this list to the cash receipts journal for the same period, thereby ensuring that a complete transaction takes place. This reconciliation should be performed by an employee who is not involved in any other aspect of the credit card receipts process.

- *Shred all documents containing credit card numbers.* If the accounting staff writes down complete customer credit card information, then there should be a procedure in place to shred the documents containing this information. Alternatively, if a customer writes payment information onto a signed sales order, then the best alternative is to lock up the accounts receivables files containing this information.

- *Bond all employees having access to credit card information.* If there is a quantifiable risk of a company suffering losses due to the theft of credit card information by an employee, a good way to mitigate this risk is to pay the annual premium for bonding insurance for anyone who handles this information.

- *Conduct security checks on all employees having access to credit card information.* It is critical to ensure that credit card information is not allowed into the hands of a third party; since the easiest way for this information to depart company premises illicitly is through the active intervention of employees, it is important to conduct security checks on all employees having access to credit card information. It is even better to conduct these reviews on an annual basis, to uncover any changes in employees' financial condition that may place them in a heightened state of risk.

- *Retain in-house transaction processing where credit card information is involved.* Though the outsourcing of accounting functions is becoming increasingly popular, it may make more sense to retain credit card processing in-house, rather than trusting this information to a third party whose security standards may not be sufficient.

- *Impose security controls on computer files containing credit card information.* An obvious control is to impose strict, multilayered security controls over any files containing customer credit card information. It may also make sense to hire a system security consulting firm periodically to locate and recommend the mitigation of any computer system security issues.

The basic process flow for credit card processing is shown in Exhibit 6.11.

Exhibit 6.11 Procedure for Credit Card Receipt Processing

Policy/Procedure Statement

Retrieval No.: CASH-04

Subject: Process Credit Card Receipts

1. PURPOSE AND SCOPE

This procedure is used by the cashier to process credit card payments through an Internet-based processing site.

2. PROCEDURES

2.1 Collect Credit Card Information (Cashier)

Verify that the customer has supplied all information required for the credit card processing, including:

- Name on the credit card
- Credit card number
- Credit card verification number
- Credit card expiration date
- Billing address

Retain the customer's phone number in case the payment is not accepted, so corrected information can be obtained.

2.2 Enter Credit Card Transaction (Cashier)

1. Access the Internet credit card processing site and log in.
2. In the Web-based data entry form, enter all customer-supplied information as well as the invoice number, the amount to be billed, and a brief description of the billing.
3. If the transaction is not accepted, call the customer and review all supplied information to determine its accuracy. As an alternative, obtain information for a different credit card from the customer. If there is no alternative, determine when the customer is paying off the existing credit card balance, note the date, store the credit card information in a locked location until that date, and then attempt to reprocess the credit card payment.
4. If the transaction is accepted, verify that a confirming e-mail has been received from the credit card processor. Then access the accounting computer system and log in the cash receipt associated with the transaction. Date the transaction one day forward if this more closely corresponds to the settlement date and corresponding receipt of cash. Enter in the Check Number field the date of credit card submission, preceded by "c/c" to indicate the type of payment and when it was processed.

2.3 Complete Related Paperwork (Cashier)

1. Stamp the invoice with a "Paid in Full" stamp, initial the stamp, enter on it the last four digits of the credit card used to make the payment, and photocopy it.

(continues)

Exhibit 6.11   *(Continued)*

---

2. Mail or fax one copy of the stamped invoice to the person whose name was on the credit card (*not* the person listed on the invoice, if any), since this person will need it as a receipt.

3. File the remaining copy of the stamped invoice in the customer file by date.

6–7 Petty Cash Controls

Though the use of petty cash is not recommended as a cash best practice, petty cash is extremely common in many corporations. The best control is to not have petty cash at all, because it is too easy for cash theft to occur. A better approach is to use procurement cards (see Chapter 2) for small purchases.

The basic process flow for petty cash is simple, so no explanatory flowchart is provided. In essence, anyone requesting a cash payment from the petty cash fund must submit a receipt as proof of expenditure and sign a document stating that he or she has received the cash. The complete procedure is noted in Exhibit 6.12. These two controls are inherent parts of the process:

1. *Require a valid receipt or receipt affidavit as proof of expenditure.* When an employee requests reimbursement from the petty cash fund, he or she must supply a receipt that contains a legible dollar amount, date, and supplier name, so there is reasonable proof that the employee has indeed made an expenditure on behalf of the company. If there is no receipt, then the employee must sign an affidavit (see Exhibit 6.14) that itemizes the same information that would normally be found on the receipt. This control ensures that there is evidence of a purchase, or at least requires an employee to fraudulently manufacture one, which may act as a deterrent.

2. *Require a receipt signature for all cash payouts.* Whenever the petty cash custodian pays out cash, the recipient must sign a "received of petty cash" form (see Exhibit 6.13), which is stapled to the receipt. By doing so, the custodian is being required to provide evidence that a third party has indeed accepted petty cash. This control is designed to keep the custodian from manufacturing receipts and directly pocketing funds without any evidence of who submitted the receipts.

Exhibit 6.12   Procedure for Petty Cash Transactions

Policy/Procedure Statement   Retrieval No.:   CASH-05
Subject: Petty Cash Transactions

1.   PURPOSE AND SCOPE

This procedure is used by the petty cash custodian to handle ongoing cash disbursements and replenish petty cash.

2.   PROCEDURES

2.1   Reconcile Petty Cash Box (Petty Cash Custodian)

1. Upon receipt of a request for cash disbursement, unlock the petty cash box.
2. Verify that the applicant has submitted an expense receipt for an amount less than the maximum reimbursable dollar value, and which contains the purchase date, dollar amount, and name of the supplier. If there is no receipt, have the applicant complete the Missing Receipt form (see Exhibit 6.14), which requires an approval signature from the applicant's supervisor.
3. Enter the date, expense description, and dollar amount on the Received of Petty Cash voucher, sign it in the Approved By field, and have the applicant sign it in the Received By field.
4. Pay the requested petty cash to the applicant.
5. Staple either the receipt or the Missing Receipt form to the back of the Received of Petty Cash voucher (see Exhibit 6.13), and file it.

2.2   Replenish Petty Cash (Petty Cash Custodian)

1. Access a blank Petty Cash Requisition form. (See Exhibit 6.15.)
2. Count all remaining petty cash and enter it in the Ending Cash on Hand field in the form.
3. Verify that the date, supplier name, expenditure description, and amount are listed on each receipt or Missing Receipt Form and that an appropriately signed Received of Petty Cash voucher is stapled to each receipt.
4. Number all the receipts and enter each one in a separate line in the Detail of Receipts section of the form.
5. Total all receipts and enter the total in the Detail of Receipts and Reconciliation sections of the form.
6. Subtract the ending cash on hand and total receipts from the standard petty cash fund balance and enter the result in the "+/- overage/shortage" field.
7. Obtain the department manager's approval signature in the Manager Approval section of the form.
8. Attach all receipt documents to the Petty Cash Requisition form.
9. Upon receipt of the requested funds, sign in the Cash Receipt Acknowledgment section of the form and give the form and attached receipts to the accounting clerk.

(continues)

Exhibit 6.12   *(Continued)*

2.3 Record Petty Cash Transactions (Accounting Clerk)

Create a journal entry document summarizing the expenses listed on the Petty Cash Requisition form as well as the amount of any shortfalls or overages. Staple the form and receipts to this journal entry and give the packet to the general ledger accountant for entry into the general ledger.

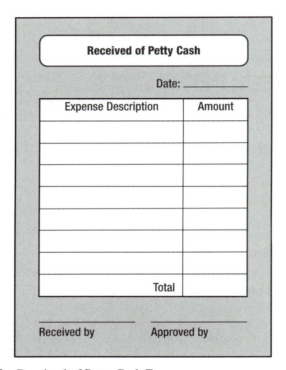

Exhibit 6.13   Received of Petty Cash Form

Though the two controls just noted are the only ones normally used for petty cash, the next audit activity is useful for ensuring that petty cash is being maintained according to the accepted procedure.

- *Conduct spot audits of petty cash.* It is possible to misrepresent the contents of a petty cash box through the use of miscellaneous receipts and IOU vouchers. By making unscheduled audits, you can sometimes spot these irregularities. Key areas to investigate during these audits are:

- ○ *IOU vouchers.* There should be no IOU vouchers in the petty cash box, since this constitutes unauthorized borrowing of company funds by employees. The petty cash custodian must be reminded that this is not allowed.

- ○ *Incomplete or suspicious receipts.* Any receipt for which there is no date or dollar amount is highly suspect and is possible evidence that an employee has submitted a fake receipt.

- ○ *Missing "Received of Petty Cash" vouchers.* If there are receipts but no Received of Petty Cash vouchers, it is possible that the petty cash custodian has used false receipts to remove cash but does not want to forge the accompanying voucher.

- ○ *Missing cash.* If the total of cash and receipts is less than the standard petty cash fund balance, then either cash has been stolen or legitimate receipts are missing.

Exhibit 6.14   Missing Receipt Form

This affidavit replaces a missing receipt form. I attest that no original receipt is available, that the expense itemized below is accurate, and that I will not seek duplicate reimbursement.

Expense description: _____

_____	_____	_____
Dollar Amount	Supplier Name	Receipt Date
_____	_____	_____
Claimant Name	Claimant Signature	Date
_____	_____	_____
Approver Name	Approver Signature	Date

Exhibit 6.15   Petty Cash Requisition

Company Name

Reporting Period: _____

Instructions

1. Count all remaining petty cash and enter in the "Ending Cash on Hand" field.
2. Verify that the date, supplier, expenditure description, and amount are listed on each receipt.
3. Number all receipts and enter in "Receipt Number" field.
4. Next to the receipt number, enter the expense type, account number, and dollar amount.
5. Total all receipts and enter in the Detail of Receipts and Reconciliation sections.
6. Subtract the ending cash on hand and total receipts from the standard petty cash fund balance and enter in the "+/– Overage/shortage" field.
7. Obtain the department manager's approval signature in the Manager Approval section.
8. Submit to Accounting for payment.

Reconciliation: Dollar Amount

Ending cash on hand	
+ Total receipts	
+/– Overage/shortage	
= Total petty cash fund	

Detail of Receipts

Receipt Number	Expense Type	Account Number	Dollar Amount

Total of all receipts _____

+/– Overage/shortage _____

= Replenishment requested _____

Manager Approval:

I have reviewed this petty cash requisition and authorize payment.

_____   _____
Signature   Date

Cash Receipt Acknowledgment:

I acknowledge receipt of the amount shown as the replenishment requested on this form.

_____   _____
Signature   Date

Any of the preceding issues should be discussed with the petty cash custodian. If repeat audits continue to find the same problems, then the problem is likely the petty cash custodian, whose control over petty cash should be rescinded. The use of a contact alarm, as described next, can deter unauthorized access.

- *Install a petty cash contact alarm.* A simple battery-powered contact alarm can be installed on a petty cash drawer that triggers a buzzer or flashing light. If the petty cash box is located in a relatively public location, this may act as a deterrent to anyone attempting to access petty cash.

6–8 Investment Controls

The process of issuing funds for an investment is unique in that every step in the process is a control point. If controls were eliminated from the process, the only step required to make an investment is for an authorized person to create and sign an investment authorization form (itself a control point) and deliver it to the bank, which invests the company's funds in the designated investment. However, as shown in the flowchart in Exhibit 6.16, there are a number of additional steps, all designed to ensure that there is an appropriate level of control over the size and duration of the investment and that the earnings from the investment vehicle are maximized.

The controls noted in the flowchart are described at greater length next, in sequence from the top of the flowchart to the bottom.

- *Create a cash forecast.* There must be some basis for both the size and duration of an investment. Otherwise, a mismatch can develop between the need for cash and its availability, resulting in liquidity problems or an excessive amount of underutilized cash. By requiring that a cash forecast be completed and approved by an authorized person, there is less risk of these problems occurring.
- *Record proposed investment and duration on cash forecast.* Though the cash forecast alone should be a sufficient control over the determination of the correct size and duration of an investment, it helps to also formally write this information directly on the cash forecast, so there is no question about the details of the proposed investment.

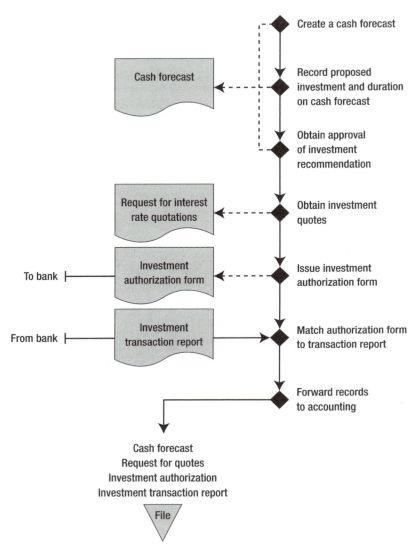

Exhibit 6.16 System of Controls for Investments

- *Obtain approval of investment recommendation.* A manager should
  sign off on the proposed investment. By placing the approval signature
  line directly on the cash forecast, the approver can review the accuracy
  of the forecast as well as the resulting investment recommendation, giving sufficient information for the approver to determine if the recommendation is correct.

- *Obtain investment quotes.* An investment officer may have a favorite bank and will continue to invest with it, even if its rates are not competitive. It is also common for the investment staff to not want to go to the effort of obtaining multiple quotes on a regular basis. By requiring people to complete a quotation sheet, this control ensures that the best investment rate is obtained.

- *Issue investment authorization form.* Banks will not invest funds without a signed investment authorization form from the company. From the company's perspective, a signed authorization also ensures that the appropriate level of management has approved the investment.

- *Match authorization form to transaction report.* The bank may unintentionally invest funds incorrectly or neglect to invest at all. By matching the signed authorization form to any investment transaction report issued by the bank, the company can verify what action the bank took as a result of the authorization.

- *Forward records to accounting.* There is some risk that a person in the investment department will alter investment authorization documents after the fact to hide evidence of inappropriate investments. To reduce this risk, require people to immediately forward a set of supporting documents to the accounting department for storage in a locked location. The accounting staff should stamp the receipt date on each set of documents received, which the internal auditors can use to determine if any documents were inappropriately delayed.

In addition to the basic process flow just noted, the next controls are also useful for ensuring that the documented investments were actually obtained and stored.

- *Periodically match the approved cash forecast, quote sheets, and investment authorization to actual investments completed.* Though all the supporting paperwork may be in order, it is still possible for an investment officer to shift funds to some other, unauthorized form of investment. To detect such transactions, the internal audit department should match all supporting documents to the actual investments made periodically, as reported by the issuing entities.

- *Assign securities custody to independent party.* It is not common for a company to physically control securities; instead, they are more commonly stored by a third-party custodian, which represents a higher level of control. If some securities must be stored on-site, then ensure that the person responsible for their physical security is not also responsible for recording the securities in the accounting records.

The procedure for initiating an investment is shown in Exhibit 6.17.

Exhibit 6.17   Procedure for Investment Transactions

Policy/Procedure Statement   Retrieval No.:   INVEST-01

Subject: Invest Funds

1.   PURPOSE AND SCOPE

This procedure is used by the treasury staff to invest funds in accordance with the corporate investment policy.

2.   PROCEDURES

2.1   Create a Cash Forecast (Financial Analyst)

1. Create a cash forecast covering the next __ weeks, including standard cash inflows and outflows and also incorporating expected capital expenditures and special adjustments.
2. Compare the new forecast to the forecast developed for the preceding week to see if there are any large variances in the weekly cash results; investigate and adjust as necessary.

2.2   Record Proposed Investment on Cash Forecast (Financial Analyst)

1. Based on the amount of excess funds projected to be available, note below each week on the forecast the proposed amount of funds to invest, the type of investment, and the duration of each proposed investment. The type of investment should be based on the approved corporate investment policy.
2. Create a copy of the forecast and file it.
3. Send the original cash forecast to the CFO.

2.3   Approve Investment Recommendation (CFO)

1. Upon receipt of the cash forecast, review it in general for errors and omissions. Have the financial analyst revise the forecast as necessary.
2. Compare the proposed types of investments to the approved corporate investment policy to ensure that they are acceptable.
3. Verify that the proposed investment duration does not exceed the approved corporate investment duration policy.
4. Sign and date the forecast in the approval block.
5. Forward the cash forecast to the treasury clerk.

Exhibit 6.17 *(Continued)*

2.4 Obtain Investment Quotes (Treasury Clerk)

1. Upon receipt of the latest approved cash forecast, print the latest Request for Interest Rate Quotations form. (See Exhibit 6.18.)
2. Verify that the banks listed on the form are approved for investments by the company.
3. Contact the banks for rate quotes on the investment type, duration, and amount noted on the cash forecast, and enter the quotes on the form.
4. Sign in the "Quotes compiled by" field in the "Approvals" block of the form.
5. Review the quotes with the CFO and enter the actual investment to be made in the "Final Investment" block of the form.
6. The CFO signs in the "Approved by" field in the "Approvals" block of the form.
7. Forward the form to the investment manager for investment placement.
8. File the cash forecast.

2.5 Issue Investment Authorization Form (Investment Manager)

1. Extract a copy of the investment form from the forms cabinet and fill it out, entering the investment type, amount, and duration noted in the "Final Investment" block of the Request for Interest Rate Quotations form.
2. Sign the investment form.
3. Fax the form to the bank quoting the highest rate on the Interest Rate Quotations form.
4. Call the firm to verify receipt of the fax.
5. Sign in the "Investment placed by" field in the "Approvals" block of the Request for Interest Rate Quotations form.
6. Create two copies of the Request for Interest Rate Quotations form and investment form, and file both copies.
7. Forward the original versions of both the Request for Interest Rate Quotations form and investment form to the Treasury Clerk.

2.6 Match Authorization to Transaction Report (Treasury Clerk)

Upon receipt of an investment transaction report from the bank, match its terms to those listed on the investment form and Request for Interest Rate Quotations form. If there are discrepancies, contact the bank to determine why, and forward this information to the CFO.

2.7 Forward Records to Accounting (Treasury Clerk)

1. Assemble the cash forecast. Request for Interest Rate Quotations, investment form, and investment transaction report into a single packet.
2. Create a copy of the packet and file it by date.
3. Forward the original version of the packet to the general ledger accountant, to be recorded in the accounting system.

Request for Interest Rate Quotations			Date: _____	
Funding Available: $_____				
	Approved Investment Vehicles			
Approved Institution	Term Deposits	Treasury Bills	Bankers' Acceptance	Other
Bank Name #1	Days Rate	Days Rate	Days Rate	Days Rate
Address	30 _____	30 _____	30 _____	30 _____
Address	60 _____	60 _____	60 _____	60 _____
Phone	90 _____	90 _____	90 _____	90 _____
Contact Name	_____	_____	_____	_____
Bank Name #2	Days Rate	Days Rate	Days Rate	Days Rate
Address	30 _____	30 _____	30 _____	30 _____
Address	60 _____	60 _____	60 _____	60 _____
Phone	90 _____	90 _____	90 _____	90 _____
Contact Name	_____	_____	_____	_____
Bank Name #3	Days Rate	Days Rate	Days Rate	Days Rate
Address	30 _____	30 _____	30 _____	30 _____
Address	60 _____	60 _____	60 _____	60 _____
Phone	90 _____	90 _____	90 _____	90 _____
Contact Name	_____	_____	_____	_____
Bank Name #4	Days Rate	Days Rate	Days Rate	Days Rate
Address	30 _____	30 _____	30 _____	30 _____
Address	60 _____	60 _____	60 _____	60 _____
Phone	90 _____	90 _____	90 _____	90 _____
Contact Name	_____	_____	_____	_____
	Start Date	$ Amount	Maturity	Rate
Final Investment	/ /	$		%

Approvals

Quotes compiled by: _____   Date: _____

Investment placed by: _____   Date: _____

Approved by: _____   Date: _____

Exhibit 6.18   Request for Interest Rate Quotations

6–9 Cash-Handling Policies

There is a wide array of policies related to cash handling, with the majority covering the investment of cash. The following 23 policies are divided into subcategories for cash application, petty cash, investment requirements, and the accounting treatment of investments.

The first three policies cover the treatment of cash upon its initial receipt at the company, to ensure that it is rapidly applied to open receivables, that errors are resolved, and that deposits are made everyday.

1. *Checks shall be posted within one day of receipt.* This policy requires the cash application staff to post received checks immediately upon receipt, which is not only useful for the collections staff, but also ensures that problem checks are addressed as soon as possible.
2. *The unapplied cash account shall be reviewed daily.* Though all cash should in theory be applied to customer receivables as soon as it is received, the nature of some payments may be difficult to ascertain, resulting in their posting to an unapplied cash account. This policy ensures that the unapplied cash account is reviewed constantly, so that unapplied cash problems are resolved as soon as possible.
3. *Cash shall be deposited daily.* When cash is retained on the company premises, there is a risk of theft, while the company also loses interest on the uninvested cash. This policy forces the company to deposit cash every day, thereby avoiding these problems.

The second block of policies addresses the use of petty cash funds, concentrating on acceptable uses of petty cash and security of the funds. They are:

4. *Reimbursements from petty cash are authorized for expenditures of up to $____ per transaction.* This policy keeps employees from obtaining large payments from petty cash funds that would otherwise have required supervisory approval prior to payment.
5. *Petty cash may not be used for these expenditure reimbursements*:
   a. Advances
   b. Gifts
   c. Personal loans
   d. Traffic citations

e. Personal expenses

f. Interest charges

This policy keeps petty cash expenditures from being made for items that would not normally be approved for payment.

6. *The petty cash fund shall be small enough to require replenishment about twice per month.* This policy establishes a rough guideline for establishing the size of a fund. Inherent in the policy is a periodic review of the fund size.

7. *Petty cash should be kept in a locked box within a locked drawer when the custodian is absent.* This policy recognizes the extreme ease with which petty cash can be stolen and so requires double locking of the storage location. It is not sufficient to require just a locking petty cash box, since the entire box can be stolen.

The next set of policies covers the types of acceptable investments, as well as their maximum acceptable duration, and the financial wherewithal of their issuers.

8. *At least $____ shall be invested in overnight investments and in negotiable marketable obligations of major U.S. issuers.* This policy forces the treasury staff to attain a minimum level of liquidity. The fixed dollar amount used in the policy should be reviewed regularly to match upcoming budgeted working capital requirements.

9. *Overnight cash balances representing ____ days of working capital shall be invested in overnight repurchase agreements.* This policy varies from the preceding policy by incorporating a variable level of cash to be invested in highly liquid investments, based on a measure (days of working capital) that will vary as the corporation changes in size. Thus, this is a somewhat more flexible policy.

10. *No more than ____ percent of the total portfolio shall be invested in time deposits or other investments with a lack of liquidity.* This policy is similar to the preceding one, except that it ignores a fixed liquidity requirement, focusing instead on a maximum proportion of the total portfolio that must be retained for short-term requirements. This policy tends to require less periodic updating as the company changes in size.

11. *The average maturity of the investment portfolio shall be limited to ____ years.* This policy is designed to keep a company from investing in ex-

cessively long maturities. The policy can be broken down into more specific maturity limitations for different types of investments, such as 5 years for any U.S. government obligations, 1 year for bank certificates of deposit, and 270 days for commercial paper.

12. *Investments in foreign commercial paper shall be limited to those unconditionally guaranteed by a prime U.S. issuer and fully hedged.* This policy is designed to lower the risk of default on investments in securities issued by foreign entities.

13. *Investments in commercial paper shall be limited to those of companies having long-term senior debt ratings of Aa or better.* This policy is designed to limit the risk of default on commercial paper investments by focusing investments on only the highest-grade commercial paper.

14. *Investments in bank certificates of deposit shall be limited to those banks with capital accounts exceeding $1 billion.* This policy is designed to limit the risk of default on certificates of deposit, on the assumption that large capital accounts equate to minimal risk of bank failure.

15. *Investments shall be made only in investments backed by U.S. government debt obligations.* This policy can be used in place of the preceding ones that specify allowable investments in nongovernment investments. This policy tends to be used by highly risk-averse companies that place less emphasis on the return generated from their investments.

16. *No single issuer shall constitute more than ___ percent of the total value of the portfolio, except federal obligations.* This policy limits the corporation's total risk associated with a single issuer. To be more comprehensive, the policy can be revised to state "no single issuer, including subsidiaries."

The next seven policies are designed to restrict management from manipulating the recording of investments to alter financial results.

17. *The board of directors shall be notified of the reasons for any significant shift in the designation of securities between the held-to-maturity, available-for-sale, and trading portfolios and the approximate impact on different categories of income.* This policy is designed to require management to justify its actions in shifting securities between portfolios, which is likely to reduce the amount of shifting, while also keeping the board informed of any likely movements of gains or losses

between the operating income and other comprehensive income parts of the income statement.

18. *The board of directors must authorize all shifts in investment designation out of the held-to-maturity portfolio.* There are specific accounting instances where the transfer of securities out of the held-to-maturity portfolio will preclude a company's subsequent use of the held-to-maturity portfolio. Accordingly, the board should be notified of the reasons for such a designation and give its formal approval before the designation change can be made.

19. *The unrecognized amount of gains or losses on held-to-maturity securities shall be regularly reported to the board of directors.* Management may designate poor-performing debt securities as held-to-maturity, in which case any changes in their fair value will not be recognized. This policy is designed to reveal any gains or losses that would be recognized if these securities were to have any other portfolio designation, so the board is aware of any "hanging" gains or losses.

20. *Debt securities shall not be classified as held-to-maturity unless sufficient investments are already on hand to cover all budgeted short-term cash requirements.* Generally accepted accounting principles already require that debt securities not be classified as held-to-maturity if a company does not have the ability to hold the securities for the required time period; this policy is more specific in stating that all anticipated cash flows be fully covered by other investments before any debt securities receive the held-to-maturity classification. The policy makes it more likely that a company will not be forced to liquidate its held-to-maturity debt portfolio prematurely.

21. *All securities purchases shall be designated as trading securities at the time of purchase.* This policy is intended to avoid the designation of an investment as "available-for-sale," which would allow management to avoid recording short-term changes in the fair value of the investment in reported earnings. The policy removes the ability of management to alter financial results by shifting the designation of an investment.

22. *All losses on securities designated as available-for-sale shall be considered permanent.* Accounting rules allow one to avoid recognizing losses on available-for-sale securities by assuming that the losses are temporary. By using this policy to require an immediate write-down on all losses, management no longer has the ability to manipulate earnings by making assumptions that losses are temporary in nature.

23. *Available-for-sale securities shall not be sold solely to recognize related gains in their fair market value.* Accounting rules do not allow ongoing recognition of gains in the value of available-for-sale securities in earnings until they have been sold, so there is a natural temptation to manage earnings by timing their sale. This policy is designed to set an ethical standard for management to prevent such actions from taking place. In reality, this is a difficult policy to enforce, since management can find reasonable excuses for selling securities when their unrecognized gains are needed for bookkeeping purposes.

Summary

Though some best practices have improved the efficiency of the cash-handling process, many of the controls needed for this process have been in existence since checks were first issued as a legal form of payment. The only demonstrable reduction in cash-related controls is achieved through the use of lockboxes, because they prevent cash and checks from ever entering the company premises.

Many controls are required for the handling of cash, since it is the most tempting of all assets to steal. However, not all of the controls presented here need to be installed; it is better to conduct a careful analysis of the volumes of different types of cash transactions being processed and concentrate the bulk of the controls where most of the cash is being handled. Even if there are modest losses from some of the lesser cash transactions, it may be more cost-effective to absorb the losses than to institute more controls.

Chapter 7

Controls for Payroll Best Practices

Overview

Payroll has been a considerable source of fraudulent activity, especially in regard to the creation of ghost employees whose pay is siphoned into the bank accounts of the perpetrators, as well as of the false boosting of reported hours worked. Of the two types of fraud, the use of ghost employees is by far the most expensive, typically resulting in ten times the expense of falsified hours worked.

In addition, payroll is an area requiring such a large volume of data collection and conversion that there is a high risk of errors being made inadvertently. Thus, in order to reduce both fraud and data errors, a variety of controls are required at key points in the payroll process. This chapter identifies controls for not only paper-based and computerized payroll systems, but also for a variety of payroll best practices, such as computerized timekeeping, payroll self-service, electronic remittances, and outsourcing.

Many of the ancillary controls listed in Section 7–1 are also useful in more automated payroll processing environments, so be sure to review that section to see what controls may be applicable elsewhere.

7–1 Basic Payroll Controls

A surprisingly large number of small companies still calculate payroll entirely by hand, especially if they have just a few employees. The flowchart in Exhibit 7.1 shows the basic process flow for these organizations, with the minimum set of controls needed to ensure that it operates properly. The small black diamonds on the flowchart indicate the location of key control points in the process, with descriptions next to the diamonds. In essence, controls

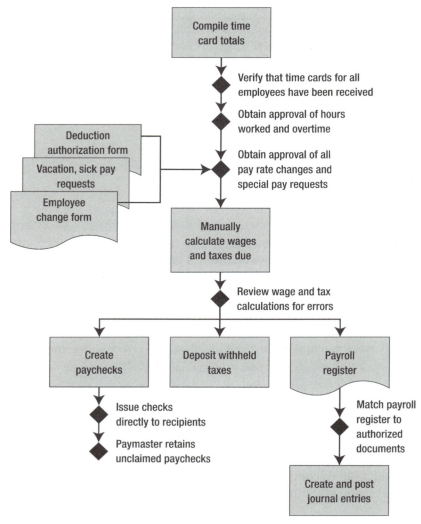

Exhibit 7.1   System of Controls for Paper-Based Payroll

are used to ensure that submitted time cards are complete, accurate, and authorized and that payroll payment and tax remittance calculations have been made properly.

A key control at the top of Exhibit 7.1 is for the payroll staff to verify against the current employee list that time cards have been received from all employees, which can rectify an exceedingly common problem. Next, the payroll staff obtains supervisory approval that the hours submitted on the time cards are correct and authorized, which uncovers inappropriate overtime claims. Once the time cards are compiled, the payroll staff next uses submitted employee change forms and a variety of pay and deduction requests to calculate the total amount to be paid. Following the initial pay calculation, a second person should verify calculations, after which paychecks are cut and payroll taxes deposited. An additional control is to hand paychecks directly to employees, verifying the identity of the recipients. Finally, the accounting staff should match the manually generated payroll register to all supporting documents prior to creating a payroll entry in the general ledger. This group of controls ensures that all employees are paid the correct amount and that pay is issued to valid employees.

The controls noted in the flowchart are described at greater length next, in sequence from the top of the flowchart to the bottom.

- *Verify that time cards for all employees have been received.* It is entirely possible for an employee's time sheet to disappear during the accumulation of time sheet data or to never be submitted. In either case, once payday comes and there is no check, impacted employees will want an immediate payment, which represents not only additional work for the payroll staff, but a sudden and unexpected additional cash outflow. To avoid this problem, always match received time cards to the current employee list and investigate all missing time cards.

- *Obtain approval of hours worked and overtime.* Employees may pad their time sheets with extra hours, hoping to be paid for these amounts. Alternatively, they may have fellow employees clock them in and out on days when they are not working. These actions can be difficult to spot, especially when there are many employees for a supervisor to track or if employees work in outlying locations. Supervisors should review and initial all time sheets to ensure that hours have been worked, though there is a risk that they will not remember what happened several days earlier in the reporting period.

- *Obtain approval of all pay rate changes and special pay requests.* Pay changes can be made quite easily through the payroll system if there is collusion between a payroll clerk and any other employee. Such changes can be spotted through regular comparisons of pay rates paid to the approved pay rates documented in employee records. It is best to require the approval of a high-level manager for all pay changes, which should include that person's signature on a standard pay change form.

- *Review wage and tax calculations for errors.* When calculated manually, payroll is the single most error-prone function in the accounting area. To reduce the number of errors, have someone other than the payroll clerk review the wage and tax calculations for errors. This does not have to be a detailed duplication of all calculations made; a simple scan for reasonableness is likely to spot obvious errors.

- *Match payroll register to authorizing documents.* The payroll clerk has complete control over the transfer of information from authorizing payroll documents into actual check payments, which introduces the possibility of fraudulent manipulation of payments. To detect such problems, a different person should compare the payroll register to authorizing documents (deduction forms, pay requests, change forms, etc.). Even if only conducted on a spot basis, the presence of this control point, if publicized, should act as a deterrent to payroll manipulation by the payroll clerk.

- *Issue checks directly to recipients.* A common type of fraud is for the payroll staff either to create employees in the payroll system or to carry on the pay of employees who have left the company and then pocket the resulting paychecks. This practice can be stopped by ensuring that every paycheck is handed to an employee who can prove his or her identity. The person handing out checks can compare the payroll register to the checks to ensure that all checks are being given to the employees. The only exception should be those cases where, due to disability or absence, an employee is unable to collect a check, and so gives written authorization for it be to given to someone else, who brings it to the absent employee.

  In cases where there are outlying locations for which it is impossible to physically hand a paycheck to an employee, a reasonable alternative is to have the internal audit staff periodically travel to these locations with the checks on an unannounced basis and require physical identification of each recipient before handing over a check.

- *Paymaster retains unclaimed paychecks.* The person who physically hands out paychecks to employees is sometimes called the paymaster. This person does not prepare the paychecks or sign them, and his or her sole responsibility in the payroll area is to hand out paychecks. If an employee is not available to accept a paycheck, then the paymaster retains that person's check in a secure location until the employee is personally available to receive it. This approach avoids the risk of giving the paycheck to a friend of the employee who might cash it and also keeps the payroll staff members from preparing a check and cashing it themselves.

A procedure listing the basic steps needed to process payroll in a paper-based environment is shown in Exhibit 7.2.

Exhibit 7.2   Paper-based Payroll Processing Procedure

Policy/Procedure Statement   Retrieval No.:   PAY-01

Subject: Basic Payroll Processing

1.   PURPOSE AND SCOPE

This procedure is used to compile time sheets, process pay changes, manually calculate wages and taxes due, create paychecks, deposit taxes, and create journal entries.

2.   PROCEDURES

2.1 Obtain Time Sheets (Payroll Clerk)

1. Obtain time sheets (see Exhibit 7.3) from all company locations. Check off the receipts against the current employee list, and contact the factory manager of each location from which no time sheets have been received or for missing individual time sheets.

2. Verify that all time sheets contain a supervisor's approval signature. Supervisors must circle and initial all overtime hours to indicate their authorization. If approval has not occurred, return the time sheets to the supervisors for their immediate review and approval.

2.2 Review Time Sheets (Payroll Clerk)

1. Add up the time on all time sheets, circling those time punches that have no clock-ins or clock-outs.

2. Review the time sheets for special work codes. If any time has been charged to family leave, jury duty, personal holiday, sick leave, unpaid leave, or vacation, circle those items.

3. Create a master review list of all employee names whose time sheets contain circled items.

4. Distribute all time sheets with circled items to supervisors, who must complete missing information and initial next to each circled item to indicate their approval.

(continues)

Exhibit 7.2 *(Continued)*

5. Upon receipt of the reviewed time sheets from the supervisors, verify that all circled items have been addressed, and then check off the time sheets on the master review list.

2.3 Review Employee Change Requests (Payroll Clerk)

1. Assemble all employee change forms and deduction authorization forms (see Exhibits 7.4 and 7.5) received since the last payroll was processed.
2. Verify that all change requests have been authorized correctly.

2.4 Calculate Wages and Taxes Due (Payroll Clerk and Payroll Clerk #2)

1. Calculate gross pay based on the most recent authorized pay rate for each employee.
2. Calculate pretax deductions, such as 401k and flexible spending account deductions. Verify that deduction goals have not been exceeded.
3. Using the appropriate IRS tax table, calculate all taxes for employees.
4. Calculate after-tax deductions based on authorized documents. Verify that deduction goals have not been exceeded.

2.5 Review Wage and Tax Calculations (Payroll Clerk #2)

1. Review all pay calculations made by the first payroll clerk, focusing on the following items:
   - Employee deductions are correct.
   - Deductions do not exceed deduction goals.
   - Pay rates are accurate.
   - The correct start dates are used for changes in pay rates.
   - Taxes are based on the correct number of employee deductions.
2. Review all possible errors with the first payroll clerk.
3. Once all errors are corrected, sign off on the calculations and return all payroll documents to the first payroll clerk.

2.6 Create Payroll Register (Payroll Clerk)

1. Itemize in the payroll register who was paid, their gross pay, tax deductions, and net pay.
2. Have the payroll manager compare the checks to the payroll register to ensure that all information was transferred correctly.
3. Initial and date all payroll change and deduction authorization forms to indicate that they were used in the payroll calculations, and file them in the employee payroll files.

2.7 Create Paychecks (Payroll Clerk #2)

1. Remove a sufficient number of blank payroll checks from the locked storage cabinet for all employees to be paid. Note the check numbers removed on a tracking sheet, which is stored in a separate locked cabinet.

Exhibit 7.2 *(Continued)*

2. Transfer gross pay, deductions, and net pay information from the payroll register to the checks, and copy the same information onto the remittance advices attached to each check.

3. Record in the payroll register, next to the pay information for each employee, the check number of the check used to pay him or her.

4. Take the payroll register and completed checks to an authorized check signer, who compares the payroll register entries to the checks and signs the checks.

5. Store the signed checks in the company safe until pay day.

2.8 Deposit Withheld Taxes (Payroll Clerk #2)

1. Remove a blank Form 8109 from the IRS-supplied booklet.

2. On the form, enter the month in which the corporate tax year ends, the dollar amount being remitted (source is the tax total on the payroll register), and contact information, and darken the square next to the type of tax being paid.

3. Create a check for the amount of the remittance.

4. Take the completed Form 8109 and check payment to the local bank and obtain a receipt for the payment.

5. File the tax payment receipt by date.

6. Send the payroll register to the general ledger accountant.

2.9 Create and Post Journal Entries (General Ledger Clerk and Controller)

1. The general ledger accountant summarizes the payroll register into a journal entry on the corporate journal entry form.

2. The controller reviews the journal entry form and initials it to indicate approval.

3. The general ledger accountant records the journal entry in the general ledger.

4. The general ledger accountant staples the journal entry form to the payroll register and files it by date.

2.10 Issue Checks (Paymaster)

1. Divide the paychecks into groups by department.

2. Go to each department and hand out paychecks to all employees showing a proper form of picture identification.

3. Upon receipt of a paycheck, each employee signs for it next to his or her name on the employee register.

4. If employees are not available, highlight their names on the employee register, and store both the register and unissued checks in the company safe.

Exhibit 7.3   Employee Time Sheet

Bi-weekly Time Sheet

Employee Name (please print) _____   Department: _____

Week Ending _____

	Start Time	Stop Time	Total Time	Work Code
Monday				
Tuesday				
Wednesday				
Thursday				
Friday				
Saturday				
Sunday				
Total				

Week Ending _____

	Start Time	Stop Time	Total Time	Work Code
Monday				
Tuesday				
Wednesday				
Thursday				
Friday				
Saturday				
Sunday				
Total				

Work Codes

F	Family Leave	R	Regular
H	Holiday	S	Sick Leave
J	Jury Duty	U	Unpaid Leave
PH	Personal Holiday	V	Vacation

Employee Signature _____

Supervisory Signature _____

Submit time sheet to your superivsor by 10 A.M. Monday following completion of period shown on time sheet.

Exhibit 7.4   Employee Change Form

Employee Name: _____   Social Security #: _____

Reason: _____

Categories	Change/New	Effective Date
Name		
Address		
Phone		
Gender		
Birth Date		
Hire Date		
Term Date		
Title		
Salary		
Status		
Married/Single		
Federal Exempt		
State Lived in		
State Worked in		
Medical Deduction		
Dental Deduction		
LTD		
STD		
Supp Life		
401k% or $		
Dependent Flex Deduction		
Dependent Flex Goal		
Medical Flex Deduction		
Medical Flex Goal		
Direct Deposit Routing #/account #		

Comments: _____

_____

_____

Authorized by: _____   Date: _____

Completed by: _____   Date: _____

Exhibit 7.5   Deduction Authorization Form

I hereby authorize that the following deductions be made from my pay:

Deduction Type	Deduction Amount	Start Date	Stop Date
☐ Cafeteria Plan—Dependent Care	_____	_____	_____
☐ Cafeteria Plan—Medical	_____	_____	_____
☐ Dental Insurance	_____	_____	_____
☐ Dependent Life Insurance	_____	_____	_____
☐ Long-term Disability Insurance	_____	_____	_____
☐ Medical Insurance	_____	_____	_____
☐ Short-term Disability Insurance	_____	_____	_____
☐ Supplemental Life Insurance	_____	_____	_____

Signature	Date

Thus far, the discussion of paper-based payroll processing has concentrated solely on the primary process flow. In addition, the next ancillary controls are designed to provide some additional degree of control over the process.

- *Continually review all outstanding advances.* When advances are paid to employees, it is necessary to continually review and follow up on the status of these advances. Employees who require advances are sometimes in a precarious financial position and must be issued constant reminders to ensure that the funds are paid back in a timely manner. A simple control point is to have a policy that requires the company to automatically deduct all advances from the *next* employee paycheck, thereby greatly reducing the work of tracking advances.

- *Require approval of all advance payments to employees.* When employees request an advance for any reason—as a draw on the next paycheck or as funding for a company trip—this should always require formal signed approval from their immediate supervisors. The reason is that an advance is essentially a small short-term loan, which would also require management approval. The accounts payable supervisor or staff should be allowed to authorize advances only when they are in very small amounts.

- *Limit access to payroll change authorization forms.* When the payroll clerk receives a signed payroll change authorization, he or she should store it in a locked cabinet until used to calculate payroll. By doing so, no one (except the payroll clerk) has an opportunity to modify the authorization document.

- *Payroll manager verifies payroll register entry.* The payroll clerk can both calculate paychecks and record this information in the payroll register, as long as the payroll manager verifies that all information was transferred correctly to the payroll register.

- *Require approval of all negative deductions.* A negative deduction from a paycheck is essentially a cash payment to an employee. Though this type of deduction is needed to offset prior deductions that may have been too high, it can be abused to increase a person's pay artificially. Consequently, all negative deductions should be reviewed by a manager.

- *Audit pay deductions.* It is useful to audit the deductions taken from employee paychecks, since these can be altered downward to effectively yield an increased rate of pay. This audit should include a review of the amount and timing of garnishment payments, to ensure that these deductions are being made as required by court orders.

- *Look for paychecks having no tax or other deductions.* A paycheck that has no tax deductions or personal deductions is more likely to be a check issued for a ghost employee, where the perpetrator wants to receive the maximum amount of cash. The easiest way to spot these checks is to create a custom report that runs automatically with each payroll and that itemizes only checks of this nature.

- *Issue lists of paychecks issued to department supervisors.* It is quite useful to give supervisors a list of paychecks issued to everyone in their departments from time to time, because they may be able to spot payments being made to employees who are no longer working there. This is a particular problem in larger companies, where any delay in processing termination paperwork can result in continuing payments to ex-employees. It is also a good control over any payroll clerk who may be trying to defraud the company by delaying termination paperwork and then pocketing the paychecks produced in the interim.

- *Match W-2 pay information to employee pay change authorizations and termination documentation.* When the payroll system prints year-end W-2 forms, match them to pay rate change authorizations for each employee. By doing so, it becomes apparent if there are any irregular pay levels. In addition, verifying pay for employees who have been terminated will reveal the existence of any employees for whom pay was issued subsequent to their departure. Though this detective control may find problems only months after a problem occurred, at least it will keep losses from growing even larger than would otherwise be the case.

- *Compare the addresses on employee paychecks.* If payroll staff members are creating additional ghost employees and having the resulting paychecks mailed to their home addresses, then a simple comparison of addresses for all check recipients will reveal duplicate addresses. (Employees can get around this problem by having checks sent to post office boxes; this control issue can be stopped by creating a policy to prohibit payments to post office boxes.)

- *Compare pay records to employee files.* A good detective control is to see if an employee human resources file exists for each check payment, on the grounds that these files typically are maintained by someone other than the payroll clerk and so represent a good independent verification of the existence of an employee. If there is no employee file, payments probably are being made to a ghost employee.

- *Prohibit payment of wages in cash.* If a company pays its employees in cash, there are additional opportunities for the funds to be stolen, which require additional controls. It is better simply to not allow cash payments. For a discussion of the controls needed for wage payments made in cash, see Section 7–2.

- *Have employees sign for paychecks received.* Though not common, an extra level of control over the payment process is to require employees to sign for paychecks received. This is not as necessary as would be the case if payments were in cash (see the next section). Generally, giving responsibility for the paycheck distribution process to a paymaster is a sufficient level of control.

- *Review paychecks for double endorsements.* If a payroll clerk has continued to issue checks to a terminated employee and is pocketing the checks, the cashed checks should contain a forged signature for the departed employee as well as a second signature for the account name into which the check is deposited.

- *Review uncashed payroll checks.* If checks have not been cashed, it is possible that they were created through some flaw in the payroll system that sent a check to a nonexistent employee. An attempt should be made to contact these employees to see if there is a problem.

- *Independently verify tax remittances.* Given the large penalties associated with late or incorrect tax remittances, some companies protect themselves by having an additional person calculate the amount of taxes remitted, and the timing and manner of remittances, to be doubly sure that remittances are handled correctly.

- *Reconcile the payroll bank account.* The payroll bank account always should be promptly reconciled, so that any discrepancies between payments made and the totals listed in the payroll register will be noted, indicating the presence of fraud. An earlier control that described how to match the payroll register to authorizing documents could be negated by false entries in the payroll register. The bank reconciliation will highlight any such false entries. This reconciliation should be conducted by someone not otherwise involved in the payroll process.

- *Compare the payroll salary budget to actual expenditures.* A very high-level control over the reasonableness of the payroll expense is to compare it to the budgeted expense, department by department. As long as the budget was designed roughly to mirror actual operations (as opposed to a stretch budget that is designed to be quite difficult to attain), this can be a reasonable indicator of problems with the payroll calculations. It is especially good for indicating the presence of ghost employees, since they will not be listed in the budget.

- *Outsource payroll processing.* A supplier of payroll processing services is responsible for remitting payroll taxes, which removes a considerable responsibility from the company; for this reason, outsourcing payroll is in itself a control point. Outsourcing is described in greater detail in Section 7–8, "Controls for Outsourced Payments."

7–2 Controls for Cash Payments

Though rare, some organizations still make cash payments to their employees. This is usually the case for day laborers, who are paid off at the end of each day, or for employees who have no bank accounts and do not wish to incur the expense of a local check cashing agency. Controls over cash payments must be strict, since stolen cash is essentially untraceable. This section itemizes the key control points needed for cash payments; however, to avoid replication, it does not list the controls shown in Section 7–1 for time sheet summarization and wage and tax calculations. The system of controls for cash payments is shown in Exhibit 7.6.

The controls noted in the flowchart are described at greater length next, in sequence from the top of the flowchart to the bottom.

- *Complete pay envelope information in ink.* By requiring pay information to be transferred onto the pay envelopes in ink, it is much more difficult for anyone to revise the pay amounts on the envelope and pocket the resulting excess cash.

- *Second clerk matches payroll register to pay envelopes.* It is possible for the primary payroll clerk to alter the amount of pay listed on the pay envelopes (as shown in Exhibit 7.8) illicitly, so that the eventual recipient of the cash can split the proceeds with the payroll clerk. To mitigate this risk, have a second clerk verify the accuracy of the pay information transferred from the payroll register to the pay envelopes.

- *Initial each verified pay envelope.* Once the second clerk has matched the payroll register to a pay envelope, the clerk should initial the envelope. By doing so, it is more difficult for anyone to substitute an entirely new pay envelope for the real one and pocket any resulting excess cash.

- *Complete bill and coin requirements form in ink.* By requiring that the form (shown in Exhibit 7.9) be completed in ink, it is much more difficult for anyone subsequently to modify the requested bill and coin amounts. If someone were to do so, they could request more cash than needed from the cashier, then modify the form again to cover their tracks and retain the excess amount of cash received.

- *Payroll manager approves the bill and coin requirements form.* The payroll manager should approve the cash request since he or she is in the best position to know the approximate amount of cash required for each

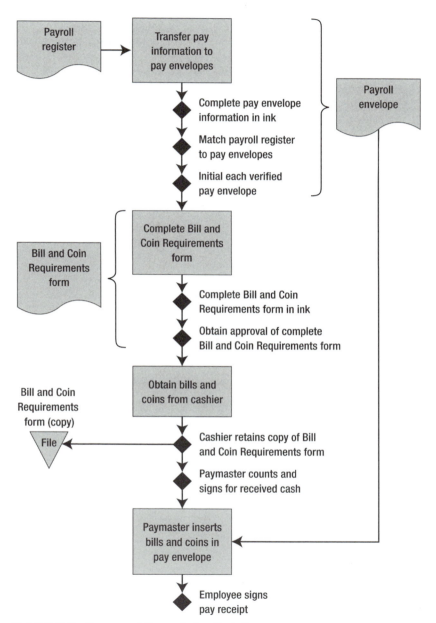

Exhibit 7.6   System of Controls for Cash Payments

payroll payment. As an added control, the payroll manager can retain a copy of the form and compare it to previous forms to see if the amounts are comparable.

- *Cashier retains photocopy of bill and coin requirements form.* Once the cashier has issued the amount of cash on the bill and coin requirements form, he or she should retain a photocopy of the form. This photocopy provides evidence of any alteration to the form that someone might make subsequent to the cash disbursement.

- *Paymaster counts and signs for received cash.* It is possible for the cashier to hand a reduced amount of cash to the paymaster and illicitly retain the difference, so the paymaster should count out the cash before signing for its receipt. This is a relatively minor control, since the paymaster still must apportion the received cash among the pay envelopes and would discover the discrepancy anyway.

- *Employee signs pay receipt.* When cash is being used for payments, it is mandatory that employees sign for the cash, using a form similar to the one shown in Exhibit 7.10. This form shows the employee the amount of money he or she has just been paid, with a signature indicating that the cash amount paid matches the total listed on the form. This approach ensures that the paymaster does not pocket any cash intended for employees.

A comprehensive cash payment procedure for payroll that incorporates the controls noted above is described in Exhibit 7.7.

Exhibit 7.7   Cash Payments Procedure

Policy/Procedure Statement   Retrieval No.:   PAY-02

Subject: Issue Cash Payments to Employees

1.   PURPOSE AND SCOPE

This procedure is used make cash payments to employees for their payroll.

2.   PROCEDURES

2.1   Transfer Payment Information to Pay Envelopes (Payroll Clerk #2)

   1. Complete all steps shown in Exhibit 7.2, sections 2.1 through 2.4. Once the payroll register is completed and reviewed, copy the pay period, hours

Exhibit 7.7 *(Continued)*

worked, earnings, tax deductions, and net pay from the register to the outside of the pay envelope. (See Exhibit 7.8.) This information must be printed on each pay envelope in ink.

2. Have a second clerk compare the payroll register to the pay envelope for accuracy, and initial each pay envelope that has been reviewed in this manner.

2.2 Complete Payroll Bill and Coin Requirements Form (Payroll Clerk and Payroll Manager)

1. Using the net pay information on the pay envelopes, complete the Payroll Bill and Coin Requirements form (see Exhibit 7.9) in ink. Enter on the form the exact amount of bills and coins needed for each employee's pay.

2. Obtain the payroll manager's approval for the requested bills and coins. The payroll manager must sign the Payroll Bill and Coin Requirements form.

2.3 Obtain Bills and Coins (Paymaster and Cashier)

1. The paymaster takes the completed and approved Payroll Bill and Coin Requirements form to the cashier.

2. The cashier counts out the correct amount of bills and coins and signs the Payroll Bill and Coin Requirements form.

3. The cashier creates a photocopy of the Payroll Bill and Coin Requirements form and files it by date in a locked location.

4. The cashier transfers the bills and coins to the paymaster, who counts and signs for the received cash.

2.4 Allocate Bills and Coins to Pay Envelopes (Paymaster)

The paymaster allocates the bills and coins to each of the pay envelopes based on the net pay listed on each envelope and locks the pay envelopes in the company safe until pay day.

2.5 Distribute Pay Envelopes (Paymaster)

1. The paymaster removes the pay envelopes from the safe.

2. Using an employee list, the paymaster sorts the pay envelopes by department.

3. In each department, the paymaster requires that each employee provide a form of photo identification before handing over a pay envelope.

4. Each employee must open and count the contents of his or her pay envelope in front of the paymaster to verify its contents and then sign for receipt of the pay envelope on the Pay Receipt form. (See Exhibit 7.10.)

5. If any employees are not present, the paymaster returns their pay envelopes to the company safe and notes their names on the employee list for daily investigation until the cash is paid.

Exhibit 7.8   Pay Envelope

Employee Name	Wilbur Smythe
Pay Period Beginning Date	May 8
Pay Period Ending Date	May 15
Hours Worked	Regular: 40 Overtime: 5
Earnings	Regular: $ 400 Overtime: $ 75
Total Earnings	$ 475
Pay Deductions	
Social Security Tax	$ 29
Federal Income Tax	$ 100
Medicare Tax	$ 12
State Income Tax	$ 47
Total Deductions	$ 188
Net Pay	$ 287 **Clerk Initials:** ____

7–3 Controls for a Computerized Payroll Computation Environment

The most common payroll system in place today involves the use of man-ually generated time cards that are then input into a payroll software system that generates gross and net pay, deductions, and paychecks. Other enhance-ments to the basic computerized payroll computation system, including computerized timekeeping, employee self-service, and electronic payments, are addressed in subsequent sections of this chapter.

   The control system for a computerized payroll computation system does not vary substantially from that used for an entirely manual system. One difference is that the computer can automatically compare the list of input

Exhibit 7.9 Payroll Bill and Coin Requirements Form

| Employee Name | | Payroll Period Ended _____May 15_____ | | | | | | | |
Employee Name	Net Pay	$20	$10	$5	$1	$0.25	$0.10	$0.05	$0.01
Anderson, John	$129.12	6		1	4		1		2
Brickmeyer, Charles	207.03	10		1	2				3
Caldwell, Dorian	119.82	5	1	1	4	3		1	2
Devon, Ernest	173.14	8	1		3		1		4
Franklin, Gregory	215.19	10	1	1			1	1	4
Hartwell, Alan	198.37	9	1	1	3	1	1		2
Inglenook, Mary	248.43	12		1	3	1	1	1	3
	$1,291.10	60	4	6	19	5	5	3	20

Payroll Manager Signature: _____ Date: _____

Cashier Disbursement Signature: _____ Date: _____

Paymaster Receipt Signature: _____ Date: _____

Exhibit 7.10 Pay Receipt

For Pay Period Ended _____May 15, 2006_____

Employee Name	Cash Paid	Date Received	Employee Signature
Barclay, David	$231.14	May 19, 2006	David Barclay
Fairchild, Enoch	$402.19	May 19, 2006	Enoch Fairchild
Harley, Jeff	$300.78	May 19, 2006	Jeff Harley
Jimenez, Sandra	$220.82	May 19, 2006	Sandra Jimenez
Nindle, Allison	$275.03	May 19, 2006	Allison Nindle

time cards to the employee master file to determine which employees have
not submitted time cards, and can even send them an e-mail notification to
turn in their time cards. It is also necessary to manually match the hours
worked as reported by the computer system to the amounts shown on individual time cards, since there is a significant risk of data entry errors by the

payroll staff. The manual step of creating and posting a journal entry for the payroll transaction is no longer necessary, on the grounds that this step typically is handled automatically by the computerized payroll system; however, if the payroll software is not integrated into the accounting software and there is no interface between the two, then a journal entry still must be created manually. The basic process flow is shown in Exhibit 7.11.

The controls noted in the flowchart are described at greater length next, in sequence from the top of the flowchart to the bottom.

- *Obtain approval of hours worked and overtime*. This is the same control used for a manual payroll system. If a computerized timekeeping system is installed (as is described in Section 7–4), then this control is replaced by automated monitoring by the time clock itself.

- *Computer reports on missing time cards*. It is no longer necessary to determine manually which current employees have not submitted time cards, since this information can be provided by the computer system itself. However, it still may be necessary to conduct a periodic audit of the employee master file to ensure that all employees listed as active have not actually been terminated (possibly indicating the presence of ghost employees).

- *Match time card totals to data entry totals*. It is quite possible to key-punch the time reported on time cards into the payroll software incorrectly. To detect these errors, have someone besides the data entry person compare the employee hours loaded into the payroll software to the amounts listed on employee timesheets.

- *Obtain approval of all pay rate changes and special pay requests*. This control does not change from the one previously described for a paper-based system. However, it can be eliminated if employee and manager self-service functions are installed, as described in Section 7–5.

- *Review payroll register for errors*. The computer system will print a payroll register once it has completed all payroll processing. This is an ideal source document for comparison to authorizing wage and deduction documents as well as the total hours listed on time cards.

- *Issue checks directly to recipients*. This control does not vary from the one described earlier for a paper-based payroll system.

- *Paymaster retains unclaimed checks*. This control does not vary from the one described earlier for a paper-based payroll system.

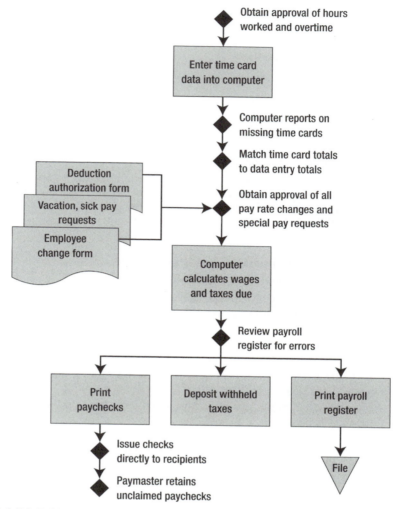

Exhibit 7.11   System of Controls for Computer-Based Payroll Processing

Exhibit 7.12 shows a complete procedure for the computerized payroll computation environment, which contains more processing detail than was shown in the preceding bullet points.

In addition to the basic controls just noted, the next controls can also be used to provide an additional level of control over the payroll computation process.

Exhibit 7.12   Computer-Based Payroll Computation Procedure

Policy/Procedure Statement   Retrieval No.:   PAY-03

Subject: Process Payroll Transactions

1.   PURPOSE AND SCOPE

This procedure is used to guide the payroll staff through the processing of a payroll cycle with the use of payroll computation software.

2.   PROCEDURES

2.1   Collect Time Cards (Payroll Clerk)

Obtain time cards from all company locations. Prior to data entry into the payroll system, obtain supervisory approval of hours and overtime worked. Supervisors must circle and initial all overtime hours to indicate their authorization. If approval has not occurred, return the time sheets to the supervisors for their immediate review and approval.

2.2   Enter Time Card Data into Computer (Payroll Clerk)

1. Access the TIMECARD ENTRY screen in the payroll software.

2. For each time card, enter the employee name and number, as well as total regular and overtime hours worked and other types of time as noted on the time card.

3. Match the total time on the screen to the total on the time card. Then stamp the time card to indicate that it has been entered in the payroll system.

4. Once all time cards are entered, run the Missing Time Cards report and notify supervisors of the missing cards.

5. Check off missing cards against the Missing Time Cards report until all have been accounted for.

2.3   Enter Other Payroll Changes into Computer (Payroll Clerk)

1. Assemble all employee change forms and deduction authorization forms received since the last payroll was processed.

2. Verify that all change requests have been correctly authorized.

3. Access the payroll software and go to the EMPLOYEE main menu.

4. Select the WAGE option, and enter the new hourly rate or annual salary amount for any employees for whom there is an authorized wage rate change document.

5. Select the DEDUCT option, and enter the deduction code and dollar amount for each documented deduction. Be sure to enter a deduction termination code for those that are of limited duration. Verify that deductions are allocated correctly to each payroll period, so that the total amount of each deduction is accurate on a monthly or annual basis.

6. Enter all manual check payments in the MANUAL PAY screen for the current period.

Exhibit 7.12 *(Continued)*

---

7. Compare the garnishments file to the detailed payroll records from the last payroll period to see if any changes are needed to current employee deductions. If so, make those changes on the GARNISHMENTS screen.

8. Print the Transaction Updates report and use it to verify that the correct entries were made.

2.4 Process and Review Payroll Calculations (Payroll Clerk and Supervisor)

1. Access the PROCESS PAYROLL screen and run the payroll calculations for the current payroll cycle.

2. Print a preliminary payroll register and compare it to source documents for accuracy. Run the payroll as many times as necessary until all errors have been eliminated from the payroll.

3. Print a final payroll register and take it to the payroll supervisor for review. If the supervisor finds no errors, the supervisor initials and dates the first page of the payroll register and files it in a locked storage cabinet.

4. Mark the date and initial each authorization document once it has been entered in the computer system and verified in the payroll register. File all entered authorization documents in the employee folders

2.5 Create Paychecks (Payroll Clerk and Check Signer)

1. Go to the payroll software and access the PRINT CHECKS option from the EMPLOYEE main menu.

2. Insert check stock into the printer.

3. Use the TEST option to print a sample check and verify that the line spacing is correct. Repeat as necessary.

4. Print the entire batch of checks.

5. Reset the printer and print all deposit advices for those employees using direct deposit.

6. Print the check register.

7. Have all checks signed by an authorized check signer.

8. Stuff all paychecks in envelopes.

2.6 Deposit Withheld Taxes (Payroll Clerk #2)

1. Remove a blank Form 8109 from the IRS-supplied booklet.

2. On the form, enter the month in which the corporate tax year ends, the dollar amount being remitted (source is the tax total on the payroll register), and contact information, and darken the square next to the type of tax being paid.

3. Create a check for the amount of the remittance.

4. Take the completed Form 8109 and check payment to the local bank and obtain a receipt for the payment.

5. File the tax payment receipt by date.

6. Notify the general ledger accountant of the amount of the tax payment.

(continues)

Exhibit 7.12 *(Continued)*

2.7 System Backup and Roll-forward (Payroll Clerk)
1. Back up the payroll database twice. Leave one copy on-site and send the other copy to the off-site storage location.
2. Reset the software to begin processing the payroll for the next pay period.

2.8 Issue Checks (Paymaster)
1. Divide the paychecks into groups by department.
2. Go to each department and hand out paychecks to all employees showing a proper form of picture identification.
3. Upon receipt of a paycheck, each employee signs for it next to his or her name on the employee register.
4. If employees are not available, highlight their names on the employee register and store both the register and unissued checks in the company safe.

- *Obtain computer-generated exception reports.* If the payroll software is sufficiently sophisticated, the programming staff can create exception reports that reveal if payments are being made to terminated employees, the amount of payments to new employees, whether negative deductions are being processed, or when unusually high base pay, hours, or overtime amounts are being processed. Any of these situations may call for a more detailed review of the flagged items to ensure that any intentional or unintentional errors will not result in incorrect payments.

- *Send a copy of all manual paychecks to the general ledger clerk.* A very common problem is for the payroll staff to create a manual paycheck and then not notify the accounting staff of the check, resulting in an unrecorded expense. The solution is to install a procedure for creating manual checks that specifically requires the payroll staff always to send a copy of every manual paycheck to the general ledger clerk, so it will be recorded in the accounting database. Since this control point may be ignored, the next control point is needed to back it up.

- *Reconcile the payroll bank account.* A key reason for conducting a regularly scheduled reconciliation of the payroll bank account is to locate manual paychecks that have not been added to the computer system.

- *Have a separate person maintain employee master records.* The computer system relies on information contained within an employee master record when it calculates payments. If the payroll clerk were to have access to the master record file, he or she could create ghost employees to whom illicit payments could then be made. Accordingly, someone besides the payroll clerk should have sole access to the employee master records file.

- *Split the time card approval and payroll processing tasks.* If someone could approve time cards and also be responsible for processing payroll, he or she could illicitly create and divert paychecks for personal use. Thus, anyone approving time cards should not have access to the payroll system.

- *Enforce at least quarterly password changes.* If there is any software requiring frequent password modification, it is the payroll system, since unauthorized access to the payroll database could result in significant losses. Passwords should be changed on at least a quarterly basis, and employees should be warned not to write down their current passwords where a third party can find them.

- *Route payroll register directly to supervisor for review.* The person operating the payroll software could create a legitimate payroll register and forward it to a manager for approval, and subsequently modify the payroll database to pay him- or herself additional funds. To avoid this, put a separate person in charge of printing payroll reports, and have this person carry the report directly to the supervisor for approval.

7–4 Controls for Computerized Timekeeping

Though many companies still use manual time sheets or punch cards, a variety of other computerized timekeeping devices are available, such as clocks equipped with scanners to accommodate employee badges equipped with magnetic, radio frequency identification (RFID), or bar-coded identification tags, Web-based time reporting, Voice over Internet Protocol (VoIP) phones with timekeeping features, and even cell phones with time reporting functionality. All these systems can be configured to automatically load timekeeping information directly into the computerized payroll computation system.

There is no need for a flowchart to enumerate the controls associated with computerized timekeeping, since the controls only involve the appropriate use of automated features within the timekeeping systems. The key controls follow.

- *Time clock controls clock-in times.* A computerized time clock can block out the hours when employees are allowed to clock in or out, thereby keeping them from clocking in for excessive hours or during incorrect shifts. This control requires extra effort to load into the computer system the exact times during which each employee is authorized to work as well as ongoing maintenance of this information.
- *Time clock requires supervisory approval of overtime.* A computerized time clock typically categorizes each employee by a specific work period, so that any hours worked after his or her standard time period will be flagged automatically by the computer for supervisory approval, possibly including a clock-out rejection unless a supervisory approval code is entered on the spot.
- *Review time clock reports for irregular entries.* A computerized time clock generates a variety of reports that itemize such information as missed punches, late punches, and overtime hours worked. These reports are a prime source of control information, and should be examined regularly by supervisors to locate incorrectly reported work hours.

Though the preceding controls are sufficient for a computerized time-keeping system, the next additional controls can bolster the overall system of controls.

- *Use biometric time clocks to eliminate buddy punching.* A common fraud is for an employee to give his badge to another employee, who uses it to clock in the first employee, even though the first employee is not on the premises. By using a biometric clock that matches either the fingerprints or hand outline of an employee, "buddy punching" is eliminated.
- *Link photo images of employees to badge scanner.* Another way to detect buddy punching is to install a camera that snaps an electronic picture of anyone at the moment they scan a badge through the time clock,

thereby linking a face to a badge. Even if the camera is not operational, its mere presence may act as a deterrent to buddy punching.

- *Require daily supervisory reviews of hours worked reports.* Even those supervisors with extraordinary memories will have a difficult time remembering which of their hourly staff members were on hand during various times of the day over the preceding weeks. To ensure a more knowledgeable review of time records, require supervisors to review hours worked at the end of every shift, using a daily timekeeping report from the computer system.

7–5 Controls for Payroll Self-Service

Self-service is becoming relatively common for employees, who can directly access the payroll system and change their address, tax deductions, benefits deductions, and related information. In addition, some companies have separate self-service systems for managers that allow them to enter pay rate changes, termination and hire dates, and similar types of information. Because these systems are based on the concept of switching the payroll staff from data entry work to process monitoring, any controls added to this process should not require manual labor by the payroll staff. Instead, the computerized self-service functions should include these automated controls.

- *Install limit checks on pay rate changes.* Managers should be allowed a budgeted maximum pay rate change per employee, after which work flow software should route any change request to a higher-level manager for further review.

- *E-mail employees with change information.* Whenever an employee uses a self-service screen to alter information, the system should send a confirming e-mail message detailing the change. This gives employees the opportunity to spot errors in their entries, while also notifying them if someone else has gained access to the payroll system using their access codes and has altered their payroll information.

- *Notify payroll staff of unauthorized state residencies.* If an employee uses the self-service feature to record a state of residence for which the company is not set up to record state income or unemployment tax remittances, the system should notify the payroll staff. The address change should also be rejected until the correct tax identification numbers have been obtained from the targeted states.

- *Require secondary approval or notification of bank account number changes.* If an employee has been terminated and another person obtains access to their self-service user ID and password, that person could alter the bank account numbers to which direct deposit payments are being made so that funds are sent to his or her personal accounts. By requiring secondary approval of these changes, or at least notification of another person, the risk of such changes occurring is reduced.

- *Link termination information to self-service access.* If an employee leaves the company, the easiest way to commit fraud is for another employee to continue making payments to that person and to intercept the payments for personal use. To avoid this problem, termination information from *any* other system in the company—pension plan, benefits, even building access codes—should be interfaced to the self-service feature and automatically shut down access to it while also notifying the payroll department that no further payments should be made, other than a termination payment.

7–6 Controls for Direct Deposit and Payroll Cards

One of the more useful best practices is to require all employees to receive electronic payroll payments, by means of either direct deposit or payroll debit cards. From a control perspective, the use of payroll cards is more advantageous to the company than direct deposit, since even the first payment made to an employee can be through the card, whereas the first direct deposit payment is typically with a check (due to the need to prenote the payment). If payroll payments by check are eliminated entirely, these controls can be stopped:

- Issue checks directly to recipients.
- Paymaster retains unclaimed paychecks.
- Have employees sign for paychecks received.

- Review paychecks for double endorsements.
- Review uncashed payroll checks.

Given the small number of controls for direct deposits and payroll cards, there is no need for a controls flowchart. The controls follow:

- *Require employee signatures and formal identification for direct deposit changes.* It is possible for someone to alter the direct deposit account information for an employee, thereby routing payments to a different bank account. This is an unlikely problem, since the employee from whom money is being taken will spot the problem and complain. Nonetheless, it is customary to at least have employees sign a direct deposit authorization form. A more extreme form of the control is to require a picture identification of the person submitting the change document.

- *Match routing and account number on employee check to submitted information.* The most common problem with direct deposit failures is when the routing or account number on the check is incorrectly entered into the payroll software. Consequently, always conduct a separate error review of this information.

- *Securely store direct deposit authorization forms.* Since the direct deposit authorization form shown in Exhibit 7.14 contains an employee's bank account number, routing number, and signature (and in some cases social security number), the company must take steps to keep this information securely stored, so that no one can use it to improperly extract funds from employee bank accounts.

- *Review report showing multiple direct deposit payments to the same bank account.* Under a direct deposit system, a payroll clerk could create ghost employees and then have their payments sent directly to his or her bank account through the direct deposit system. This type of fraud is easily detected by running a custom report in the payroll software that shows only employees for whom more than one direct deposit payment has been made as part of a single payroll cycle. An even more effective control is to run the same report for multiple payroll cycles, in case a canny employee only creates ghost employees who are located in different pay cycles.

The procedure for creating a direct deposit transaction is shown in Exhibit 7.13.

Exhibit 7.13   Direct Deposit Procedure

Policy/Procedure Statement	Retrieval No.: PAY-04

Subject: Issue Direct Deposit Payments to Employees

1.   PURPOSE AND SCOPE

This procedure is used by the payroll clerks to issue direct deposit payments to employees.

2.   PROCEDURES

2.1   Update Rejected Prenotes (Payroll Clerk)

1. Review the preceding period's report of rejected prenotes. Verify that replacement bank routing number and account number information has been received for these rejected items.

2. If there is no replacement routing information, contact the employees whose information was rejected and remind them to submit replacement routing information. Also, set the payment flag in the computer system to "payment by check" until the replacement information has been received.

2.2   Update Direct Deposit File with Employee Changes (Payroll Clerk)

1. For employees wanting to alter their direct deposit information, issue to them the Direct Deposit Authorization form. (See Exhibit 7.14.) In particular, they must enter the bank routing number and account number in the appropriate fields, as well as attach a voided check to the bottom of the form. It is not allowable to attach a deposit slip to the form.

2. Verify that the bank routing and account number information on the bottom of the check matches the information entered by the employee in the middle of the form. If there is a discrepancy, always use the information on the check.

3. Require formal photo identification by the employee requesting the direct deposit update, and match the signature on the photo identification to the signature on the Direct Deposit Authorization form.

4. Enter the updated information in the employee master file in the computer system. Write the entry date on the Direct Deposit Authorization form and initial the document.

5. Securely store the Direct Deposit Authorization form in the employee file. Verify that the filing cabinet containing employee records is locked.

2.3   Issue Direct Deposit Data to Bank (Payroll Clerk #2)

1. Three business days prior to the pay date, run the audit report showing the presence of multiple direct deposit payments being made to a single bank account. If these payments are occurring for unrelated parties, notify both the internal audit department and the controller of the issue as a possible ghost employee situation.

Exhibit 7.13   *(Continued)*

2. Reformat the direct deposit file into the format needed for acceptance by the processing bank.

3. Access the bank's direct deposit Web site and upload the reformatted file.

4. Verify that the bank has received the information and that there are no errors in it. Print the screen showing the bank's acceptance, and store the screen print in the direct deposit payroll file by date.

2.4 Distribute Payment Notifications (Payroll Clerk)

1. Print remittance advices for all employees being paid by direct deposit.

2. Stuff all remittance advices in envelopes.

3. Include the direct deposit remittance advices with any regular payroll checks, batch the envelopes by supervisor, and deliver them to supervisors for delivery to employees.

7–7 Controls for Electronic Remittances and W-2 Forms

In addition to issuing electronic payments to employees, it is also possible to issue electronic remittance advices and W-2 forms to them. The most common approach is to post this information in PDF format in secure accounts on the Internet. There is no asset control problem with these best practices, since there is no potential loss of assets. However, there is a risk of employee pay information becoming available to anyone who gains access to the online accounts. The next control is necessary to mitigate this risk.

- *Require user ID and password access to remittance and W-2 accounts.* Anyone accessing electronic remittance or W-2 information over the Internet must be required to set up user identification and password information to access the accounts. To lock down access to this information even more tightly, it may be necessary to require periodic password changes.

7–8 Controls for Outsourced Payroll Processing

Many companies do not process their payrolls at all. Instead, they send time-keeping and pay rate information to a third party, who processes the payroll, sends back paychecks to the company for distribution, and remits taxes on

Indicate status change	Effective Date:
☐ Start ☐ Stop ☐ Change	_____/_____/_____

Name (Last, First, Middle Initial): please print	Social Security Number:

Financial Institution Name:

Bank Routing Number (must be 9 numbers—see sample check below) ☐☐☐☐☐☐☐☐☐☐	Account Number ☐☐☐☐☐☐☐☐☐☐☐

Type of Account:	Deposit Amount:
☐ Checking (staple a voided check to the bottom of this form)	$_____Amount in Checking
☐ Savings (contact your financial institution for its routing number)	$_____Amount in Savings

I authorize _____ to direct funds to my account in the financial institution listed above. I understand that the authorization may be discontinued at any time. If any of the above information changes, I will submit a new authorization agreement. I understand that if I close an account without notifying the company, funds payable to me will be returned to the company, which will delay payment to me.

Employee Signature:

Work Phone:	Date:

Notes:
- Once submitted, direct deposit usually begins on your second paycheck.
- Payments should appear in the account at your financial institution on the scheduled pay date.

Attach a Voided Check Below:

John Q. Public
55 Elm Street
Anywhere, CO 01234   9000

Pay to the order of_____   *VOID* $ _____

_____Dollars

Routing	Account	Check
Number	Number	Number
: 123456789 :	554403401	9000

Exhibit 7.14   Direct Deposit Authorization

behalf of the company. Generally speaking, the use of payroll suppliers reduces the level of control needed over the payroll process, especially if the company elects to have the supplier make payments to employees with direct deposit; by doing so, no controls over the handling of checks are needed.

The essential process flow is shown in Exhibit 7.15. The process differs from that of an in-house computerized system in only a few areas. First, any

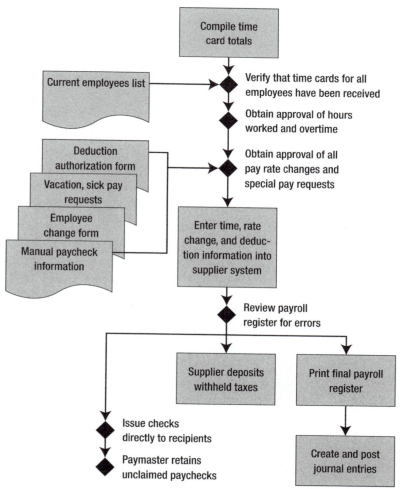

Exhibit 7.15   System of Controls for Outsourced Payroll Processing

special payments outside regularly scheduled pay cycles are handled with manual checks, which must be entered into the supplier's payroll system as part of the next pay cycle. Also, the supplier handles all tax remittances, check printing, and direct deposit payments.

The controls shown in the exhibit are not described in more detail, since they merely repeat controls already described in the manual payroll processing section. In addition to these basic controls, the next supplementary controls can be added.

- *Request verification of all tax remittances.* Though payroll suppliers have an excellent record of making tax remittances on behalf of a company in a timely manner, there is a slight chance of this not occurring. If so, the more paranoid controller may wish to request verification of all tax remittances, or at least until the supplier has established a history of handling remittances reliably.
- *Route all paychecks through a single company contact.* Some payroll suppliers will mail employee paychecks to a variety of company locations, for local distribution. However, there is a significant risk that some paychecks will be mistakenly batched together and sent to the wrong location. To avoid this problem, it is sometimes better to require that all paychecks be sent to a single location, where they can be batched and reissued by company staff to all company locations.

7–9 Payroll Policies

The next eight policies are useful for enforcing payroll-related controls. The first five policies are targeted at employees in general, enforcing various rules that reduce the amount of data entry and tracking work by the payroll staff. They are:

1. *Hourly employees must submit an approved time sheet by the designated date and time in order to be paid as part of the regular payroll cycle.* Though difficult to enforce, this policy puts the burden of time sheet submission on individual employees rather than the payroll staff.
2. *The company does not make purchases on behalf of employees.* This policy keeps the payroll staff from having to track a series of periodic deductions from employee pay in order to cover the cost of items pur-

chased by the company for employees. From a control perspective, it also eliminates the risk to the company that an employee will leave the company prior to paying back the funds expended for the purchase.

3. *The company does not issue advances on company pay.* This policy keeps the payroll staff from having to manually enter pay deductions into the payroll system to offset pay advances, thereby reducing the risk that deductions will be incorrectly entered or not entered at all.

4. *Employees shall not be allowed to carry forward more than __ hours of vacation and sick time into the next calendar year.* This policy ensures that there is no risk of excessive vacation or sick time payouts to a departing employee that would otherwise occur through the ongoing accumulation of earned vacation and sick time.

5. *All employees shall be paid by direct deposit or payroll card.* This policy is useful for switching 100 percent of employees to electronic payments, thereby avoiding several control problems associated with making check or cash payments.

The next two policies are strictly control-oriented, requiring secure storage of employee files and enforcing the segregation of certain tasks.

6. *Pay-related authorizations shall be stored in a central employee file.* This policy ensures that access to all pay-related authorizations can be restricted easily, while also reducing the likelihood that authorization documents can be lost. Authorizations should cover such items as pay rate changes, benefits, tax withholdings, and changes in employment status.

7. *No employee can be responsible for both processing payroll and distributing pay.* This policy ensures that proper segregation of duties keeps anyone from creating a paycheck, recording it, and then pocketing the funds. This policy is mandatory if payments are made in cash but is not necessary if payments are distributed electronically.

The final policy is a general requirement to remit tax payments in a timely manner.

8. *Payroll taxes shall be remitted in full on a timely basis.* Though obvious, this policy makes it clear to the payroll manager that taxes must be remitted in the full amount and on time, with no exceptions. Late tax

remittances can entail large penalties and late fees, as well as personal liability by company officers in some states, so this is a major policy to enforce.

Summary

The traditional paper-based payroll process can be totally replaced by employee self-service, automated timekeeping, computerized payroll processing, and electronic payments. This chapter addressed the controls for each of these best practices, resulting in a vastly more streamlined and automated control system. The best overall approach to controls when payroll has been converted to a front-to-back electronic system is to assign the payroll department overall responsibility for locating and correcting transactional errors, while the internal audit department conducts periodic control reviews to ensure that the payroll staff is itself following required controls in an acceptable manner.

Chapter 8

Controls for Fixed Assets Best Practices

Overview

There are few best practice enhancements to the basic fixed asset–related objectives of properly approving fixed asset acquisitions, valuing and depreciating them, and disposing of them in an orderly manner. Consequently, this chapter focuses on a single methodology for accomplishing these objectives. Given the significant size of a company's investment in fixed assets, a considerable amount of control information is provided here. There are 24 controls, 6 procedures, and 11 supporting policies, all designed to provide a proper level of control over all fixed asset transactions.

8–1 Fixed Asset Controls

This section contains two dozen controls that can be applied to the acquisition, valuation, and disposal of fixed assets. Of this group, 13 are considered primary controls and are included in the flowchart in Exhibit 8.1. The remaining 11 controls either do not fit into the various fixed asset transaction flows or are considered secondary controls that can bolster the primary controls as needed.

In essence, the system of controls for an asset acquisition requires that initial funding approval come from the annual budget, as well as additional approval through a formal capital investment form just prior to the actual acquisition. There should also be a postinstallation analysis of how actual project results compared to the estimates shown in the original capital investment form. The key controls used once an asset is installed are to tag it, assign specific responsibility for it, and ensure that any asset transfers are approved by the shipping and receiving managers. Finally, asset disposition

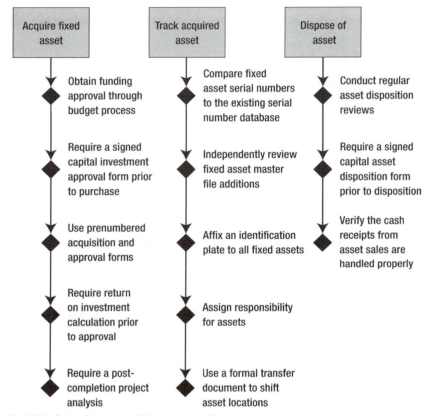

Exhibit 8.1   System of Fixed Asset Controls

controls call for regular disposition reviews to ensure that dispositions occur while assets still retain some resale value, a formal disposition approval process, and proper tracking of any resulting receipts.

The controls noted in the flowchart are described at greater length next, in sequence from the top of the flowchart to the bottom for each of the three types of fixed asset transactions.

- *Obtain funding approval through the annual budgeting process.* The annual budgeting process is an intensive review of overall company operations as well as of how capital expenditures are needed to fulfill the company's strategic direction. As such, capital expenditure requests should be included in the annual budget, thereby ensuring that they will be analyzed in some detail. Expenditure requests included in the approved budget still should be subjected to some additional approval at the point of actual expenditure, to ensure that they are still needed. However, expenditure requests not included in the approved budget should be subjected to a considerably higher level of analysis and approval, to ensure that there is a justifiable need for them.

- *Require a signed capital investment approval form prior to purchase.* Given the significant amount of funds usually needed to acquire a fixed asset, there always should be a formal approval process before a purchase order is issued. An example is shown in Exhibit 8.2. Depending on the size of the acquisition, a number of approval signatures may be required, extending up to the company president or even the chair of the board of directors.

- *Use prenumbered acquisition and disposal forms.* If the company uses a manual system for fixed asset acquisitions and disposals, then it should acquire a set of prenumbered acquisition and disposal forms. By doing so, it can keep track of form numbers to ensure that none is lost prior to completion. This is also a good way to ensure that employees do not attempt to submit multiple acquisition authorization forms for the same asset, allowing them to order duplicate assets and make off with the extra items. For this to be a fully functional control, someone must be assigned the task of storing the forms in a secure location and monitoring which form numbers have been released for use.

- *Require return on investment calculation prior to approval.* Given the considerable size of some fixed asset investments, a reasonable control is to calculate the estimated return on investment to see if the investment exceeds the corporate hurdle rate. The return calculation can involve a variety of approaches, such as the payback period, net present value, or internal rate of return. All three calculations are included in the capital investment proposal form shown in Exhibit 8.2.

- *Conduct a postcompletion project analysis.* Managers have been known to make overly optimistic projections in order to make favorable cases for asset acquisitions. This issue can be mitigated by conducting regular reviews of the results of asset acquisitions in comparison to initial predictions and then tracing these findings back to the initiating managers. This approach can also be used at various milestones during

Exhibit 8.2 Capital Investment Approval Form

Name of Project Sponsor:	H. Henderson	Submission Date:	[Date]

Investment Description:

Additional press for newsprint.

Cash Flows:

Year	Equipment	Working Capital	Maintenance	Tax Effect of Annual Depreciation	Salvage Value	Revenue	Taxes	Total
0	-5,000,000	-400,000		800,000				-5,400,000
1			-100,000	800,000		1,650,000	-700,000	1,170,000
2			-100,000	320,000		1,650,000	-700,000	1,170,000
3			-100,000	320,000		1,650,000	-700,000	1,170,000
4			-100,000	320,000		1,650,000	-700,000	1,170,000
5		400,000	-100,000	320,000	1,000,000	1,650,000	-700,000	2,570,000
Totals	-5,000,000	0	-500,000	2,400,000	1,000,000	8,250,000		1,850,000

Tax Rate:	40%
Hurdle Rate:	10%
Payback Period:	4.28
Net Present Value:	**(86,809)**
Internal Rate of Return:	9.4%

Approvals:

Amount	Approver	Signature
<$5,000	Supervisor	
$5–19,999	General Mgr	
$20–49,999	President	
$50,000+	Board	

Type of Project (check one):

Legal requirement	
New product-related	
Old product extension	Yes
Repair/replacement	
Safety issue	

the construction of an asset to ensure that costs incurred match original projections.

- *Compare fixed asset serial numbers to the existing serial number database.* There is a possibility that employees are acquiring assets, selling them to the company, then stealing the assets and selling them to the company again. To spot this behavior, always enter the serial number of each acquired asset in the fixed asset master file, and then run a report comparing serial numbers for all assets to see if there are duplicate serial numbers on record.

- *Independently review fixed asset master file additions.* A number of downstream errors can arise when fixed asset information is entered incorrectly in the fixed asset master file. For example, an incorrect asset description can result in an incorrect asset classification, which in turn may result in an incorrect depreciation calculation. Similarly, an incorrect asset location code can result in the subsequent inability to locate the physical asset, which in turn may result in an improper asset disposal transaction. Further, an incorrect acquisition price may result in an incorrect depreciation calculation. To mitigate the risk of all these errors, have a second person review all new entries to the fixed asset master file for accuracy.

- *Affix an identification plate to all fixed assets.* If a company acquires assets that are not easily differentiated, then it is useful to affix an identification plate to each one to assist in later audits. The identification plate can be a metal tag if durability is an issue, or can be a laminated bar code tag for easy scanning, or even a radio frequency (RFID) tag. The person responsible for tagging should record the tag number and asset location in the fixed asset master file.

- *Assign responsibility for assets.* There is a significant risk that assets will not be tracked carefully through the company once they are acquired. To avoid this, formally assign responsibility for each asset to the department manager whose staff uses the asset, and send all managers a quarterly notification of what assets are under their control. Even better, persuade the human resources manager to include "asset control" as a line item in the formal performance review for all managers.

- *Use a formal transfer document to shift asset locations.* If the preceding control is implemented that assigns responsibility for specific assets to department managers, then the transfer of an asset to a different department calls for the formal approval of the sending and receiving department managers. Otherwise, managers can claim that assets are being shifted without their approval, so they have no responsibility for the assets.

- *Conduct regular asset disposition reviews.* Fixed assets decline in value over time, so it is essential to conduct a regular review to determine if any assets should be disposed of before they lose their resale value. This review should be conducted at least annually, and should include representatives from the accounting, purchasing, and user departments. An alternative approach is to create capacity utilization metrics (which is most easily obtained for production equipment) and report on utilization levels as part of the standard monthly management reporting package; this tends to result in more immediate decisions to eliminate unused equipment.

- *Require a signed capital asset disposition form prior to disposition.* There is a risk that employees could sell off assets at below-market rates or disposition assets for which an alternative in-house use had been planned. Also, if assets are informally disposed of, the accounting staff probably will not be notified and so will continue to depreciate an asset no longer owned by the company, rather than writing it off. To avoid these problems, require the completion of a signed capital asset disposition form, such as the one shown in Exhibit 8.3.

- *Verify that cash receipts from asset sales are handled properly.* Employees may sell a company's assets, pocket the proceeds, and report to the company that the asset actually was scrapped. This control issue can be reduced by requiring that a bill of sale or receipt from a scrapping company accompany the file for every asset that has been disposed of.

The preceding controls were primary ones required as part of the basic fixed asset transaction flows. In addition, the next ancillary controls either are general controls that operate outside of any specific transaction or are designed to provide additional risk mitigation.

- *Segregate responsibilities related to fixed assets.* If the person purchasing an asset also receives it, there is a considerable risk that the person will alter the purchasing documents to eliminate evidence of the

Exhibit 8.3   Capital Asset Disposition Form

Issuing Department Name: _____

Department Manager Signature: _____

Step 1: List all equipment being dispositioned in the following spaces:

Tag Number	Item Name	Model Number	Serial Number
1.			
2.			
3.			
4.			
5.			

Step 2: Check one of the action categories listed below (limit of one):

☐ **Return to Seller**

Supplier RMA Number: _____

Shipping Supervisor Signature: _____

Date: _____

☐ **Lost/Stolen**

Insurance Claim Number Filed: _____

Risk Manager Signature: _____

Date: _____

☐ **Transfer to Another Department**

Department Name: _____

Receiving Manager Signature: _____

Date: _____

☐ **Trade-In**

Purchase Order Number: _____

Shipping Supervisor Signature: _____

Date: _____

☐ **Cannibalize for Parts**

Purchasing Manager Signature: _____

Warehouse Manager Signature: _____

Date: _____

☐ **Disposal**

Administrative Officer Signature: _____

Warehouse Manager Signature: _____

Date: _____

Copies: (1) to Accounting, (2) Department Receiving the Assets, (3) Issuing Department

receipt and then steal the asset. The same concern applies to several aspects of fixed assets transactions. A control over this situation is to segregate these types of responsibilities:

- ○ Fixed asset acquisition
- ○ Fixed asset transaction recording
- ○ Custody of the fixed asset
- ○ Fixed asset disposal
- ○ Reconciliation of physical assets to accounting records

- *Restrict access to the fixed asset master file.* The fixed asset master file contains all baseline information about an asset and is the source document for depreciation calculations as well as asset location information. If people were to gain illicit access to this file, they could make modifications to change depreciation calculations (thereby changing financial results) as well as modify locations (possibly resulting in theft of the assets). To avoid these problems, always use password controls to restrict access to the fixed asset master file.

- *Restrict facility access.* If the company owns fixed assets that can be easily moved and have a significant resale value, there is a risk that they will be stolen. If so, consider restricting access to the building during nonwork hours and hire a security staff to patrol the perimeter or at least the exits.

- *Install an alarm system to detect RFID-tagged assets.* If the company has especially valuable fixed assets that can be moved, then consider affixing a RFID tag to each one and then installing a transceiver near every building exit that will trigger an alarm if the RFID tag passes by the transceiver.

- *Reconcile fixed asset additions with capital expenditure authorizations.* A good detective control to ensure that all acquisitions have been authorized properly is to periodically reconcile all fixed asset additions to the file of approved capital expenditure authorizations. Any acquisitions for which there is no authorization paperwork are then flagged for additional review, typically including reporting of the control breach to management.

- *Increase the capitalization limit.* A key problem with fixed asset tracking is that it involves a considerable amount of additional paperwork as well as ongoing depreciation calculations, which may so overwhelm the accounting staff that they are struggling to keep up with the paperwork rather than focusing on proper control of the assets themselves. This recommended control may seem counterintuitive, but increasing the capitalization limit reduces the number of assets designated as fixed assets, thereby allowing the accounting staff to focus its attention on the proper approval, tracking, and disposition of a smaller number of large-dollar assets. Thus, oversight of smaller assets is abandoned in favor of greater inspection of large-dollar asset transactions.

- *Conduct a periodic fixed asset audit.* The internal audit staff should schedule a periodic audit of fixed assets, reconciling the on-hand inventory to the accounting records. Given the considerable quantity of fixed assets that many companies maintain, it is acceptable to focus on the 20 percent of fixed assets that typically account for 80 percent of the invested cost of all fixed assets. An example of a report suitable for a fixed asset audit is shown in Exhibit 8.4.

- *Verify the fair value assumptions on dissimilar asset exchanges.* Accounting rules allow one to record a gain or loss on the exchange of dissimilar assets. Since this calculation is based on the fair value of the assets involved (which is not stated in the accounting records), the possibility exists for someone to artificially create an asset fair value that will result in a gain or loss. This situation can be avoided by having

Exhibit 8.4 Fixed Asset Audit Report

Location	Tag Number	Description	Model No.	Serial No.	Inoperable?	Tag Missing?
Accounting	05432	Dell laptop	Dim 43	IE75J	Yes	
Accounting	05021	HP laptop	HP 312	06M14	Yes	
Engineering	04996	Compaq server	CQ 007	MK14J		
Engineering	04985	IBM server	A31	A09J5		Yes
Engineering	04900	Quark license	Ver 4.0	MM047		
Engineering	04730	Office license	Ver. 2004	F4KQW		
Engineering	04619	Windows license	Ver. XP	9M4G7		
Production	01038	50 ton press	G42	Z9G2K		Yes
Production	01004	150 ton press	G90	V12L9		

an outside appraiser review the fair value assumptions used in this type of transaction.

- *Test for asset impairment.* There are a variety of circumstances under which the net book value of an asset should be reduced to its fair value, which can result in significant reductions in the recorded value of an asset. This test requires a significant knowledge of the types of markets in which a company operates, the regulations to which it is subject, and the need for its products within those markets. Consequently, only a knowledgeable person who is at least at the level of a controller should be relied on to detect the presence of assets whose values are likely to have been impaired.

- *Verify that correct depreciation calculations are being made.* Though there is no potential loss of assets if incorrect depreciation calculations are being made, it can result in an embarrassing adjustment to a company's financial statements at some point in the future. This control should include a comparison of capitalized items to the official corporate capitalization limit to ensure that items are not being inappropriately capitalized and depreciated. The control should also include a review of the asset categories in which each individual asset has been recorded, to ensure that an asset has not been misclassified and therefore incorrectly depreciated.

- *Verify that all changes in asset retirement obligation assumptions are authorized.* A company can artificially increase its short-term profitability by altering the assumed amount of future cash flows associated with its asset retirement obligations. Since downward revisions to these assumptions will be reflected in the current period's income statement as a gain, any changes to these assumptions should be approved prior to implementation.

8–2 Fixed Asset Procedures

The handling of fixed assets requires the use of several rigidly defined procedures to ensure that transactions are recorded and valued properly. Each procedure describes its purpose and scope, what positions are responsible for completing each step, and the specific tasks needed for completion. The procedures are listed in the next table.

Exhibit Number	Procedure Description	Exhibit Number	Procedure Description
8.5	Capital proposal evaluation	8.8	Test assets for impairment
8.6	Record fixed asset payment	8.9	Gain/loss recordation for asset disposal
8.7	Depreciation calculation	8.10	Fixed asset audit

8–3 Fixed Asset Policies

Due to the large investments involved, a number of policies are needed to supplement the fixed asset controls noted earlier in this chapter. The first set of three policies addresses the company's investment in assets, covering the initial asset acquisition, a formal review of payback, and ongoing asset valuation.

1. *Management must approve all asset additions through a formal review process.* This policy requires the management team to follow a formal review process that requires both the use of cash flow analysis and a hierarchy of approvals depending on the size of the proposed expenditure.
2. *Capital investment results shall be reviewed annually.* This policy requires a company to compare the actual results of a capital investment to what was predicted in its capital investment proposal form. The intent is to highlight incorrect assumptions that may still be used for other capital investment proposals, which can then be corrected to ensure better ongoing capital investment decisions.
3. *Periodically review all fixed assets for impairment.* This policy ensures that the accounting staff will regularly compare the book value of all fixed assets to their fair value, and write down the book value to the fair value if this is the lower amount.

The next two policies establish responsibility for each fixed asset, so that managers are more likely to maintain a close watch over assets.

Exhibit 8.5   Capital Proposal Evaluation Procedure

Policy/Procedure Statement	Retrieval No.: FA-01

Subject: Capital Proposal Evaluation Procedure

1. PURPOSE AND SCOPE

This procedure is used by the financial analyst to verify the assumptions, cash flows, and net present value of all capital proposals.

2. PROCEDURES

2.1 Verify Assumptions (Financial Analyst)

1. Review each submitted capital expenditure form to ensure that all fields have been completed. If not, return the form to the sender, with a note regarding the missing information.

2. Review all assumptions with the person submitting the form. If they vary significantly from assumptions used for previous approved capital budgets, or if there are reasonable grounds for doubt, modify the underlying numerical data.

2.2 Verify Cash Flows (Financial Analyst)

1. Review all itemized cash flows listed in the form with the project manager, purchasing staff, sales staff, and anyone else with a reasonable degree of knowledge regarding the amount or timing of the cash flows.

2. Adjust the amount or timing of cash flows in the capital expenditure analysis based on the preceding cash flow review.

2.3 Calculate Net Present Value (Financial Analyst)

1. Obtain the cost of capital from the controller, and use this to discount the stream of cash flows noted in the capital expenditure proposal. Verify the calculation against the net present value listed in the form.

2. If the project seems unusually risky, also recalculate the net present value using a higher discount rate, to be determined by the controller.

2.4 Issue Recommendation (Financial Analyst)

1. If the net present value is positive, issue a favorable project recommendation to the controller and project sponsor.

2. If the net present value is negative, but the type of project listed on the Capital Investment Proposal Form is a "Legal requirement" or "Safety issue," then issue a favorable project recommendation to the controller and project sponsor.

3. If the net present value is negative, but the type of project listed on the Capital Investment Proposal Form is "New product-related," "Old product extension," or "Repair/replacement," then issue an unfavorable project recommendation to the controller and project sponsor.

Exhibit 8.6   Record Fixed Asset Payment Procedure

Policy/Procedure Statement   Retrieval No.:   FA-02
Subject: Record Fixed Asset Payment Procedure

1. **PURPOSE AND SCOPE**

This procedure is used by the accounts payable (A/P) clerk to record payments for fixed assets.

2. **PROCEDURES**

2.1 Determine Payment Coding (A/P Clerk)

1. Match the received supplier invoice to the authorizing purchase order and receiving documentation.
2. Determine if an asset purchase exceeds the corporate capitalization limit. If so, code the purchase into the appropriate asset account. If not, contact the assistant controller to verify which expense account is to be charged for the purchase.

2.2 Record Fixed Asset Payable (A/P Clerk)

1. Open the payables module and create a payables transaction. Charge all costs on the supplier invoice related to the asset itself, including freight and delivery fees, shipping insurance, sales taxes, and installation costs, to the designated asset account.
2. Open the fixed assets register and enter the asset's name, asset class, and location within the company. Also enter the fixed asset tag number, if available. The system will automatically assign a depreciation calculation method and period to the asset based on the asset class to which it was assigned.
3. Verify that the amount listed in the fixed asset register matches the amount entered for the purchase transaction.

2.3 File Supporting Documents (A/P Clerk)

1. Copy the supplier invoice, attach the remittance advice and receiving documents to it, and file these documents in the payables folder.
2. File the original supplier invoice with all supporting authorization documents by asset class in the fixed assets storage cabinet.

Exhibit 8.7   Depreciation Calculation Procedure

Policy/Procedure Statement   Retrieval No.:   FA-03

Subject: Depreciation Calculation Procedure

1.   PURPOSE AND SCOPE

This procedure is used by the general ledger accountant to ensure that the correct depreciation type and period is used for each capitalized asset.

2.   PROCEDURES

2.1   Determine and Record Asset Type (General Ledger Accountant)

1. Compare the type of asset to the company policy statement on asset types in the accounting policy manual.
2. Go to the fixed assets register in the computer database and enter the asset under the correct asset category.

2.2   Set Depreciation Parameters (General Ledger Accountant)

1. When adding the asset to the database, set the number of years of depreciation in accordance with the standard listed in the company policy statement on asset types.
2. Set the first-year depreciation at the half-year convention.
3. Set the depreciation method as the _____ method.

2.3   Print and Store Depreciation Information (General Ledger Accountant)

1. Print the transaction and store it in the fixed asset records manual.
2. Print the depreciation register and verify that the system has calculated the depreciation expense for the newly added asset correctly.

Exhibit 8.8   Test Assets for Impairment Procedure

Policy/Procedure Statement	Retrieval No.: FA-04

Subject: Test Assets for Impairment Procedure

1.   PURPOSE AND SCOPE

This procedure is used by the fixed asset and general ledger accountants to determine if the fair value of a fixed asset has dropped below its book value and to adjust the book value down to fair value if this is the case. Most assets have book values clustered near the corporate capitalization limit and therefore are so small that impairment testing would not result in significant asset valuation changes. Accordingly, this procedure is designed to test the values of only the largest assets.

2.   PROCEDURES

2.1   Select Assets for Testing (Fixed Asset Accountant)

1. Sort the fixed asset register by declining net book value (e.g., original purchase price less accumulated depreciation).

2. Select for impairment testing those 20% of the listed assets containing 80% of the total book value of the asset register.

2.2   Determine Level of Impairment (Fixed Asset Accountant)

1. Determine the total undiscounted cash flows expected to be generated from each of the selected assets (including net salvage value), and list this amount next to their net book values.

2. Compare the net book value figure to the undiscounted cash flow figure, and highlight those assets for which the book value is higher.

3. For the highlighted assets, determine the amount of the variance between the net book value and the undiscounted cash flow figure, and record an adjustment in the general ledger for this amount.

2.3   Update Accounting Records (General Ledger Accountant)

1. Enter in the general ledger the reduction in value of the impaired assets.

2. Reduce the net book values of all adjusted assets in the fixed asset register to match the amount of their undiscounted cash flows.

2.4   Revise Depreciation Calculations (Fixed Asset Accountant)

Calculate depreciation based on the new reduced book value figures, and adjust any recurring depreciation journal entries to include these changes.

Exhibit 8.9   Gain/Loss Recordation for Asset Disposal Procedure

---

Policy/Procedure Statement   Retrieval No.:   FA-05

Subject: Gain/Loss Recordation for Asset Disposal Procedure

1.   PURPOSE AND SCOPE

This procedure is used by the fixed asset and general ledger accountants to calculate the gain or loss on the sale or disposal of any capital assets.

2.   PROCEDURES

2.1   Summarize Asset Sale Information (Fixed Asset Accountant)

1. Receive documentation from the purchasing department regarding the sale of assets. This should include a signed Asset Disposition form that authorized someone to sell an asset. If the document is not signed by an authorized person, return it with a note asking for the appropriate signature. The document should be accompanied by a copy of the bill of sale and a copy of the check or other document that shows proof of the amount paid.

2. Once the sale documentation is complete, go to the fixed asset database and call up the record for the asset being sold. The easiest way is to conduct a search based on the name of the asset, though the documentation may contain the asset number or tag number, which can also be used to find the correct record.

3. Write down the original asset cost and total accumulated depreciation, which is located in the record in the fixed asset database.

2.2   Calculate Gain or Loss on Sale (Fixed Asset Accountant)

1. Subtract the sale amount and accumulated depreciation from the original asset cost. If there is a positive amount left over, this is a loss on the sale of the asset. If there is a negative amount left over, this is a gain on the sale of the asset.

2. Obtain a journal entry form and complete it for the gain or loss transaction. The asset's original cost goes in the "Credit Column," while the accumulated depreciation amount goes in the "Debit Column." The sale amount is a debit to cash. If there is a gain, this is recorded as a credit. A loss is recorded as a debit.

3. Forward the completed journal entry form to the general ledger accountant.

2.3   Update Accounting Records (General Ledger Accountant)

1. Access the fixed asset database and record the sale of the asset. Print the fixed asset report after this transaction is recorded, and compare the total for the account to the general ledger, to ensure that the information is recorded in the same amounts in both locations.

2. File one copy of the gain or loss calculation in the journal entry book and one in the permanent file documenting the addition or removal of fixed assets.

Exhibit 8.10   Fixed Asset Audit Procedure

Policy/Procedure Statement   Retrieval No.:   FA-06

Subject: Fixed Asset Audit Procedure

1.   PURPOSE AND SCOPE

This procedure is used by the internal audit staff, fixed asset accountant, and purchasing manager to verify the existence of fixed assets in the locations listed in the computer system.

2.   PROCEDURES

2.1   Conduct Fixed Assets Audit (Internal Audit Staff)

1. Obtain a list of all assets that are scheduled to be reviewed.
2. Check off all assets on the list as they are found and their tag numbers matched to the list.
3. Draw a line through any information to be changed, and write corrections above it.
4. Note on the report if an asset is inoperable or subject to disposition.
5. Note on the report if any asset tags are missing.
6. Note on the report if any assets are confirmed as being eliminated or transferred.
7. Note on the report any assets that cannot be located.
8. Confirm the results of the audit with the responsible department manager, and have the manager sign the report.
9. Send a copy of the report to the fixed asset accountant and the purchasing manager.

2.2   Update Records (Fixed Asset Accountant)

1. Upon receipt of the audit report, access the fixed asset master file and update location codes, descriptions, and tag numbers for any information changes identified during the audit.
2. Create replacement asset tags for all assets noted on the report as having missing tags, and affix them to the assets.
3. For all assets that cannot be located, update their location code to Missing. Print a report showing all assets designated as Missing, and send it to the responsible manager for additional research.
4. Print a complete asset report for the audited area containing all updated information, and send it to the responsible manager(s).
5. Match all items listed on the report as having been disposed of to the file of approved Capital Asset Disposition forms. If there is no authorizing form for a disposition, notify the responsible manager and refer the matter to the controller.

(continues)

Exhibit 8.10 *(Continued)*

2.3 Update Pending Disposition Records (Purchasing Manager)

1. Upon receipt of the audit report, review all assets noted as being inoperable or subject to disposition. Discuss the need for disposition with the manager responsible for the asset.
2. If disposal appears prudent, complete the Capital Asset Disposition form and forward it for approval.

1. *Fixed assets that are lost or stolen must be replaced with funds from the responsible department.* This policy is designed to firmly affix responsibility for each asset to a specific department manager. If the asset disappears, that manager must use internal department funds to replace it.
2. *All asset transfers and disposals require management approval.* This policy brings any asset movements to the attention of the accounting department, which can then record the revised asset locations in the accounting records. The policy also allows review of the proposed prices to be obtained from the sale or disposal of assets.

The next six policies address fixed asset–record-keeping requirements, so that the accounting staff records additional information only for assets exceeding a fixed minimum amount, securely maintains adequate records, makes accurate valuations, and records assets that are physically present.

1. *All assets with a purchase price exceeding $_____ shall be recorded as fixed assets.* This policy reduces the amount of paperwork associated with fixed asset tracking by shifting smaller assets into the expense category.
2. *The capitalization limit shall be reviewed annually.* This policy requires the controller to verify that the existing capitalization limit represents a reasonable balance of minimized record keeping for fixed assets and not an excessive amount of charges to expense for lower-cost assets.
3. *A detailed record shall be maintained of each fixed asset acquired.* This policy forces you to centralize the record keeping for each asset, making it much easier to identify, locate, cost, and determine the warranty provisions associated with each one.

4. *Copies of property records shall be maintained in an off-site location.* This policy reduces the risk of lost records by requiring a periodic shifting of record copies to a secure outside location.
5. *All asset valuations associated with dissimilar asset exchanges shall be reviewed by an outside appraiser.* This policy prevents the accounting staff from intentionally creating gains or losses on asset exchange transactions by assuming incorrect asset fair values.
6. *Conduct an annual inventory of all fixed assets.* This policy requires the internal auditing or accounting departments to compare the record of fixed assets to their actual locations, typically resulting not only in adjustments to their recorded locations, but also a determination of the need to dispose of selected assets.

Summary

The largest set of fixed asset controls relates to the *acquisition* of fixed assets; given the sometimes massive costs required to install fixed assets, it is entirely appropriate to install rigorously enforced controls over the acquisition process. The next most important controls are over the fixed asset recording and depreciation calculation functions, since incorrect entries can result in significant alterations to the level of reported financial results. Finally, the level of control exercised over asset disposition can vary substantially by company, based on the life span and resale value of the assets involved. If assets deteriorate quickly and have minimal resale value, then the level of control over dispositions may be cursory at best. Substantial long-term assets with significant resale values may call for the use of in-depth and multilayered control systems to ensure that they are properly utilized and eventually disposed of at the maximum possible prices.

Index

DATE DUE
